Rita Carter is an award-winning science and medical writer who contributes to, among others, *The Times*, *New Scientist* and the *Independent*. Having in the past worked as a TV presenter, Rita continues to appear in the media as an authority on science and gives lectures throughout Europe and the US.

By Rita Carter

Mapping the Mind
Consciousness
The People You Are

The People You Are

Rita Carter

ABACUS

First published in Great Britain in 2008 as *Multiplicity* by Little, Brown
Reprinted 2008, 2010, 2011
This paperback edition published in 2014 by Abacus

A CIP catalogue record for this book
is available from the British Library.

ISBN 978-0-349-13996-8

Typeset in Minion by M Rules
Printed and bound in Great Britain by Clays Ltd, St Ives plc

Papers used by Abacus are from well-managed forests
and other responsible sources.

MIX
Paper from
responsible sources
FSC® C104740

Abacus
An imprint of
Little, Brown Book Group
100 Victoria Embankment
London EC4Y 0DY

An Hachette UK Company
www.hachette.co.uk

www.littlebrown.co.uk

For RH, with thanks from all of us

Contents

Priests, possession and Mesmer's plural pianist ▪ Pierre
Janet and the vanishing furniture ▪ Multiple Personality
Disorder – the first wave ▪ Ego-states and hidden
observers ▪ Modern MPD – a manufactured madness? ▪
Looking inside the multiple brain ▪ So what is a
personality, anyway?

Majors, minors and micros ▪ The big 'I am' – developing the
sense of self ▪ The children in the child ▪ How situations
create personalities ▪ Searching for the essential self ▪ The
trouble with personality tests ▪ Sharing the stage

Memory, experience and 'I-memories' ▪ State-dependent
recall ▪ How memories fit together – the brain-wide web ▪ The
brain as building site ▪ Dissociation ▪ Adaptive dissociation ▪

Preface

This book was germinated during a spot of light relief after a heavy dinner. The meal had been a tricky one. It was a formal do that marked the end of a three-day medical conference and I was stuck up the far end of the table next to an eminent ear, nose and throat specialist who had earlier delivered a mind-numbingly technical lecture in an unrelieved monotone. Our conversation (blocked sinuses) had stalled and I was itching to go. Before I had a chance, however, the master of ceremonies announced an after-dinner entertainment.

A nondescript man in a crumpled tuxedo walked into the room and did a few magic tricks. Then he asked us all to stand up. 'Now close your eyes,' he said, 'and put your hand out in front of you. Make it into a fist and imagine it is clutching a bunch of gas-filled balloons.' Pause. 'Think of the balloons pulling upwards,' he continued, 'pulling their strings tight, tugging and struggling to fly away.' Pause. 'Up, they are pulling, up and up and up, dragging your hand towards the sky.' Pause. 'How hard they pull. Feel your hand is being pulled up and your arm is being stretched . . .'

Around this point I opened my eyes to see what was happening. I noticed my own arm had risen a few inches and so had most others. But here and there, dotted among the diners, I saw people whose arms were pointing straight up to the ceiling. Some of them were reaching so high they were standing on tiptoe, their bodies taut and straining, fists clenched, heads thrown back, looking for all the world as though they were about to be borne aloft. To my surprise I saw that the ENT specialist at my side was among them.

One by one the more obviously entranced audience members were brought forward to entertain us. A prim-looking woman did an excellent imitation of Mick Jagger, a knee man relived his sixth birthday party, and a distinguished liver consultant seemed wholly persuaded that he had come out by mistake in his pyjamas. Each one performed like a seasoned comic, including the ENT doctor who became a Martian invader who happened to have landed on a nudist beach. 'Blogdrachnop!' he spluttered, twitching his eyebrows like twin antennae. 'Channy tom der kump? Glup!'

Apart from how funny it was (you had to be there), the thing that really riveted me about this spectacle was the utter transformation of the performers. It seemed for all the world as though the banal patter of the hypnotist had released in each of them a previously hidden personality. In some cases, the difference was so marked that it was almost impossible to believe the two were generated by the same brain.

You have probably seen enough vaudeville hypnotism to know that this happens. But have you ever wondered how? Could it be that we all have an uninhibited entertainer within us, capable of acting out any role that is suggested? If so, where are they lurking when not on show? Do we have to be hypnotised to release them, or might we switch from one to another in other circumstances too? And what about the roles they played? Was the six-year-old birthday boy just a public performance or did the man's feelings match the goggle-eyed excitement displayed on his face? Was the gyrating Mick Jagger impersonator looking out at the world through her own eyes, or with the jaded perception of an aged rock star?

These questions took root in my mind and I knew they would nag away at me until I found some answers. I thought I knew where to start looking. In my 1998 book *Mapping the Mind* I examined some of the brain mechanisms – the laying down of personal memories, for example – that produce our sense of identity. Then, in my subsequent book *Consciousness*, I looked at the weird effects that can occur if these mechanisms cease to work in the normal way. One of them is the breakdown of our usual sense of 'oneness'. Instead of having a single, consistent identity, a person behaves, and may feel, as though they are one personality now, and then another and, perhaps, yet another – each with a separate name, personality and set of personal memories.

The mental state that produces entirely separate personalities, or 'alters', is a seriously dysfunctional condition and it seems at first to be too bizarre to have anything to do with 'normal' people. But, watching those utterly sane and sensible medical folk going through their party pieces at the behest of the hypnotist, it occurred to me that they looked very much like people switching from one alter ego to another. Could the brain-state produced in them by hypnosis be in some way similar, I wondered, to the condition that causes the dramatic mental 'shape-shifting' seen in people with identity disorders?

Then I started thinking about other personality transformations I had seen – switches that occurred in everyday situations rather than in response to hypnotism. There was the boss I once suffered, who ran his department with cold, impersonal efficiency but turned into a lurching, sentimental moron after his end-of-day dose of alcohol. The so-together female colleague who fell into inarticulate giggles whenever a man paid her a compliment. The girlfriend who always ran any show – except in her own home where she turned into a doormat for her vile husband. The devoted family man who turned out to have a twice-a-week gay cruising habit. The shy-as-a-mouse academic who when asked to deliver a quick talk on her area of expertise ended up hogging the microphone for two hours.

And then, of course, there is me: a finicky perfectionist half the time and a reckless ignorer of detail the other half. A party-pooper one week, queen of the night the next. Careful plate-watcher on Wednesday, fridge-emptying gannet come Sunday. Could inconsistencies of character such as these also be seen as a form of mental multiplicity?

With this question in mind I took a fresh look at what recent brain research has revealed about human memory and our sense of personal identity. I found that by thinking of each person as a group rather than as a single, unchanging personality many familiar but previously puzzling things made much more sense. In particular, certain features of our memory system that are generally treated as unrelated phenomena clicked together like pieces of a jigsaw. The way that we can remember some things at some times and not at others, for instance, is entirely understandable if you think of each person as a vessel in which different personalities – each carrying their own 'bag' of memories – come and go. So is the way our behaviour alters in response to different situations and different people. And it removes the mystery of why so many of us display entirely contradictory character traits: introvert and extrovert generous and mean, ambitious and lazy . . .

Then I started to talk to people about their own experience. Were they aware of major shifts of perspective, emotion and attitudes within themselves? Did they ever look back on things they had done and wonder what on earth they had been thinking? Had they observed sudden changes of behaviour and demeanour in others? Had they ever met a friend and found they were talking to a stranger?

As I got better at framing my questions the stories tumbled out. Almost everyone I asked recounted some example of what could be interpreted as personality switching, either in themselves or in others. Those stories form the backbone of this book and I am grateful to all those friends, acquaintances and strangers who shared them with me. Combined with the scientific evidence that is emerging about the way our brains create a sense of identity they have persuaded me that personalities, or selves, do not come one to a person, but are created by that person in as many forms and as great or small a number as is required. Multiplicity of mind is not some strange aberration but the natural state of human being. Furthermore, our ability to shift and change has evolved because it is potentially useful – and today, more than ever, we need to *make* use of it. I hope this book will help you to do that.

One division that is commonly seen in an individual is between a personality that likes to get a good grasp of a subject before trying to apply it, and one that prefers to try a thing in practice first and then go back to see how and why it works. This book is designed to work for both because it is itself divided into a first part that is mainly explanatory and a second part that is practical. You can either read it in the conventional way, from start to finish, or begin with Part II and come back to the first part later.

In Part I the first chapter starts by charting the curious history of multiplicity, from its roots in superstition, through the discovery of hypnosis, to modern-day brain-imaging. Chapter Two describes the shifting 'inner landscape' of mind on which our personalities are built. It explains why conventional personality tests fail to capture the full complexity of human beings, and why the search for an 'essential' or 'authentic' self is doomed to failure.

Chapter Three explains the mechanism by which personalities are created in our brains, and how and why some live a separate existence from their neighbours. Chapter Four explains why multiplicity is becoming more visible, its potential benefits, and likely problems. Finally, Chapter Five introduces the main types of personality: anxious parents, frightened children, stereotypes, rebels and shadows.

Part II is practical. It shows you how to identify and get to know the members of your own 'inner family' and to see how their different skills, knowledge and ways of looking at the world can be used to the advantage of you all. For those who read this part first I have provided back references to various explanatory passages in Part I in order to prevent repetition.

It includes a new tool, the Personality Wheel, which I have designed to give you a graphic representation of your various personalities and to show, at a glance, how they interact and contrast with one another. Finally, there are a number of exercises that will help to get your personalities communicating with one another, and, I hope, encourage them to work together as a team. My hope is that by showing you how to tease apart the different people you are, you will be in a better position to get your act together in a world where, increasingly, people feel they are falling apart.

Introduction

Hi there! Thanks so much for looking in!

Yeah, hi. Have a nice read.

Book covers are all so attractive aren't they? You just can't tell if they're any good without looking inside!

Sure. Dog-earing the pages ... leaving finger marks on the jacket ...

How about I tell you a bit about what we're doing in here?

Must you use that breakfast-newsreader-on-speed voice? It grates.

Shut up. I'm trying to draw this person in.

(Mimics) 'Hi there!!!! Book covers are all so attractive aren't they ...'

People like a bit of warmth.

They probably find your hysterical ingratiation as nauseating as I do.

(Fading ...) You always stop me when I get enthusiastic.

Just as well or you'd rabbit away for ever.

Hey! There's someone *reading* this!

Sorry about that, and thanks for staying. The exchange above is, I'm afraid, fairly typical of the sort of thing that goes on in my head and it is unlikely that yours will be quite like it. The experience of internal conflict is probably familiar though, because most people talk to themselves,[1] and the conversation often takes the form of argument. You may experience it just as a vague murmur in the back of your mind, or it might be a deafening cacophony of conflicting thoughts, belief and feelings. A lot of people hear the words spoken aloud. This was once assumed to signify madness, but attitudes towards it have changed dramatically in the past few years and it's now known that many voice-hearers simply have an interesting glitch in their auditory cortex which causes thoughts to manifest as external speech.[2]

My own family of voices are not audible and I have never doubted that they are products of my brain. They are nevertheless distinct, individual, and often unpredictable, each one chipping in with its own opinions and ideas. Usually the conversations are small-change squabbles: '*Go on, buy those heels – they're sooo cool!*' pipes up some remnant of a teenager as we pass a shoe shop. '**Call that footwear?**' growls another one of me. '**Anyone wearing those deserves to break an ankle.**' Such internal disputes have occasionally reduced me to dithering indecision about things I would have preferred to be single minded about. 'Look! – *a little country cottage with a For Sale board! You could have hens!*' '**Sure, and mice. And no espresso for forty miles.**' '*But look at the roses!*' '**And the mud.**' . . . and so on . . . and on . . . until the moment for action is long passed.

The undermining potential of internal conflict is obvious and this book is in part aimed at helping you to get it under control. But it is also designed to help you nurture and benefit from what – for reasons I will explain – I am calling multiple selves.

Certainly I benefit from my own. There are times when some long-slumbering entity leaps in to my mental arena like the arrival of Superman. For example, struggling, once, to order a particular confection in a Parisian bakery, a voice I did not know was in me interrupted my gauche gesticulations with a confident request for *un choix de viennoisserie*, then threw in a comment about the weather in fluent French just for fun. Where did it come from? If you asked me now, or, indeed, minutes before that incident I would tell you I do not speak French. My schoolgirl vocabulary deserted me years ago. Yet there it was! On demand! Similarly, when I have been distracted my hand has been known to doodle shockingly accurate caricatures even though 'I' can't draw. Most startlingly, the shy mouse who has been known to sit silently in an English minicab while knowingly being driven forty miles in the wrong direction is visibly identical to the woman who, incumbent in a New York taxi, barks directions at the driver at every intersection. The origins of this tough cookie remain obscure; I just know she takes over the moment I set foot on American soil. To her I owe memories of Manhattan which – left to my English self – would never have been made.

Have you finished talking about yourself? You are meant to be explaining about this new edition.

Yes, thank you (even one's less kindly voices are sometimes useful). This is indeed the second edition of this book. It was first published as *Multiplicity: The New Science of Personality*, and the ideas in it emerged from my previous studies of human memory and consciousness.

Increasingly these phenomena are being shown to be fragmentary, intermittent and many-stranded, and I argue in this book that the 'self' reflects this; we are not consistent and singular individuals but a cluster of personalities, each with different strengths and weaknesses. Rather than striving for integration, however, I believe it is more useful for us to identify and get to know our inner families, listen to their voices, and allow each to do what it does best, for the good of all.

After the publication of the first edition, scores of readers wrote to say that *Multiplicity* had allowed them, some for the first time, to be themselves – many, various, good, bad and complicated – rather than just the one self that had at some time been elected as the 'real' one. Others expressed their relief at finding that they were not alone in having opinions, moods, thoughts and sometimes memories and knowledge which changed along with the ebb and flow of circumstance. A few had worried that the character changes they experienced were a sign of instability or madness. Relieved of that fear they found a freedom for the first time to exercise their personalities to the full. Many people told me that the stories in these pages were almost identical to their own – the description of emotional changes they detected in themselves with different sets of people; the behavioural transformations that occurred when they switched from one language to another, and the double or triple lives they led – not in a bad way, but in a way that allowed them to move easily between differing worlds and enjoy the benefits of each.

You too may discover that you have within you a range of perspectives and skills that until now you have barely used. The exercises in the second half of this book will, I hope, help you to discover them, and put them to use in much the way that you would deploy a multi-skilled workforce.

So I really hope you'll enjoy it, as well as finding it really, really useful . . . and maybe you will find it fun to do the exercises with your friends . . . and then there's the Personality Wheel which is a wonderful way of showing you exactly which personality is which and how they relate to one another . . .

(Sigh)

The People
You Are

PART I

CHAPTER 1

A Brief History of Our Selves

The idea of there being two or more selves in a single body sounds crazy. Look carefully, though, and you will see that the evidence for human plurality is all around us and always has been. We glimpse it wherever people talk to ancestors, divine wisdom from spirit guides, receive messages from personified gods, consult oracles, get 'taken over' by the souls of the dead or tune in to an 'inner helper'. It is on view when we act out a part, take on roles, live up to expectations and reinvent ourselves. More commonly, but less obviously, it shows in day-to-day shifts of feeling and behaviour. When someone says 'I don't know what got into me', or 'I just wasn't myself', they are implicitly acknowledging the existence of a self other than the one who is speaking.

Most of our greatest philosophers, psychologists and therapists have recognised the essential multiplicity of the human mind. In ancient Greece, Plato saw the psyche as a three-part affair consisting of a charioteer (the rational self) and two horses (one the spirit and one the 'appetite'). In the fourth century St Augustine wrote of his 'old pagan self' popping up at night to torment him. Shakespeare's characters endlessly morph from one identity to another. Serious cases have been made to attach the label of Multiple Personality Disorder to Hamlet, Othello, Macbeth and several others.

In the twentieth century, Freud's enduring id, ego and superego model introduced the idea of a horizontal split between the conscious and unconscious mind, and Jung's theory of archetypes held that there are separate, powerful entities within the unconscious. The influential 'object-relations' school of psychiatry taught that external 'objects' could be internalised and become personalities of a sort, and Transactional Analysis, developed in the 1950s by Eric Berne, was based on the concept of three inner beings: child, adult and parent.

The idea that each of us is made up of often conflicting multiple personalities was stated most clearly, perhaps, by the Italian psychologist Roberto Assagioli who founded a form of therapy called Psychosynthesis. 'We are not unified,' he wrote. 'We often feel we are because we do not have many bodies and many limbs, and because one hand doesn't usually hit the other. But, metaphorically, that is exactly what does happen within us. Several subpersonalities are continually scuffling: impulses, desires, principles, aspirations are engaged in an unceasing struggle.'

Twenty years later American psychologist John 'Jack' Watkins and his wife Helen pioneered 'ego-state therapy', which envisages our personalities as a 'family of self', and uses hypnotic techniques to bring them out. Around the same time California psychologists Drs Hal and Sidra Stone started to develop a therapeutic system called 'Voice Dialogue', between inner personalities.*

In parallel with this, neuroscientific investigation strongly suggests that there is no 'essential self' to be found in the human brain. The more we learn about the workings of that amazing organ the more we see that each of us is just a bundle of learned and/or biologically programmed responses that click in as and when the situation demands. As Robert Ornstein, Professor of Human Biology at Stanford University, put it: 'The mind contains a changeable conglomeration of "small minds" . . . fixed reactions, talents, flexible thinking . . . and these different entities are wheeled into consciousness and then usually discarded, returned to their place, after use.'[1] Since he wrote that, imaging technology has made it possible to watch this kaleidoscopic brain activity on a computer

---

*Ego-state therapy, Pychosynthesis and Voice Dialogue are all still going strong, and details of how to track down therapists trained in these disciplines can be found at the back of this book.

screen. Brain scans of extreme multiple personalities have even shown the neurons associated with one personality turn off, like an electric light, and another lot turn on, as a person changes in demeanour, behaviour and in what they can remember. Even in the dry prose of scientific reporting the researchers speak of different 'selves' within a single brain.[2]

Despite all this, personality shifting is still seen as something weird and spooky – a manifestation of spiritual possession rather than a natural physiological phenomenon. Even the language of possession persists. Describing the process of composing, for example, songwriter David Gray says: 'You start off by tinkering around with a few sounds and having a really good time. But when you get deeper into it and your demands get greater and more ambitious something rears its ugly head. You become possessed.'[3]

Yet multiplicity has a long history of scientific investigation, albeit much of it entangled with superstition.

Priests, possession and Mesmer's plural pianist

In the latter part of the eighteenth century cases of possession were generally dealt with by exorcism. One of the most celebrated exorcists of the day was a Catholic priest called Father Johann Gassner, who practised in Switzerland. His technique involved swinging a metal crucifix in front of his subjects while chanting ritual incantations.

While Father Gassner became famous for his victories over demons another flamboyant character, an Austrian physician called Franz Anton Mesmer, was struggling towards a natural (rather than supernatural) explanation for the healing powers of person-to-person interaction. At that time there was much interest (as there is today) in mysterious 'forces' and 'fluids' and 'energies'. And (again, as today) it was often difficult to distinguish between superstitious nonsense and the cutting-edge of scientific discovery.

Mesmer believed he had discovered 'animal gravitation' (later 'animal magnetism') – a mysterious life-giving substance or energy that flowed through countless channels in the body and could be influenced by magnets. Illness, according to Mesmer's theory, was caused by blockages of the flow, and these could be released by 'crises' – acute attacks of whatever the ailment might be. A person with asthma, for example, might be cured in the course of a severe asthma attack, while someone with epilepsy might be cured during a seizure.

Mesmer believed the magnetic flow joined everyone together in an invisible force field, and that physicians could therefore help restore their patients' health by using the harmonising influence of their own magnetic flow. One way to bring this about was for the physician to make 'passes' – sweeps of the arm over the patient's body – to induce a healing crisis and rebalance the patient's energy.

Animal magnetism was widely regarded as a scientific breakthrough, and Mesmer's treatment was reputed to have remarkable effects. Wrong though it turned out to be, the theory behind it was at least rational, given the biological knowledge of the time. And it chimed happily with the mood of enlightenment that was sweeping Europe.

Meanwhile, for the same social climatic reasons, Father Gassner and his theatrical exorcisms were coming under critical scrutiny. In 1775 Mesmer was asked to observe Gassner at work and give his opinion to the Munich Academy of Sciences. Mesmer noted the rhythmic swinging of Gassner's crucifix, and presumably saw some parallel with his own 'passes'. He concluded that Gassner's often dramatic healing effects on the possessed were brought about by the priest's powerful animal magnetism and his deployment of the metal crucifix. Although Mesmer observed that he thought Father Gassner was entirely sincere in his beliefs, his report more or less finished off the priest's career.

Mesmer's own practice, by contrast, flourished. His theory became increasingly sophisticated and over the years he invented elaborate paraphernalia to aid healing sessions. One of his techniques, for example, was to seat patients around a vat of dilute sulphuric acid and then get them to hold hands while the healing force – facilitated, somehow, by the acid – passed through them. The set-up was similar to a séance – more similar, in fact, than Mesmer knew because with hindsight it is clear that, as with spiritual mediums, most of his success was due to the power of trance, suggestion and belief.

A couple of years after bringing Johann Gassner's career to an end Mesmer met someone who unwittingly triggered a crisis in his own life. Maria-Theresa von Paradies was an eighteen-year-old pianist, singer and composer who had been born into elevated social circles in Europe and became a favourite of the Austro–Hungarian Empress. Maria-Theresa had been blind since infancy, but, despite the attentions of Europe's leading eye specialists, no cause or cure for her condition had been found.

In Mesmer's care, Maria-Theresa regained her sight. However, with the cure came a disaster: she completely lost her ability to compose and play music. Not only was this a tragic loss of talent; for her parents it meant a disastrous loss of money, because Maria-Theresa received a generous artistic scholarship from the Empress. Much to the girl's distress, her parents took her away from Mesmer, upon which her blindness promptly returned.

Mesmer's reputation never fully recovered after this episode and, although he made a number of high-profile comebacks, by the time of his death in 1815 he had been practically forgotten by the outside world.

Mesmerism did not die with its inventor, though. It continued to flourish in different guises, and eventually, stripped of its cosmic fluid, it laid the foundations of modern hypnosis. Although Mesmer himself did not realise it, his 'passes' and trance-inducing healing sessions were the means of accessing and manipulating brain-states that were not usually conscious. By hypnotising Maria-Theresa he had 'turned on' a personality that could see, but 'turned off' the pianist. In at least one crucial way the two states were different personalities.

The term 'hypnosis' comes from the Greek *hypnos*, meaning sleep. It was coined by a Scottish physician, James Braid, in the 1840s. He chose it because he thought at first that 'Mesmerised' subjects were asleep. Later, though, when more familiar with the state, he concluded it came about from extreme narrowing of attention and tried to rename it as 'monoideism'. This, as we will see, is a pretty accurate description of what happens, but by the time Braid came up with it the technique was being used under the name of hypnosis by hundreds of physicians as well as a growing number of entertainers and quacks. It was too late to change, and to this day we are stuck with the rather misleading notion of hypnosis as a form of slumber.

Pierre Janet and the vanishing furniture

Hypnotic techniques were refined throughout the nineteenth century and various verbal inductions ('Look into my eyes', etc.) came to be used in addition to the sort of rhythmic movements that Mesmer had stumbled upon. Most practitioners, though, had no real idea of what was happening in the hypnotic state. Braid was on the right track when he proposed that hypnosis altered attention. But it was a French physician – Pierre Janet – who realised that in some circumstances it could effectively switch off one personality and switch on another.

Janet theorised that the human brain can generate many different ways of seeing and responding to the world – mind-states that he called 'existences'. Only one existence is generally conscious at any time and a person might therefore be entirely unaware of the existences within themselves that are not currently conscious. In a hypnotic trance, however, a person can be easily induced to switch their attention from one to another, and in doing so, bring the second existence into consciousness and put the other out of it.

Janet's theory emerged from hundreds of experiments in which hypnotised subjects underwent extraordinary transformations. Entranced volunteers would be told by him, for example, that when they opened their eyes, they would not see any furniture in the room. The subject would then come round, be asked if they saw any furniture, and dutifully reply that they did not. If asked to walk around the room, however, they would carefully skirt around the table and chairs. When Janet asked why they had taken such an indirect route they would offer some weak explanation or simply say that they did not know. Asked specifically if they did it to avoid the furniture, the subjects would hotly deny such an absurdity.

Janet also discovered that it is not necessary to take a person through a hypnotic ritual in order to access a secondary 'existence'. He developed what he called the 'method of distraction', which involved first engrossing his subject in some fascinating task, or getting them to engage in an intense conversation with a third party and then whispering a command or question in a voice so quiet that the subject would not consciously notice it. The 'second self', however, clearly received the subliminal message, because the subject's body would signal a 'reply' with unconscious movements, such as raising an arm. Janet found that he could even place a pencil in the person's hand and they would write a response, all the while continuing their task or conversation as though entirely oblivious to what their hand was doing.

Janet used the French word *disaggregation* to describe the separation of 'existences'. His explanation was that the human mind consisted of many elements and systems, each of which can combine with others to form complex states. Some of them draw others to them – including certain memories – and so become centres for distinct personalities. These successive 'existences' may interact with external reality and develop further by absorbing and retaining new impressions. They might even develop higher psychological functions such as desires and ambitions, and – crucially – a sense of self, so that when they became conscious they feel (as well as behave) like an autonomous person.[4]

This description of what we would now call multiple personalities cannot be bettered today. The main difference between Janet's ideas and those held by many contemporary psychologists is that Janet recognised multiplicity as a normal, albeit often hidden, state of mind, whereas today it is generally assumed to exist only in people who are ill. The nearest translation, in modern English psychology, of *disaggregation* is 'dissociation' – defined as the separation of mental processes, thoughts, sensations and emotions that are normally experienced as a whole. And this term is usually used – wrongly, I shall argue – to mean a psychiatric disorder.

Severe dissociation can certainly be disturbing and destructive but, as we will see later, it is not in itself abnormal. Rather it is a manifestation of the extraordinary flexibility of the human psyche and is often perfectly healthy or even beneficial. Far from being pathological, the separate 'existences' which it helps to create and maintain can help us cope with the complexity of modern life and exploit the opportunities it offers.

Multiple Personality Disorder – the first wave

Although Mesmer did not, apparently, interpret what he was seeing in Maria-Theresa as the switching from one personality, or 'existence', to another, a pupil of his, the German physician Eberhardt Gmelin, was soon to do so in another patient. In 1791 Gmelin reported the case of a young German woman who regularly transformed into a French aristocrat: '[She] suddenly "exchanged" her own personality for the manners and ways of a French-born lady, imitating her and speaking French perfectly and speaking German as would a Frenchwoman.' These 'French' states repeated themselves. In her French personality, the subject had complete memory for all that she had said and done during her previous French states. As a German, she knew nothing of her French personality. With a motion of his hand, Gmelin was easily able to make her shift from one personality to another.[5]

With that Gmelin kicked off what in recent decades has become the highly contentious history of Multiple Personality Disorder (MPD). Throughout the nineteenth and into the twentieth century there was a steady trickle of reports of dual or multiple 'consciousnesses'. Some of the more sensational ones became known beyond the medical profession; their stories were published in popular magazines or written up by the patients themselves, just like the modern *Three Faces of Eve* and *Sybil*.

There was Mary Reynolds, who alternated between being 'buoyant, witty, fond of company and a lover of nature' and 'melancholy, shy and given to solitary religious devotions', and Felida X whose three different personalities each had their own illnesses. One of them even had her own pregnancy, unknown, at first, to the others.

Then there was the most famous of all, the pseudonymous Christine Beauchamp, whose numerous different personalities would, according to her therapist, 'come and go in kaleidoscopic succession, many changes often being made in the course of twenty-four hours'.[6]

In 1906, Harvard Medical School hosted an international conference on MPD, but this, it turned out, marked the high point of the first surge of interest in the condition. Over the next thirty years interest died away, perhaps because MPD was eclipsed by the new fashions of 'hysteria' and 'neurosis'. In 1943 one eminent psychiatrist declared that MPD was 'extinct'.

The announcement, however, turned out to be premature. A second wave of MPD was to erupt in the late seventies, and would turn out to be far more controversial than the first. In the meantime, though, the idea of multiplicity went seriously out of fashion.

Ego-states and hidden observers

Therapeutic hypnosis fell out of favour, too, but a few academics and practitioners continued to research and apply it. One of these was Professor Ernest Hilgard, a psychologist at Stanford University. By 1975 Hilgard had already pioneered the use of hypnosis in pain relief, and as part of his teaching, he routinely demonstrated to his psychology students how to induce hypnotic dissociation. One such session led to the discovery of a phenomenon he called The Hidden Observer.

Hilgard did a conventional hypnotic 'induction' on one of his students, lulling him by suggestion into a state of relaxation and compliance. He then told him that, on feeling a touch on his shoulder, he would become unable to hear anything. Another touch would bring his hearing back to normal. Sure enough, after the first touch, the student ceased to respond to questions or remarks and he didn't jump when two blocks of wood were banged together right next to his ear. Hilgard explained to the other students that the subject was, effectively, deaf. Yet his ears are fine, objected one of them. The sounds must be getting into this brain so at some level he *must* be hearing.

Hilgard decided to test this idea. He spoke quietly to the hypnotised student, observing that there are many systems at work in the brain – those governing digestion and blood pressure, for instance – which respond to the environment but of which we have no conscious knowledge. Perhaps, he suggested, there was such a system at work in the student now, processing sounds, but not offering them to his conscious mind. Then he asked: If there is a part of you which is hearing and understanding these words, please would it raise a finger?

When, after a few seconds, the subject's index finger lifted, it came as a surprise to everyone – including, it seemed later, the subject himself. Hilgard restored the student's normal hearing by touching him again on the shoulder. The lecturer then asked his subject to describe what he had been aware of from the time of his induction into hypnosis.

The student had little to report: he hadn't been able to hear anything from the time of the induction until now, he said, and the session had thus been rather boring. To keep himself occupied he had been working on a mathematical problem. Then, he said, he felt his finger lift. He had no idea why. Fascinated by this turn of events, Hilgard put the subject back in a trance and suggested to him that there were two 'parts' within him, one of which had heard everything that went on in the prior session, while the other part was deaf. Hilgard said that he would touch the student's arm in a particular way, and that would be the signal for the hearing part to talk to him. A second touch would signal the return of the part that had been deaf.

At the pre-arranged signal the student duly described things he had heard in the previous session. The instructor's voice, the students' remarks, the banging of the blocks – it had all been perfectly clear. 'This part of me responded,' he said, 'so it's all clear now.' At the second touch, however, he told the same story as before: he had not heard a sound.

Hilgard discovered that such a Hidden Observer could be created under hypnosis in almost anyone. He subsequently used the phenomenon to enable people who were unable to tolerate anaesthesia to undergo surgery. Before the operations he would hypnotise them and tell them they would not feel the knife, but that a Hidden Observer would feel it for them. After the operation they duly said they had felt nothing. But when Hilgard put them back into hypnosis and addressed the Hidden Observer directly it spoke freely of the excruciating pain that it had suffered.

Around the same time Jack Watkins – one of the few therapists who had continued to work on MPD through the middle part of the century –

discovered that under hypnosis alters could be brought out in people who had displayed no obvious signs of them in their normal waking state. In the early 1970s Watkins met his wife Helen, another hypnotherapist, who was then working with disturbed college students. Helen, too, noticed that under hypnosis her clients would quite often reveal different personalities. She found that these covert ego-states, as they called them, were often responsible, in one way or another, for the students' problems and that the best way to deal with them was to treat them as separate entities. As Helen describes them: 'Ego-states may be large and include all the various behaviours and experiences activated in one's occupation. They may be small, like the behaviours and feelings elicited in school at the age of six. They may represent current modes of behaviour and experiences or, as with hypnotic regression, include many memories, postures, feelings, etc., that were apparently learned at an earlier age.'

The Watkinses recognised that ego-states were similar in content to Hilgard's hidden observers and also to the alters found in their MPD patients. In one study, wrote Helen: 'when Hilgard's "hidden observers" were activated in normal college students as hypnotic subjects, further inquiry into their nature and content elicited organized ego-states. We . . . consider that hidden observers and ego-states are the same class of phenomena. They represent cognitive structural systems that are covert, but are organized segments of personality, often similar in content to true, overt multiple personalities.'[7]

The Watkinses, however, noted a clear distinction between the ego-states found in normal people and the alters in their MPD patients. Ego-states did not 'take over' their hosts entirely because, as the Watkinses put it, the boundaries between them were permeable. Instead of being entirely cut off from each other, they shared memories and acknowledged each other's existence.

Modern MPD – a manufactured madness?

In the late 1970s and 80s, MPD made an explosive comeback. By then known more widely as Dissociative Identity Disorder (DID), the term which replaced Multiple Personality Disorder in the US *Diagnostic and Statistical Manual* (which lists psychiatric conditions and their symptoms).*

Between 1985 and 1995 some forty thousand cases are estimated to have been diagnosed – twice as many as in the entire preceding century. Some therapists claimed the disorder affected at least one per cent of the population.[8] The apparent discovery of thousands – maybe millions – of MPD/DID cases was fantastically controversial because the condition was by then closely associated with cruelty in childhood and particularly with sexual abuse. The implication of such an epidemic was that child abuse was far more pervasive than anyone had dreamed. Either that, or an awful lot of people were lying, deluded or both. The atmosphere surrounding the issue became so heated that more or less everyone concerned was forced to take a stand in one of two opposing camps.

Sceptics claimed (and many still do) that MPD/DID is a bogus condition created by a collusion (usually unwitting) between unhappy 'patients' and over-zealous therapists. The patients – encouraged by a climate in which self-revelation and victimhood is a matter of pride rather than shame – look for a framework in which to express some vague psychic discontent. Therapists see in such people the exciting possibility of a (relatively) rare and strange condition and, often without realising what they are doing, encourage them to act out being various other personalities. They then induce these manufactured entities to fabricate stories of childhood abuse which are presented as 'recovered' memories.

The opposing theory is that children who are repeatedly abused learn to 'go away' in their heads when the situation becomes intolerable. Their brains continue to respond to what is happening but the experience is not integrated with the personal memories that contribute to the child's

---

*The name-change in the US coincided with a slight change in the diagnostic criteria, but it is thought to have been made mainly to allay criticism from sceptics who thought 'MPD' gave the condition too much credence. 'DID' suggests identity confusion, rather than any genuine separation, so patients were henceforth treated for the delusion of multiplicity rather than for the condition itself. The other major psychiatric handbook, however, *The International Classification of Diseases*, which is widely used outside the US, still refers to MPD. In this book I will usually use the term Multiple Personality Disorder (MPD) rather than DID.

major identity. Instead it is stored in the brain as a separate little package of bad feelings and horrible memories. These remain unconscious until another traumatic episode triggers them into life. Each time the nasty memories are revived they collect more experiences, so repeated 'outings' gradually turns the package of trauma-related responses into a complex entity with a distinct personality. It might give itself a name and develop its own opinions and ambitions. Such personalities usually remain rather two-dimensional and childlike because while they are unconscious they are not (usually) privy to what is happening, and thus tend not to learn much beyond their small, traumatic world.

So which is right? The answer, I think, is that it is not an either/or situation. There is certainly persuasive evidence to show that memories of childhood abuse 'recovered' from apparently traumatised alters can be false.[9] But the reality, or otherwise, of the events that are recounted by a personality have no bearing on whether the personality itself is 'real'. Remembering things wrongly, or lying about past events does not mean a personality doesn't exist – it just means it has got things wrong or is lying!

As for the charge that personality switching is 'just acting', the problem is that there is no sharp division between 'being' a character and acting it. Of course, it is possible to affect a role – deliberately acting and speaking in a way that is quite at odds with your inner thoughts and feelings. Equally, though, if you are totally immersed in a part your thoughts, perceptions and feelings *become* those of that character. In this state your behaviour is an honest reflection of your inner self, and as I'll explain in a moment it therefore seems reasonable to describe it as the adoption of a different identity rather than an act.

Until recently there was no objective way of knowing whether a change in someone's behaviour corresponded to an alteration in their subjective identity. The only way to assess whether someone with MPD was acting was to look at their behaviour and guess. But that is no longer the case. Brain-imaging technology has made it possible to see inside a person's head and observe the neural machinations that produce sensations, thoughts and feelings. The generation of their inner life can be displayed on a screen for all to see.

Brain-imaging shows what is going on in a person's mind by signalling which parts of the brain are active. When one part flares up a person feels angry and another creates fear. Hunger is produced by one lot of neurons, lust by another. A true statement is marked by a different pattern of activity from a lie. You can even see, by looking at a scan of a person's brain, whether they are looking at a face, or a cat, or a house.[10]

When the inner workings of MPD patients' brains are displayed what we see is a pattern that suggests very strongly that alters are not just acts. As one set of behaviours disappears and another takes its place the neuronal patterns in their brain change in tandem with the altered demeanour. The brain scans even suggest that different memories are available to each personality.

One study, for example, involved eleven women, each of whom seemed to have two distinct states of being. In one state they claimed to recall some kind of childhood trauma while in the other they denied any such memory. The women's brains were monitored while they listened to tape recordings of someone reading out some of their own previously related recollections. One of the recordings described the traumatic memory. When the women were in their 'non-traumatised' personality the parts of their brains which would be expected to respond to a personal anecdote remained quiet. In other words, they registered the information as though it was something that had happened to someone else. When they switched to the other personality, however, the trauma story stirred a flurry of activity in the brain areas associated with a sense of self. Instead of just registering what they were hearing, they *identified* with it, remembering the story rather than just recognising it. Just as the women's behaviour suggested, their two personalities had different autobiographies.[11]

Another imaging study was done on a forty-seven-year-old woman who could switch from one personality to another more or less on cue. During the transition from one to the other the part of the brain that processes memories momentarily closed down, as though it was shutting off one 'bag' of memories while switching to another.[12] A third study of personality-switchers found that their brainwave coherence – a measure of which neurons are firing in synchrony – was completely different in each of their personalities. This suggests that the subjects were thinking and feeling quite differently in each state.[13] No such changes were seen in actors trying to mimic the condition, nor in the subjects themselves when they were asked to act out a change of identity. Taken together these studies suggest that alters do not just behave differently – their brains think, feel and recollect things differently too.

Most people now being diagnosed with MPD have a number of alters, rather than just one, which are combined in what is conventionally called a 'system'. There are endless variations: some make angry, aggressive alters to protect the children, or friends to alleviate the loneliness, or torturers who mimic the abusers. Some people have only child alters, but others go on making new personalities, which may be any age. Most MPD systems contain at least one member of the opposite sex. Some include animals.

Usually at least one member in a system is in some way disruptive, and the behaviour of alters – promiscuity, self-harm, addiction, aggression, phobias – is often what first brings people with MPD to the attention of a therapist. However, the crucial thing about the disorder, which distinguishes it from normal multiplicity, is not the nature and behaviour of the alters but the fact that they do not share a common memory. Although some personalities may share information there is always a communication 'gap' in an MPD system. The normal 'household', as multiple systems are sometimes called, is open-plan, while in people with MPD at least some of the personalities live in watertight compartments.

One reason for the spectacular rise in MPD diagnoses in the 1980s and 90s is that the Watkinses' careful distinction between alters and ego-states was often ignored: 'Too many practitioners today are hypnotically activating covert ego-states and announcing that they have discovered another multiple personality,' lamented Helen Watkins in 1993. For every true case of MPD that was diagnosed there were probably many whose normal multiplicity was uncovered by hypnosis and mislabelled.

This book is not for or about people with MPD – it is about the normal multiplicity which is common to us all. But understanding a little about that extreme form of multiplicity may help us to understand our own selves because, although the behaviour of people with this condition seems bizarre they are probably not as different from the rest of us as we like to believe.

The strangeness of MPD arises from a mistaken assumption: that we start with a single, whole personality. MPD is thus assumed to be the result of this single personality being 'smashed'. As I hope to show you, though, personalities do not come ready-plumbed in every baby, one to each body. An infant comes equipped with many built-in drives and individual genetic leanings but its personalities still have to be constructed from the building blocks of experience. You might think of a newborn's mind as a building site with a unique form – dips and hillocks, obstacles and pitfalls, soft spots and rocky areas. These influence and constrain what is erected on it, but they do not dictate it.

So what is a personality, anyway?

Before we go further, it is probably a good idea to clarify what I mean when I refer to personality. We don't usually stop to ask what someone is talking about when they use the word because it seems obvious. Yet there is no single accepted definition of it in psychology, and dictionaries are not particularly helpful. Mine gives several definitions. The main one is 'the sum of a person's mental and behavioural characteristics by which they are recognised as being unique', while another is 'the distinctive character of a person that makes them attractive'.[14] Obviously these are quite different things. Your dictionary may say something else again.

If we were to accept the definition of personality as 'the sum' of a person's characteristics it would, of course, rule out the possibility of them having more than one. But it would also make the word meaningless – just another term for a 'person'. And a moment's thought will show that we don't really think of personality that way. If we did, phrases such as 'that remark was out of character' and 'she was a different woman after her illness' would be incomprehensible.

So I am using personality to mean something which I think is closer to the way the word is actually used. A short definition might be: *a coherent and characteristic way of seeing, thinking, feeling, and behaving.*

The crucial word is 'characteristic'. By my definition a personality has a certain style or pattern to it – something that binds the thoughts, feelings and acts into a distinctive 'set' which is consistent enough to allow us to say about any part of it, 'Oh! that's typical of Linda!' or 'That sounds like me!'

A personality might, for example, have a whole bunch of ideas and behaviours that could be thought of as personal ambition. It might be determined to be the best at its job, the winner of every competition, the most competent sportsperson, the top salesman. It might like to travel fast, in straight lines, get angry with people who get in its way, forget to take time off, and try to bully its children to be more like itself. The personality may not do all these things (God forbid!) but it *could*, because they are not in conflict with one another. Another personality might believe that personal success is really not important at all. It might drift happily along in a non-demanding job, meander along country lanes rather than drive ferociously along motorways and allow its children to do exactly what they like. Although it is unlikely, both these personalities could exist in the same person. However, there would have to be some separation between them simply because the brain-states which generate rampant ambition and those that produce worry-free relaxation are too different from each other to occur at the same time. For the person to function normally, without perpetual inner conflict, her two personalities would have to take turns at being 'on stage'. When one was active the other would have to be unconscious.

Either/or brain-states operate at every level of cognition, from complex thoughts and behaviours to simple visual perceptions. If two experiences are entirely at odds with one another, the brain has to choose to be conscious of one or other, and the best it can do by way of entertaining both is to switch rapidly between them. The simplest example of this is a thing called the Necker cube (below).

The box is drawn in such a way that the front panel could either be to your left and angled down, or to your right and up – both interpretations are equally 'correct'. Even when you know that, though, your brain will only allow you to see one at a time . . . it just can't 'do' both patterns simultaneously. You probably know of other visual illusions that work in much the same way: the shapes which switch between being twin profiles and a vase, or the drawing that looks like a pretty girl when it is seen one way and an old hag the other.

This inability to see things in two ways simultaneously occurs throughout the brain, including areas concerned with thoughts and emotions. When we are listening intently to one conversation, the areas of brain concerned with attending to, and processing information from that source effectively turn down the volume of any other noise in the room. That is why people in conversation often fail to notice background music that would seem quite loud if heard alone, or ignore the call to dinner when they are concentrating on a TV programme. Similarly, with emotions the fear-generating areas of the brain are inhibited when the parts that create serenity are active, and the sadness part is quietened when the parts that create pleasure are triggered.

The see-saw effect is not absolutely cut and dried, of course; at times we are all aware of mixed emotions and conflicting thoughts. But when our conflicting beliefs, desires or urges become conscious simultaneously we have to take a conscious decision to act on one or the other. We have to decide between 'I want to smoke' and 'I don't want to die of cancer', 'I want to stay up and party' and 'I want a decent night's sleep'. At least at the level of behaviour we cannot 'be' more than one personality at a time. We have to switch from one to another.

Some people (though very few) go through life without ever confronting the lifestyle equivalent of a Necker cube. The situations they encounter offer them no choice of response – there is only one way to interpret them, one way to react, one way to be. Or they may meet situations that offer options and simply fail to see them. These people do not harbour other 'existences', they really are what they feel themselves to be – single and 'whole' personalities.

Most of us, though, do not find life to be like this. We endlessly encounter situations that can be seen and responded to in myriad different ways. For most of us the options presented to us are increasing – life is getting more, not less, complicated. Hence we switch from one way of seeing things to another, one way of being to another. And as we do it we accumulate an inner family of selves – Janet's 'existences' – which take turns to 'be' the self of the moment.

Rest assured, though – we are not talking Jekyll and Hyde. Although our personalities are, by definition, distinguishable from one another, in most of us they are more like conjoined twins than entirely separate individuals. Just being subjected to the same sensory stimuli blurs the dividing line between them. Their co-existence in the same body means they necessarily share so much that it may be difficult to spot exactly where one starts and another ends.

For this reason personality switches may easily be overlooked. The only giveaway may be a slight change of voice, the use of a slightly different vocabulary, or perhaps a subtle alteration in the way a person stands or laughs. For example, the wife of a Church of England vicar once told me: 'When Gerry is with our friends he is a full six feet tall. But when he puts on his dog collar he shrinks half an inch. The vicar in him feels embarrassed about looking down on people so he somehow becomes compressed. He laughed at me when I pointed it out and said it's nonsense – but one day I'm going to find a way of measuring him and I know I'll be right!'

Like Gerry, it is tempting to scoff at the suggestion that we shift from personality to personality. From inside it just doesn't feel like that – most of us have a strong and enduring sense of being a single, more or less unchanging entity: the 'I' I am now is the same 'I' I will be tomorrow. If you look carefully at human behaviour, however, you find this sense of certainly is misplaced. The next chapter examines the shifting and sometimes blurred landscape of our personalities, and shows how our fond notion of inner stability, consistency and unity has been shown, time and again, to be a myth.

CHAPTER 2

The Landscape of Mind

One of the flight paths taken by aircraft heading from London to North America carries you first up the spine of Britain, then in a north-westerly arc over the Highlands and islands of Scotland. On a clear day you can look down and see the landscape spread out beneath you like a full-colour, three-dimensional atlas.

During the first part of the journey England spreads out like a gently undulating quilt, all of a piece until it is punctuated by velvety hills marking the beginning of the Highlands. These soon give way to mountains and plunging valleys bordering broad seaways as the coastal lochs carve their way into the mainland. Then you are looking down on islands, scattered like pieces of a massive jigsaw puzzle. Some of them are connected to the mainland by causeways, and you may just make out a ferry tramping between others. On the larger islands you can see spreading settlements, industrial chimneys and public buildings. On the smaller ones, scattered roofs tell of a lonelier existence.

If you were to liken your inner landscape to one of those views, which would it be? Do you feel your personality to be 'all of a piece', a consistent, clearly bounded and densely woven fabric of thoughts and emotions? Or are you aware of a more complex geography: a central hub, perhaps, but also outlying areas which others rarely see, and far flung places whose existence is just a rumour, even to you?

Surprisingly little work has been done into the way that we visualise our inner landscape, particularly the extent to which we think of ourselves as separate personalities. You only have to listen to people speaking to realise that on one level we know they are there: 'That's the schoolteacher in him coming out' we might say of someone who, uncharacteristically, launches into a lecture. Or 'I was a real tart that night!' But because we do not yet have a well-developed model of healthy multiplicity we tend not to see it even when it stares us in the face.

The English therapist John Rowan, one of a very few psychologists who recognise multiplicity as normal, reckons that most people have four to nine 'subpersonalities', as he calls them. 'More than nine and I begin to suspect that some of them are simply aspects of others, and should be grouped with them,' he says. 'Fewer than four and I begin to wonder if sufficient attention has been paid to the less visible ones.'[1]

Other researchers have looked at the 'self-aspects' or 'self-schemas' that people hold. These are not quite the same as personalities but they are similar. Most of these studies have been done on students.* These suggest that we vary enormously in the degree to which we feel ourselves to be one or many. In one study the volunteers ranged in their reported number of 'selves' from one to twenty, with an average of seven.[2]

Our inner landscape is constantly changing. Various personalities form, change, fade away, reform, merge, shrink and grow. In young people its shape changes rapidly, like clouds blown about on a windy day, but over the years a more settled pattern emerges. Typically, in my observation, it might consist of one, or perhaps two, of what I will call 'major' personalities, plus a handful of 'minor' characters and any number of fragmentary 'micros'.

Majors, minors and micros

A major is a fully fleshed out character with thoughts, desires, intentions, emotions, ambitions and beliefs. Minors are less complex (though often very strong) personalities which 'come out' in particular situations. Micros are the building blocks of personalities – individual responses,

---

*Students are the guinea pigs of social psychology, being numerous, cheap, easy to capture and often normal.

thoughts, ideas, habits. Micros may be as tiny as a physical or vocal tic or a repeated intrusive thought, emotion or desire which stands out in contrast to a person's normal behaviour.

Compatible micros tend to get attached to one another to form minors, which in turn coalesce into majors. Most people retain a smattering of free-floating micros such as the odd verbal tic or some mild and inexplicable phobia.

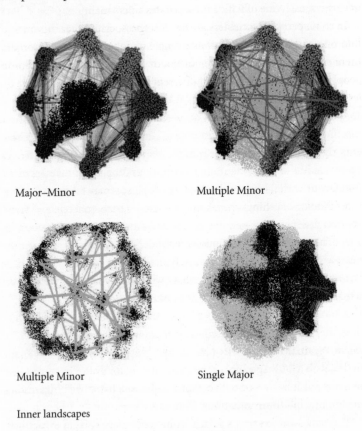

Major–Minor

Multiple Minor

Multiple Minor

Single Major

Inner landscapes

Some people have one major and several minors (top left) while others have varying numbers of minors (top right and bottom left). A few have just one almost wholly integrated major (bottom right).

Personalities cohere as a result of experiences connecting up in the brain, forming a 'web' that holds our memories (this process is explained in detail in Chapter Three). If everything that happened to us was bound tightly together we would develop just one, densely integrated web. But few of us end up like this because another process, dissociation, ensures that dissimilar experiences are only loosely connected, or perhaps not connected at all. Hence the things that happen to us get bound together in clusters, each one of which incorporates a personality.

In some people the clusters are so closely associated that they merge into one and the person exhibits a single major personality. In others there may be one large cluster (a major) and several minors. Some people just have minors – lots of different personalities that are more or less all equally active.

A major is built up from a dense web of experiences that have bound together over a very long period. It may include bits of the person's parents that they absorbed as children, characteristics borrowed from siblings, ideas from the dominant culture and behaviour designed to find favour with friends and colleagues. A person may take in an entire way of looking at things from someone else – a perpetual sense of anxiety from their mother, perhaps, or a friend's quirky sense of humour, or a set of beliefs adopted from the dominant religious dogma. Majors may include a very wide range of characteristics but they cannot contain *conflicting* characteristics. One might be, say, hard-working and extrovert, or hard-working and introvert, but not extrovert *and* introvert.

Minors tend to be more idiosyncratic than majors because, by definition, they have not fitted together with enough others to merge into a major. A minor may consist of just a small clutch of responses – enough to deal with a fairly specific type of event. It may, for example, consist just of a compulsion to argue with certain people, or a habit like binge-eating or smoking in certain situations.

You may need to know a person quite well before you get to see their minors. You may think you know someone very well, then share an unfamiliar situation – a holiday with a work pal, say – and suddenly get a glimpse of a personality you never knew existed. If you only ever see someone in a particular type of situation – when they are in charge, perhaps, or when they are with their partner – you may be familiar with *only* one of their minors, and be surprised to discover that other people, who know them in quite different contexts, seem to know a completely different person.

Minors may be quite complex, or extremely narrow in their focus, and although they may not do much, they may be very distinctive. Some exist to do just one thing – domestic chores, or driving, or looking for things to buy. While they are active much of the world around them is neglected. 'I must have been dreaming,' mutters our major personality when it returns to remove the laundry from the dishwasher or apologise for cutting a friend in the street.

Major personalities are more often in evidence than minors – indeed it is the greater range of experience they accumulate by being 'on stage' most of the time that makes them major. Because a person's major is the one that other people usually see it tends to be regarded, both by itself and by others, as the person's 'real' self.

The big 'I am' – developing the sense of self

With a very few exceptions (which we will come to later) people normally feel as though they are just one. The conviction persists even in those who have quite dramatic personality switches. The recognition that there is more than one self in a single body might be quite obvious to an outside observer, but the subjective illusion of singularity is so strong that each personality invariably claims ignorance of any other.

Hence when we are in our extrovert personality we accept invitations to future parties without a qualm, thinking we are always in the mood for a get-together even if history recounts that we often have to drag ourselves to such events and hate them when we arrive. When we tell the boss to get lost we see ourselves as decisive, strong and brave. We forget that we also contain a frightened, insecure person who needs the money. During periods of elation it seems ridiculous to think that we have it in us to be depressed

Just occasionally, however, our comfortable conviction of unshifting singularity is undermined. It happens when two or more of our personalities become active at the same time. If we don't understand what is going on the feeling may be deeply unsettling, and the active personalities will launch into battle, scuffling to take control of the person's behaviour. Usually this results in a dominant personality shouting down a less strident one, even if the quieter one is talking more sense. And when several personalities come out together their clamour is interpreted as doubt, indecision and confusion.

Most of the time, though, the illusion of singularity remains undisturbed. It is created by a powerful trick of the brain, which ensures (in most of us) that only one personality is fully conscious at any time – rather as only one view of the Necker cube is experienced in any one moment. It is socially useful, for reasons we'll see in Chapter Five, that people believe themselves to be singular, so the illusion is heavily supported by social convention.

The sense of singularity is part of a larger sense of self – a whole bag of cognitive tricks which kick in throughout childhood. The crucial development is the ability of a child to see itself from the outside – an 'object' that can be seen (and judged) by others and that continues through time. She realises, for example, that she continues to exist even while she is asleep, and that the 'me' of the moment – hungry, say – is connected with the person that was not hungry at all three hours ago and the person who will not be hungry in half an hour, after tea. Hence the 'me's of the moment – the hungry me of now, the angry me of yesterday, the sleepy me of later – get strung together in a single, continuous thread.

For many years, however, this thread of self is a fragile creation and any small shift in emotion or attention can break it. Hence when five-year-old Mandy puts on Mum's high-heels and strides down the hallway 'being' a supermodel there is little or no connection in her head with the tomboy Mandy who fought her brother for possession of the rocking horse the day before; or the studious Mandy who spent all morning trying to learn her alphabet.

The children in the child

Children may also fail to recognise their personalities as themselves, seeing them instead as external, autonomous entities, commonly referred to as imaginary companions (ICs). Skippy – the creation of my friend Pat's daughter, Amy – is a fairly typical IC. He arrived suddenly, when Amy was four, complete with a firm set of dietary foibles. Every mealtime for more than a year Pat was coerced into laying a place at the table for Skippy and woe betide her if she served up something he didn't like. Once, when I was there, Pat slithered a token portion of strawberry ice cream on to Skippy's plate. 'Don't give Skippy pink ice cream!' screamed Amy. 'He'll sick it up all over the table!'

Children who create imaginary companions were once assumed to be lonely or socially incompetent. Their invisible playmates were regarded by adults (if they knew about them) as sad substitutes for 'proper' social interaction which were dumped as soon as the child got real friends. This theory no longer stands up, not least because nowadays it is more common for children to report having imaginary companions than not. In the 1930s, about one in nine children admitted to an IC, but by the 1990s it was one in three. Now it is more than two-thirds, and the ICs do not necessarily disappear with age or increasing social engagement. Research by Dr Marjorie Taylor, a psychologist at the University of Oregon, and her colleagues found that having an imaginary companion is at least as common among school-age children as it is among preschoolers.

Imaginary companions described by the children came in a fantastic variety of guises, including invisible boys and girls, a squirrel, a panther, a dog, a seven-inch-tall elephant and a 'hundred-year-old' GI Joe doll. Some children reported having multiple and serial imaginary companions. The number of imaginary companions described by children ranged from one to thirteen different entities.[3]

Not all imaginary companions are friendly – they can be quite uncontrollable and even aggressive. One of their functions may be to act as a vehicle for experimental personalities – minors which the child wants to try out at a safe distance before adopting internally. Having placed them in the IC the child can observe how this or that response goes down in the outside world. Does Skippy get into trouble for not accepting pink ice cream? Is a naughty IC able to get away with it? The child can try out all sorts of social behaviours vicariously, safe in the knowledge that, should the IC do anything disastrous, the child itself is safe from the consequences.

Traditionally ICs are thought of as a thing of childhood – if an adult admitted to one they would probably be viewed with some suspicion. Writers and actors, however, have a special licence to create external minors for others' amusement, and the degree to which the characters appear to break free from their creators is often regarded – probably correctly – as a measure of the artist's talent. Marjorie Taylor's team interviewed fifty fiction writers, ranging from an award-winning novelist to scribblers who had never been published, and found that forty-six had invented characters who had subsequently taken over the job of composing their life stories. Some of them also resisted their creators' attempts to control the narrative. Some fictional folk wandered around in the writers' houses or otherwise inhabited their everyday world. The writers who had published their work had more frequent and detailed reports of these personalities seeming to break free of their creator's control, suggesting that the faculty of projecting personalities into the external world really is a measure of creative expertise.[4]

One common way that children reveal a sense of being multiple is by speaking of 'we' instead of 'I' or referring to themselves in the third person. Adults are usually very quick to 'correct' these errors (as they see them) and the effect of this is to encourage children towards the adult illusion of singularity.

'J' is one of a very small number of adults who does not have a sense of being alone in his body. It may be that he has hung on to a sense of multiplicity which most of us have discarded.

'When I was a kid I thought everyone experienced lots of different people,' he says. 'Then I started to have rows with my mother because she thought I was playing around with her when I told her things like "I can't do that because Jay wouldn't like it" or "Chrissy is crying again".

Eventually my parents packed me off to a therapist and I cottoned on pretty quickly that if I didn't want to get some freaky psychiatric label I should start talking as though I was a single.'

As J discovered, forcing children to use the word 'I' makes it much more difficult for them to sustain their multiple selves: 'When you talk like a singlet you tend to think of yourself as one. I can see how, if you are pressed into acting like an "integrated" person, you could start to think you really are alone in your skin. But the guys in my family [household] never went away, even when I tried to shut them out, and as soon as I was away from home I let them talk freely again.'

Ariel, us, and several other children were working at the art table, making a collage out of buttons glued to construction paper. I was absent-mindedly gluing buttons to the paper, while Ariel seemed to have a pattern to her work. On her paper were red and green buttons, red on the right, green on the left. Each hand seemed to be working independently. Suddenly she let out a howl, tore up her paper and ran to her 'hide out'. I followed her, so I could find out what went wrong.

'I get so mad at him!' (When she said 'him', I assumed it was her 'imaginary' friend Sam.)

'I can see that. Sam made you very angry.'

'I didn't want any green buttons on my side. I just like red,' she said, stamping her foot. And then: 'But I want green! Only green! And *she* never lets me do it.'

I looked at Anise and Jennifer, who are with me when we work with children. I could not believe what I was hearing. 'Well, maybe you can make two pictures, one with red and the other with green,' I suggested, 'and you could help each other out.'

She/they sniffled, and nodded. 'OK.'

– incident in a classroom, reported by a teacher's assistant

Most of us succumb much more easily to the insistence that we are singular. Up to the age of about twelve children's personalities seem to rub along fairly happily together, but as they grow up people come under increasing pressure to settle for being one personality or another. 'What are you going to be when you grow up?' they are asked. 'Which subjects do you want to study?', 'Are you mathematical or artistic?' These questions do not necessarily come from adults. The child's own developing personalities want answers to these things, too, so the pressure comes from inside as much as out.

During adolescence, after several years of relatively smooth operating, the brain undergoes a major rewiring exercise. Many of the changes take place in the frontal lobes, which are responsible for maintaining our conscious sense of self, as well as for rational thought, emotional control and the behavioural constraints we think of as our conscience. They also play an important part in the formation of our notion of what we are like.[5] One effect of this seems to be that personalities that had until then been operating more or less independently start to compete for dominance, and what had been a murmur of different but co-existing viewpoints erupts into a shouting match. This, for example, is how one fairly typical teenager describes herself:

I'm responsible, even studious every now and then, but on the other hand I'm a goof-off too, because if you're too studious, you won't be popular. I don't usually do that well at school. I'm a pretty cheerful person, especially with my friends, where I can even get rowdy. At home I'm more likely to be anxious around my parents. They expect me to get all As . . . I worry about how I probably should get better grades. But I'd be mortified in the eyes of my friends. So I'm usually pretty stressed-out at home, or sarcastic, since my parents are always on my case. But I really don't understand how I can switch so fast. I mean, how can I be cheerful one minute, anxious the next, and then be sarcastic? Which one is the real me?[6]

Construction work continues in the frontal lobes of the brain right up the age of thirty or so. Well before this work is complete, though, most people, if asked, will offer a fairly coherent description of themselves. Instead of the confusion and contradictions admitted by the teenager, the young adult gives a clear and tidy account of their strengths and weaknesses, attitudes and beliefs. The message is clear: this person knows who they are and where they are going.

Close observation of adult behaviour, however, shows that we are not nearly as consistent or well-defined as we like to think. Rather we change, constantly, to suit whatever situation we happen to be in. When a situation calls for us to please or impress, for example, most people obligingly slip into an appropriate personality. The changes are not just outward – mere behavioural concessions to necessity. We change inwardly too.

In an experiment carried out by psychologist Kenneth Gergen students were given what they were told were self-descriptions of people they would be partnering in a project. Half of them were given biographies which spoke of failure, low self-esteem and self-loathing. The other half were given self-assessments that described the author as brilliant, confident and attractive. The students were then asked to give a description of themselves in return.

By far the majority of the students responded with tales of themselves which mirrored the self-assessment of their putative partners. Those who thought they were being partnered by insecure, incompetent people said that they, too, were far from perfect. Those that thought they were being put with someone brilliant, however, found all sorts of positive qualities to report about themselves and very few bad ones.[7]

This in itself is hardly surprising. What is, though, is that the students were not simply presenting, like a gift, the personalities they thought would go down best. They actually seemed to hop into them, abandoning whatever personality was there before and becoming this personality that matched the situation so obligingly. They sincerely believed that they were giving a neutral and honest description of their 'real' personality.

How situations create personalities

The extent to which people will switch personality to match what is required of them was dramatically demonstrated almost half a century ago in a series of extraordinary experiments. First, the maverick psychologist Stanley Milgram horrified the world by showing that a majority of perfectly ordinary, usually benign citizens could be transformed into apparently sadistic torturers just by placing them in a situation where they felt such behaviour was demanded of them by a figure of authority.

Milgram's most famous experiment, which was first published in 1963, involved asking volunteers to give people increasingly severe electric shocks as penalties in a laboratory situation which the volunteers thought was about studying memory and learning. In fact the 'victims' of the shocks were stooges who were just pretending to be in pain, and the study was actually about just how far ordinary people would go in obedience to authority. Milgram was staggered to find that more than 60 per cent of his subjects were prepared to subject their fellow citizens to shocks that would make them scream with pain.

A man we will call 'B', for example, continued to deliver what he thought were electric shocks to another volunteer even after the victim was seen to 'resist strongly and emit cries of agony'. According to the study report, B related to the experimenter in the laboratory coat in a 'submissive and courteous fashion, and did his work with robotic impassivity' even though the 'learner' begged him to stop. At the 330-volt level, B was told the learner was no longer physically capable of answering the questions. Annoyed, B is reported to have said: 'You better answer and get it over with – we can't stay here all night.' This ruthless commander personality then switched to a craven minion as he turned to the white-coated experimenter and asked: 'Where do we go from here, Professor?'

The experiment was repeated in other places and with other groups of subjects, including some selected from particular professions. The results were worst (that is, the highest percentage of testers went all the way to 450 volts) with a group of nurses.[8]

Then, in 1968, the psychologist Walter Mischel published a book which analysed the results of hundreds of studies in which people's character profiles were matched against their actual behaviour in different situations. For example, schoolchildren and students were rated on personality tests for the trait of 'honesty', and then observed in a variety of situations where their honesty was actually put to the test. They were, for example, placed in situations where they could steal money or cheat in an exam, and seem likely to get away with it.

The results showed the character assessments that had been made on the basis of the children's behaviour in one situation did practically nothing to predict how they would behave in another. A child who stole money would not be much more likely to cheat in an exam than one who did not.[9]

Next, in 1971, the Stanford Prison Experiment found that in just six days ordinary students could be turned into monsters by being cast – quite arbitrarily – in the role of 'guard' in a simulated prison situation where their 'prisoners' were fellow students. The study's designer, Professor Philip Zimbardo, recalled: 'My guards repeatedly stripped their prisoners naked, hooded them, chained them, denied them food or bedding privileges, put them into solitary confinement, and made them clean toilet bowls with their bare hands . . . Over time, these amusements took a sexual turn, such as having the prisoners simulate sodomy on each other.'

He concluded: 'Human behaviour is much more under the control of situational forces than most of us recognize or want to acknowledge.'

Milgram agreed: 'The social psychology of this century reveals a major lesson,' he declared. 'It is not so much the kind of person a man is as the kind of situation he finds himself in that determines how he will act.'[10]

The conclusions of the Stanford and Milgram studies have since been validated time and again, including in several real-life situations such as the inhumane behaviour of US soldiers with regard to their captives at Guantánamo Bay. A meta-analysis of twenty-five thousand social psychology studies carried out by researchers at Princeton University concluded that almost everyone is capable of torture and other evil acts if 'cued' by the situation.[11]

Of course, everyone knows that people behave differently in different situations. The conventional view of this, though, is that people are showing different sides of a single self rather than 'being' entirely separate personalities. The distinction may sound rather academic, but it actually signifies a profoundly different view of what we are.

The 'many-sides' view holds that although people may change on the surface, deep down in each of us there is a solid, singular and unchanging 'authentic' self. A visual metaphor of this model would be a cut gem turning slowly in the light. Its angled surfaces sparkle in turn as the light changes, but in the centre there lies an unchanging core.

Multiplicity, on the other hand, recognises that we consist only of our 'faces' – there is no 'real' self lurking behind them. One self may look back on the embarrassing doings of another and bewail them. In some people one personality may even watch another and bewail their actions as they occur. But the bewailer is no more 'authentic' than the bewailed – it is just that in retrospect we *prefer* to identify with one cluster of characteristics than another.

This is not a popular idea. We badly want to think of others, and ourselves, as essentially unchanging beings. Useful and beneficial though it might be, our shiftiness makes us uneasy. Hence we embark on an inevitably hopeless and unending quest for our 'real' selves.

Searching for the essential self

This search for authenticity is one of several misconceptions that lie behind our enduring enthusiasm for astrology. Type 'star signs' into Google and – as I write this – you get more than forty-two million results. By the time you come to read this there will probably be millions more. Presumably the people who visit these sites think they are getting meaningful information. Can so many be wrong?

Actually, yes. Astrology is almost certainly nonsense. Yet it often seems startlingly accurate, because people unconsciously change their ideas of themselves to match what the stars have decreed they are like. So desperate are we to discover a 'real me' that it seems we will willingly identify with any Real Me that is on offer.

Professional sceptic James Randi sometimes demonstrates this by walking into a college classroom posing as an astrologer and casting horoscopes for all the students. He then asks the students to read and then rate each one for accuracy. Invariably, the overwhelming majority give the results a high accuracy rating, claiming they reflect their personalities to a tee. Randi then gets the students to pass the horoscopes around, at which point they discover that every horoscope is exactly the same. Although the wording seems to refer to very definite, individual-sounding characteristics, it is actually so vague that every student can identify with it.

You can do the same experiment for yourself: pluck any astrological 'character reading' from a website or magazine, take off the star sign then offer it to people saying it has been drawn up for them, personally, based on their birth-date. Even people who are sceptical of astrology will invariably express amazement at how much of it seems to be accurate.

The desire to pin down an 'essential' personality also fuels the expanding industry that offers 'scientific' personality testing. Many personality tests are little more use than a zodiac reading. These are the five-minute coffee-break distractions – a selection of patterns to choose from, or a dozen questions to answer, the results of which are obvious. The scientifically sanctioned end of the business, however, is a serious matter. Psychometric testing – which includes personality profiling – is used routinely in almost every branch of industry to help select employees. In the US alone, one estimate of its worth, in terms of people employed and tests sold, is $400 million a year.[12] It is also used by psychiatrists and psychologists to aid medical diagnosis, and by various other agencies who have power to regulate our lives. The result of a personality test could, in theory, determine whether you are fit to fly a passenger plane, give evidence in court, or adopt a child. Given the potential power of personality testing, we might hope it has more to recommend it than astrology. Certainly a few of the personality tests – generally the longest and priciest – are scientific instruments in that they have been tested over many decades and hundreds of thousands of people.

The trouble with personality tests

If there is no such thing as a 'real' you to discover, though, what is it that these tests are revealing? To answer this we need to look quite closely at the tests themselves. Personality tests fall into two groups: those that put people into categories or types, and those that measure personality traits. Many of them effectively combine the two.

The Myers-Briggs Type Indicator (MBTI) is the most widely employed and influential personality test. It is used by psychologists and psychiatrists, employers, educators and sociologists to test more than two million people every year. The MBTI consists of a lengthy and complex questionnaire which is meant to be given to people by qualified assessors, trained to interpret the results. These take the form of identifying a person as one of sixteen different psychological types.

Most of those who take it think their MBTI result reflects something 'authentic' about them. The US National Research Council, a subgroup of the National Academy of Sciences, investigated the test's impact in advanced training programmes for US Army Officers and found that 84 per cent of those who took it thought the MBTI gave a 'true' and 'valuable' assessment of their character.

Yet the objective reliability of the test – that is, the extent to which it yields the same results each time a person takes it – does not measure up to its popularity. The NRC report cited a review of eleven studies of MBTI test-retest outcomes that showed that as few as 24 per cent of respondents – and no more than 61 per cent – were put in the same type as before when they took the test a second time.[13] In other words, like Randi's universal star sign, the MBTI types are loose enough for a person to slip on one, then another, and believe both are tailor-made.

The second type of personality test does not attempt to put people into types, but instead describes them by where they lie on various dimensions, each of which defines a particular personality trait. Trait theory is based on the idea that characteristics that matter in daily life have come to have words attached to them, and the more important they are, the more likely they are to be expressed by a single word. So, for example, there is a whole range of behaviour that is generally approved of by other people: kindness, sympathy, considerateness – all of which can be brought together under the umbrella word of 'goodness' or 'niceness'.

Of course, a person could be kind without being considerate, or sympathetic without being kind, but generally speaking if a person rates highly on one of the measures, they will be expected to rate highly on the others. By rating a person on the single dimension of 'niceness', therefore, you are saying a whole lot of things about them very economically. Over the years psychologists have whittled down the number of dimensions required to give a more or less complete picture of a personality to just five:

Openness to Experience
Conscientiousness
Extroversion
Agreeableness
Neuroticism

'Goodness' or 'niceness', you will see, is not among the 'Big Five'. In fact, apart from extroversion, the dimensions are probably not characteristics that anyone would arrive at intuitively. Nevertheless, years of number-crunching has shown that when all the descriptions that fall under their umbrella are taken into account (e.g. when you include under extroversion the degree to which a person is talkative, outgoing, sociable and so on) these five dimensions contain nearly everything that can be said of a personality. By assessing where each testee lies on the five dimensions – where they are between, say, agreeableness and disagreeableness or extroversion and introversion – you are therefore meant to have a complete, if crude, picture of them.

Trait testing is a fuzzier sort of test than the type testing. Rather than saying that a person who scores high on, say, conscientiousness will indeed be conscientious whenever they are tested, they predict that a person will be conscientious *most of the time*. This gets around the problem that the MBTI Johnnies posed when a person slid from one type to another because it doesn't presume to tell you what your core self is – just what the likelihood is of you being like this or that. Someone might be conscientious, say, 80 per cent of the time and careless 20 per cent; extrovert on one in four occasions and a shrinking violet on the others.

But what on earth does it mean to say that there is an 80 per cent probability that a conscientious person will behave conscientiously? Are personalities prone to off-days – failing to hit their targets sometimes, like second-rate snooker players? And what if the person displays an entirely different personality 20 per cent of the time? If that is not their personality showing, what on earth is it? Someone else's?

Multiplicity, obviously, makes sense of this, just as it makes sense of the 'slippage' in the type testing. A person with a conscientious major personality will display that trait just so long as their major is active. When a minor takes over who does not share that trait it will temporarily disappear. As our circumstances change, so do our personalities.

Big Five testers seem slowly to be coming around to this idea themselves, although they don't express it in quite that way. They have found that the predictive value of trait testing is hugely improved when people are invited to do the test within a frame of reference. This means that they are instructed to put themselves mentally into a particular role or situation and answer the questions from that perspective only. If a person is doing the test as part of the selection procedure for a job, for example, the candidates are instructed to answer the questions 'as though they are in the working environment'. In addition, questions such as 'do you become irritable if a person is late to meet you?' may be rephrased to ask: 'would you issue a reprimand if an employee is late for a meeting without good excuse?'

Tests that are given with instructions like these are proving to be much more effective at predicting the behaviour of a person when they are in the same frame of reference as the one they were in when they did the test. For example, when people did a Big Five test in each of several roles – friend, student, employee, lover and child – they rated differently on every one of the dimensions in each role. In the 'friend' mode, they were more extroverted, in the student role they were more neurotic and less agreeable, in the employee role they were more conscientious and in the romantic role they were more open to experience.[14]

In other words: the friend is a different personality from the student, and the student is different from the employee. They don't call it multiplicity (yet) but that is what this new testing implies.

Sharing the stage

While most of us slip-slide, sequentially, from one train of consciousness to another, a few people remain simultaneously aware of more than one personality. Instead of feeling themselves to be just the one, they are privy to the thoughts and feelings of 'back room' personalities running as a parallel stream of consciousness alongside the thoughts and feelings of the one that is in charge of behaviour. This unusual state of mind is known as co-consciousness, and although few of us will ever experience it completely, a little of it might help us all.

Alex is one such person. He works as an estate agent, and to his friends he is an entirely regular guy with a fairly conventional view of life. In a way this assessment is absolutely right. Alex *is* conventional. His main concern is to sell more houses than his competitors, make money and establish a materially secure lifestyle.

What his colleagues do not know, however, is that the Alex they recognise is only one of eight, quite separate Alexes which his brain is generating at any moment. While Alex-1 is 'out', these other personalities look on as though from the wings, each one harbouring their own thoughts. And when Alex leaves work, he steps into the wings himself, and allows another of his household to take control of their body.

Sometimes it is Alexander who emerges, the slightly pompous, tweed-clad ex-public school boy who takes his fishing rods to visit his parents in the country. Sometimes it is 'A', the lager-drinking couch potato who can tell you the details of every goal scored by his football team in the last three seasons. Occasionally it is Alex-the-cook, who will spend an entire day preparing a special meal for a few friends. Once in a blue moon it is the Alex that gets blindingly drunk and then drives too fast through city streets.

Alex has never been diagnosed with any sort of psychological disorder. Far from being pathological, his multi-streamed mental life works perfectly well because the various members of the group are in close and constant communication. Their continuous multi-way inner conversation allows them to pool their memories so there are no memory gaps. And they share tasks, by arrangement, to ensure that the 'front' or 'active' personality is the one best able to manage current circumstances. The only problem is Alex-the-drunk, but the other Alexes are working on him.

Co-consciousness sounds, at first, simply impossible, just as MPD tends to sound impossible to someone who is unfamiliar with it. Certainly it is very difficult to imagine what it is like to be aware of being more than one 'self' at the same time. If you think about it, though, you may realise that you, too, have had glimpses of how it feels. One co-conscious multiple describes it like this:

> Imagine being in a theatre, in front of the stage. From that viewpoint, you can see all the actors and props up close and first-hand. Now picture standing at the very back of this large theatre, what the view from this vantage point might be. You could still see and hear everything, however it would not be as lucid or meaningful as it was in front of the stage.
>
> For the multiple, being in front of the stage is similar to being out and in control of the body, and being in the back is similar to experiencing what is taking place externally, from the inside.

The degree to which co-conscious multiples feel they are simultaneously 'inside' each of their backstage personalities varies. Sometimes they are aware of a household member's thoughts as 'silent knowledge' and sometimes they manifest as internal voices. Teresa, one of a large co-conscious household, says: 'Sometimes I get a whole flash, or a shift in perception, where I see/hear/taste/smell/feel a piece of memory really strongly that is also not related to anything near by that I can see. I interpret this as getting information from someone else.'

Other members' thoughts (as opposed to sensory perceptions) manifest mainly as voices inside her head. Such voices should not be confused with the voices that plague schizophrenics. Those, for the people who hear them, are usually indistinguishable from the voices of people 'outside'.

'My own thoughts might run something like this: Gee, I really like that dress. But we're really low on cash right now so I won't get it,' explains Teresa. 'But I also "hear" other voices in my head. Sometimes they are talking to me, or relevant to the situation at hand. Sometimes, though, they're not – it's like eavesdropping on someone, or catching pieces of a TV show when you're doing something else. Occasionally I even hear discussions between other people, so it's like hearing a conversation. To me, all the voices are fairly distinct, although sometimes they go into what I think of as "neutral" which means I can't figure out who they are.'

Teresa also experiences the others' emotions, though these, she says, are less easy to distinguish from her own than thoughts.

'Usually they aren't related to anything I see in front of me and have a vaguely . . . untrue feeling to them,' she says. 'It's hard to explain, but it's like a paler version of a real feeling.'

Even if this does not accord at all with your normal waking experience, you might recall something like it occurring in your dreams. The illusion of unity is maintained by activity in the brain's frontal lobes, and during sleep these are effectively turned off, or down. One effect is that our critical faculties – among them the bit that usually says 'Hey! Something odd is happening here!' – are not very active. Hence dream narrative is often so bizarre – it gets past the usual 'reality check'. Another effect is that in dreams we may find ourselves to be both an actor and an observer in a situation, seeming to inhabit two characters' minds at the same time. The feeling may just be one of knowing what is in another mind as well as your own. Or it may be more complete than that; a feeling of actually looking out through two pairs of eyes.

In one of my own recent dreams, for instance, I was sitting on a bank fishing, and at the same time I was under the water watching the fish swim up to the bait. Never mind what (if any) psychological significance this may have – the important thing about it for me is that in the dream I experienced two distinct streams of consciousness. My ability to do this, even if only in sleep, persuades me that the sense of multiplicity that some people claim is their normal state is as real to them as the sense of singularity is to the rest of us

Living co-consciously may not be easy, what with the clamour of competing voices and the constant negotiating between personalities. In some ways, though, co-conscious multiples may function better than what they describe as singlets because, effectively, they are able to draw on the combined talents of several people, rather than just on one. Romy, a member of another co-conscious household explains:

Not many of us – individually – are more intelligent than the average person. But what happens is that everyone brings their own skills and abilities to the body for the time that they are out, and so we seem more intellectually able because we bring such a variety of skills with us. I myself am very technically inclined, and the courses I've been doing at the college have been a breeze for me. But if one of the others happens to get out, they can stare blankly at the page, knowing that I (Romy) know this stuff, and being able to access that yes, we have seen it before and it is in Common Knowledge, but they don't have a damn clue what to do with it! And I, in turn, could not write poetry or draw a portrait to save my soul, but there are some amazing poets and artists who share this body, making it seem like we all have those skills. So it's not a matter of multiples being superior so much as that the combination of skills in any system/household can make it seem like we're able to do and understand a whole lot more.

As this account suggests, it is not enough just to share information, it is also important that the personality best suited to a particular task comes out, on cue, to do it. Some households seem to have more control over this than others. 'Our work involves doing a whole range of completely different things,' says Jo, the 'spokesperson' for a household which owns and runs an interior décor shop:

First thing we have to do each week is check the stock lists on the computer, and that is really painstaking, detailed stuff. Personally I would be hopeless at it, but Immy (another household member) is great at it. Then we have to check on the product displays. That's a job I share with P; we both have a talent for making stuff look pretty; showing it off to best advantage.

People who know us well can always tell which of us has done a particular display, though, because we have different styles. I like to spread the goods out so you can see at a glance what's there, but P likes to do it more artistically. He'll take three or four contrasting fabrics and drape them over the back of a chair as though they've just been discarded there. I can feel myself itching to straighten them out; tidy it up and show the patterns more clearly, but if I do that we can get locked into a tussle, with me arranging them one way, then P sneaking back and rearranging them, and then me doing it again . . . we wasted a lot of time doing that until we came to this arrangement: I do it for a couple of weeks, then P does it.

Student multiples sometimes send different personalities to different classes, or to take different exams. 'Carly did all my history papers last year,' says a member of one household. 'We ended up with straight As. But Carly never comes out on social occasions so people get really puzzled when something to do with history comes up in a conversation and I don't have anything to say about it.'

Another way in which co-conscious people have an advantage over others is that if they have a problem personality among them, they are able to conduct a multi-way conversation with it, in which all sides can be heard together.

Part II of this book describes how you can get a conversation going between personalities even if you currently experience them only as a muted burble rather than a clear stream of parallel consciousness. It will also help you to identify your personalities as individuals, with their own interests and quirks. First, though, let's look at the way that personalities are made.

CHAPTER 3

Mechanisms of Mind

Memory, experience and 'I-memories'

We tend to think of memories as a replay of past events – a personal library of documentary film footage which we can select and watch at will. In fact it is not like that, because memories are not events but *experiences*.

To recall a past episode in your life is to reconstitute the mind-state you were in at the time. Part of this is, literally, sensational. That is, it includes the experience of seeing, hearing, tasting and so on. These are the components we tend to think of as 'events'. Along with them, though, you also reconstitute (in part at least) the thoughts, emotions and behavioural responses you were generating at that moment. These are the 'I' component of memories – the bits that become the habits of mind which cluster into personalities. Because they are bound together with the sensational part of each experience, when you reconstitute something that you saw or heard you also reproduce the personality *to whom* it happened. More of this in a moment.*

*Of course, you never normally reconstitute a previous brain-state in its entirety. If you did you would have no way of telling the memory apart from the original experience. The only possible exception to this is the intense flashbacks suffered by people suffering from Post-Traumatic Stress Disorder. These can be so similar, subjectively, to the original experience that the person is unaware of the present and acts as though they are back in time.

No two people ever have exactly the same experience. You and I may both think we remember Belinda's wedding, but I remember my experience of it and you remember yours and the two may be very different. Even if the facts of the matter are accurately recalled by us both (as far as we can tell) the emotional 'colouring' of our recollections will probably be different because event memories include at least a trace of the mood we were in at the time the memory was laid down. Details will be different, too, because each one of us notices slightly different aspects of an unfolding scene. At Belinda's wedding we may both have noted that Hermione was wearing a particularly flamboyant hat. But your eye may also have been caught by the fall of a rose petal from a table decoration, while mine might have picked up the sound of a glass breaking at the far end of the room. Even if we didn't consciously register these fragmentary experiences they may have triggered a cascade of other memories in each of us. The rose petal may have reminded you of a funeral, and thus may have subtly clouded your mood for a few minutes. The glass breaking might have reminded me of a car accident I was in, and so infected the moment with a tiny trace of fear.

We are able to recall past experiences, complete with their idiosyncratic details, because they are encoded in the flesh, rather as a tune may be etched into the surface of an audio disc. A memory (and the personality incorporated in it) thus has a physical basis – it is 'there', in your brain, even when it is out of mind.

This is how it works. Each moment of experience is generated by electrical activity created by rapid on–off firing of individual cells. Firing is a sort of mini-explosion which occurs only in nerve cells, or neurons. If one neuron fires strongly and frequently enough it has a knock-on effect on its neighbours. Sometimes the effect is inhibitory – it signals them *not* to fire. But at other times it causes a whole bunch of neighbouring neurons to start firing in synchronised bursts like a line of chorus girls kicking their legs in sequence to create a Mexican wave. These flurries of organised activity are our sensations and thoughts and emotions. Gentle flutterings pass unnoticed, but if a bout of synchronous firing is rapid, energetic and sustained it becomes conscious. And activity that is particularly energetic or sustained –

whether conscious or not – causes the neurons involved to change, physically.

These changes are minute – a matter of subtle rearrangement of individual molecules. Their effect, though, is profound, because it is this that creates memory. The tiny alterations in cells strengthen the links between simultaneously firing neurons in such a way that in the future when one fires its original 'dancing partners' are likely to fire too. The process is known as Long Term Potentiation (LTP), and is summed up by the T-shirt slogan: 'Neurons that fire together, wire together!' So, as you can see, the more a particular group of neurons get to dance together, the more the physical changes in them encourage them to do it again.

A memory, then, is a brain *habit* – a pattern of neural firing that the brain produces easily because it has done it before. Some memories are episodic – that is, when they are active they partially reconstitute the experience of a previous 'episode' in our lives. Over time they change, and large parts of them fade away altogether. Sometimes the parts that fade are the 'I' components, leaving only the factual bits – so-called 'semantic memories'. The residue of a distant geography lesson, for example, may be some arcane fact about the gross national product of Ecuador. Or the factual elements may be lost leaving only an emotional or 'I-memory' – a sense of paralysing boredom in the face of anything remotely geographical, perhaps.

These free-floating 'I-memories' can be thought of as micro personalities, and those that are similar to one another – the boredom with geography and a similar sense of boredom with, say, maths – might join up to make a 'bored with schoolwork' minor. Minors, in turn, may coalesce into a major. For example, if you smoke when you drink the pattern of neuronal firing (micro) which is your smoking habit is activated simultaneously with the neuronal pattern that is your drinking habit (another micro). Let's say you limit your drinking to Friday nights when you don't have to get up to go to work the next day. The micro which is the thought 'Thank God it's Friday! Let's relax!' thus occurs at the same time as the drinker/smoker micros. Relaxing, for you, might mean dancing all night. For someone else it might involve slumping in front of the TV. So you will probably develop a Friday night/drinking/smoking/dancing habit while they get a Friday night/drinking/smoking/slumping habit. To which might be added 'dressing up' or 'dressing sloppily', and so on. Little by little a small nexus of habits may grow into a whole way of seeing, thinking, feeling and behaving so that what begins just as a cluster of memories becomes, in time, a fully fledged personality. It may become hugely complex, complete with intentions and ambitions. The Friday night dance, for example, may become an all-consuming way of life with which you, and other people, come to identify yourself. In other words, the clubbing 'you' may become your major personality. Or it may remain a skeletal little minor who comes out for a few hours only, and returns to sleep the moment you leave the club.

Given that personalities are made of memories, and no two people ever have the same experience, it is easy to see how different personalities arise in different people. But how can two (or more) distinct personalities co-exist in a single brain? After all, you may suppose, they have shared a lifetime of experience.

In fact our various personalities do not share the same experiences. Or, at least, they do not share the same experiences *equally*. Although they are products of the same brain, they are not generated by the same brain processes.

It is a little like one of those advertising signs made of thousands of light bulbs: turn on one set and it blazes out 'Pepsi-Cola!' Turn on another and it says 'Drink Coke!' Some of the light bulbs may be common to both (the 'Co' in 'Cola' and 'Coke', for example, overlap) but the messages are still quite different.

The switch from one neural pattern (Coke!) to another (Pepsi!) is clean enough in some people to be visible on a brain scan. But you don't need fancy laboratory equipment to be aware of these internal shifts even when they are far more subtle than those detected (so far) by brain-imaging.

State-dependent recall

If you examine your inner life carefully you will almost certainly find that your memories of some things are clear and intense while others are vague and gappy. Your schooldays may have been reduced to a few snap-shots perhaps, or last year's summer holiday may seem, after only a few weeks back at work, like a distant dream. Vague memories, however, tend to become quite clear if you put yourself back in a state that is similar to the one you were in when they were laid down. This curious phenomenon is known as 'state-dependent memory'.

A classic experiment demonstrates in neatly quantifiable terms just how potent state-dependent memory can be. Volunteers were asked to learn a string of words one day and then recall them the next. Half of them were given a stiff drink before the learning exercise while the other half did the memorising sober. Next day both groups were given alcohol before being asked to recall the words. The drink, as you might expect, undermined both groups' ability to recall the list and neither of them did as well as a third group who were sober both when they learned and when they recalled the list. But what you might not expect is that the group who were drunk on both occasions did better – more than twice as well, in fact – than the group who had learned them while they were sober but tried to remember them when they were drunk.[1]

In other words, it wasn't the fact they were drunk when they learned the words that prevented the volunteers recalling them sober so much as the fact that they were in a different brain-state. If you think of each state as a different personality you can see why – the words were stashed in the bag of memories laid down by the drinker and were not therefore fully available to the sober one.

Other studies have shown that other mind-states, such as moods, are also associated with their own bags of memories. People remember more happy memories when they are happy themselves, and more sad ones when they are sad. Furthermore, when a person is in a particular mood they experience the world in a way that matches it. Experiences that chime with the mood – the sight of spring flowers in the sun when you are feeling bright, the glimpse of a person crying when you are sad – capture attention more than things which go against it. Both types of events may be happening, but the person will only *notice* the ones that resonate with how they feel.[2] Mood-congruent processing, as this is known, ensures that each mind-state is not 'polluted' by experience or perceptions that would dilute its character. So, in time, each mood – happy, sad, angry, scared – accumulates its distinct memories as well as its characteristic way of seeing the world. The sunny mood, for example, gets to have a big collection of sunny associations, so it develops an optimistic attitude and sees itself as a happy person. Moods thus become minors. A mood may even be the central kernel around which a person's major grows.

Once you are tuned into it you can see state-dependent memory and mood-congruent processing at work in all sorts of situations. Sandy, for example, recounted to me the odd transformation she experienced when she looked after her grandchild.

This competent middle-aged woman spent more than a decade caring, full-time, for her children before building a successful career as a marketing manager. A little while ago her eldest daughter had her first child. It had been a complicated pregnancy and the daughter was exhausted by the time the child arrived, so Sandy took a month off work and moved in with her daughter to help with the new baby.

'It took a lot of persuading to get me to do it,' she says. 'Not so much because I didn't want to but because I really thought I had forgotten how to look after a baby; the time when I was a new mum seemed like another lifetime – a distant blur of broken nights and milky stains. Yet the moment I held that baby it was as though I had been looking after my own just yesterday.'

State-dependent memory is often concealed from us because when we are in one state we rarely need to call on the experience held by another state. On holiday, for example, we may not realise how out of touch we have become with our working personality until we run into a work colleague and find, for a moment, that we can't place them. Sandy found that once the mum in her re-emerged, her bag of work memories were almost entirely inaccessible.

'I had a crisis call while I was at my daughter's from the person who was standing in for me at work. She wanted to know in what order to do things during a training session. I had run those training sessions every fortnight for five years, but at that moment, standing with the baby in one arm and the phone in the other, I couldn't remember how I started the sessions or what came next. The knowledge had just gone.'

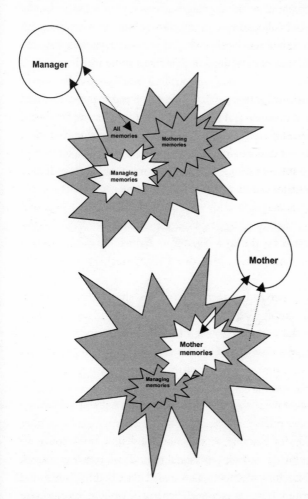

While Sandy is Manager (top) her experiences are bound with other 'Managing memories' in the Manager's 'bag'. She still has access to other memories, but they are not as bright or easy to recall. When she bcomes Mother (below) her previous 'Mothering memories' become clear, but her access to others are compromised.

How memories fit together – the brain-wide web

Memory recall fluctuates in all of us, but more so in those of us, like Sandy, who have developed very clearly distinguished personalities. The reason for this is that memories are encoded in the brain in a web, or a net-like way. You could think of each element of a memory (the sight of a particular hat, say) as a node, or knot in a fishing net, connected to others by strings. When a memory comes to mind it pulls on all the strings leading out from it, and the memories at the other end get jogged. The jogged memories in turn jog those they are connected to, and so on. The further away you go from the initial recollection the weaker the jogging effect. But so long as two memories are part of the same net there is the possibility that one will bring to mind the other.

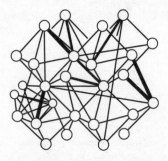

Memories are stored as though in a three-dimensional network: some are connected very strongly and directly and some are not directly connected at all. So long as they are all part of the same network, however, when one is jogged the effect is felt, however faintly, by all the rest.

In order to get linked up with others and thus woven into the network, memories have to share something. This shared material is the 'strings' that bind them together. Things that happen at the same time are usually linked automatically by their shared time-slot. Hence the memory of Hermione's hat is bound to the memory of Belinda's wedding. And if it happened to be raining at Belinda's wedding, that too will get attached. The nodes in the net are the events and the string that links them is their shared timing.

This little cluster of new experiences slots into the net by joining with other memories that share something with them. The wedding bit of it connects to all the other weddings you have been to. Rainy weddings get doubly attached. And the rain bit links up with, say, memories of rainy holidays.

The links take off far and wide . . . the purple of Hermione's hat may get linked via its colour to a skirt you once foolishly bought and never wore. Which in turn may link to a little guilty memory about pretending not to have any change when a charity collector shook a collecting tin at you as you left that same shop on another occasion. The rattling of change may link to some distant recollection of a baby's rattle, and the guilt may remind you that you have still to buy Belinda a wedding present . . . Rain, of course, has countless connections – with rainy picnics, rainy walks, rainy journeys . . .

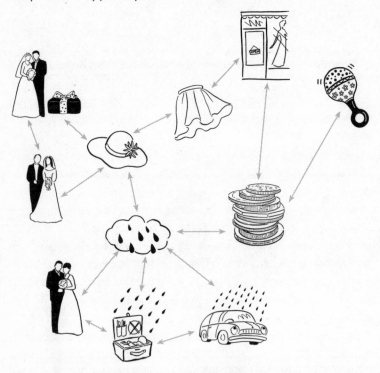

You can see that providing every experience has *some*thing in common with what has gone before – timing, colour, location, sound, emotion – you end up with a vast network in which everything is connected to everything else. Hence if one memory is jogged, the others will feel it too, with its immediate neighbours feeling it most.

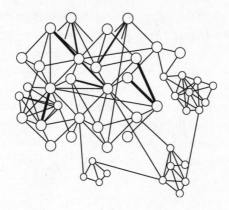

Most of us end up with a memory web that could be represented by the pattern above (though infinitely more complicated!). Although everything is connected to everything else, the memories are clustered or 'bagged' together. When a single memory is activated, therefore, it tends to trigger its associated memories, but has very little effect on distantly connected ones.

The interconnectivity of all our experiences normally ensures that when a situation jogs to life one particular set of responses we continue to have access (should we need it) to a wider web of recollections, including autobiographical information like our name, where we live, what day of the week it is and why we are in a particular place at that particular moment. The neural firing patterns which encode this background may not be active enough to make it conscious, but they are poised to burst into life given a cue. If someone asks you for your address, for example, the firing pattern that incorporates that information will strike up instantly.

Imagine, though, that you had one cluster of memories that had somehow failed to get connected up with the rest of your memory web. Most of the time you would be unconscious of it because there would be no strings running to it from your daily experiences, and thus nothing would usually shake it into life. Conversely, on the rare occasions when it *was* jogged into consciousness, there would be no strings running back to your everyday experience so your consciousness would be *limited* to that memory – if someone asked you for your address you would not be able to retrieve it. If the memory cluster is a small one it might not contain *any* autobiographical knowledge. You would not even know who you are.

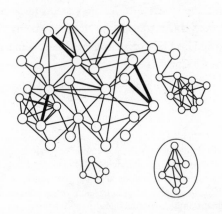

If a small cluster of memories fails to bind into the web (ringed, left), the personality incorporated in them is isolated. When the memories in this isolated cluster are jogged the personality that is activated no longer has access to the recollections which give them their Major identity.

This, essentially, is what happens in people with the 'Who am I?' type of amnesia that features in so many thrillers. Their most recent experiences are not woven into the larger part of their memory web so they are marooned in the here-and-now without a bridge to the rest of their life. The condition is very similar to that of a person with MPD, except that in the latter case the person is marooned in a detached bit of their *past* life.

In adults only memories of very extreme experiences are likely to be disconnected with the rest. This is because most experiences, even very novel or nasty ones, connect with *some*thing that has happened to the person in the past just because they have been around long enough to accumulate lots and lots of experiences. Children, though, have far fewer stowed experiences to link new events with, so much more of what happens to them is, initially, at least, free-floating.

Take, for instance, Tom – just sprung to life, miraculously, with an entirely clean slate for a memory. He has various genetic dispositions, of course, and in real life they would have a great influence on what follows. Just now, though, for the sake of simplicity we are going to ignore them. The important thing is that Tom has no learned responses other than those that are pretty much common to all human beings.

So let's give Tom his first experience. We'll start with a nice one: Tom is given a puppy for Christmas.

This makes Tom very happy, so the puppy experience incorporates 'I-memories' that add up 'Happy Tom'. Next Tom is taken to the seaside and this makes him happy too. So the 'I' bits of the two experiences – happiness – overlap.

It is not just any old happiness, though – this is *Tom*'s happiness. In fact – as happiness is so far all that Tom has ever been, it *is* him: Happy Tom. Every experience he has had, and every memory he can have, so far, brings out this single personality. Tom's next experiences are happy too: a first flight in a plane and a big bar of chocolate. So now he has a cluster of memories which all produce Happy Tom. The Happy Toms share so many brain-states that they are effectively bound into a single personality.

You can see from this that if Tom's experiences continued in this vein – every one of them giving him unalloyed joy – he would develop just one rather limited personality. He would be what I am calling a 'Single Major' – a completely integrated self with no ragged edges or threadbare patches in his memory net.

But let's make Tom's life a little more real. He gets sent to school and hates it. He gets a cold: horrid. He gets attacked by the school bully. Scary. He has to do homework. Boring. And the coalition of these experiences, bound by their common unpleasantness, creates a new entity: Unhappy Tom.

Now we have two quite separate Toms – Happy Tom, with his little bag of memories, and Unhappy Tom, dragging around his rotten baggage. The Tom who is 'there' at any moment depends entirely on which situation he finds himself in: seaside, aeroplanes, chocolate and puppies jog out Happy Tom, and school, illness, bullies and homework bring out Unhappy Tom. The two Toms can't access each others' memories because there are no connections between them, so Unhappy Tom does not even know that Happy Tom exists and vice versa. When the situation changes from one that brings out Happy Tom (playing with his dog, for example) to one that calls up Unhappy Tom (going to school) the switch is clean and sudden. It is as though one actor leaves the stage and another sweeps in from where it has been waiting its cue in the wings.

As Tom grows up, however, he accumulates more experiences, many of which create links between the previously disjointed memories. The seaside visit and the journey to school might be linked by a trip in the family car. Tom might get bored ('Are we there yet?') or car-sick during both trips, and thus the two otherwise very different events would both be associated with Unhappy Tom as well as with Happy Tom. The experience of his first flight, though happy, may include a bout of turbulence which makes him frightened. This would link it to the fright he got when he was beaten up at school. Tom might do his homework on his computer and punctuate the slog with surreptitious spells of online gaming which connect back to the Happy Tom.

Already you can see that all Tom's memories are interconnected. Rattle any one of them and Happy Tom and Unhappy Tom will both vibrate. Some of the memories, though, shake up Unhappy Tom more than Happy Tom and vice versa. Cue 'school', for example, and the more you shake it the more Unhappy Tom comes to life. Cue 'chocolate' and Happy Tom is the one who becomes most active. Tom does not have Multiple Personality *Disorder* because his personalities retain some connection to one another. When Happy Tom is out, Unhappy Tom is still quietly purring along, unconsciously, ready to perk up and take over if jogged to life by a situation which resonates with his particular bag of memories.

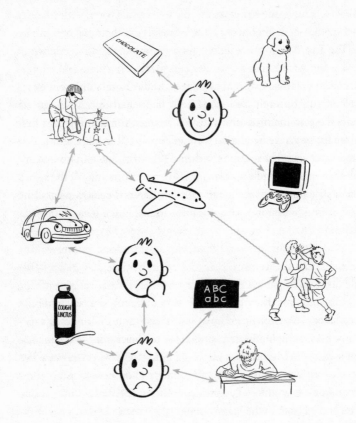

The brain as building site

In real life Tom's inner landscape would develop in a much more complicated way because his reactions to the things that happened to him would be idiosyncratic, right from the start, due to his unique genetic inheritance.

Experiences, as we have seen, are not things that happen to us but our *responses* to those things – the sensations, emotions and thoughts that our brain produces in response to events. Our responses depend largely on our previous experiences, which in turn depend on the ones before that and so on. But they also depend to some extent on the way we are *made*. For example, the structure of a persons' visual cortex – the density of their colour-encoding neurons, say – will affect their perception of a visual image even *before* the sight is recognised and assessed in terms of what it is and what it means.

Hence an identical external event can produce quite different experiences in two different brains. If Tom happened to have a genetic inheritance that inclined him towards anxiety, for example, his first flight might not have been a mixture of fun and fear but unmitigated terror. Flying would have connected with school bullies and homework rather than puppies and chocolate and so his personalities would take a different shape from that of a naturally less nervous person, even if the two of them (somehow) were subjected to identical environmental influences.

Genes do not only influence the way people respond to events, they also influence the *range* of responses they have. Some people are naturally emotionally stable, so however diverse the external events that happen around them their experiences tend to share a similar emotional tone or 'colour'. Magnolia, perhaps. Others have quite dramatically varying responses, plunging from bubbling joy to abject misery. When they are happy they are conscious *only* of happiness and when they are sad they can imagine no other way to be. These same people tend to get utterly caught up in the events of the moment. Their attention is like a narrow beam of light which illuminates target mental events intensely, but casts a shadow over everything else.

Dissociation

'Slicing up' the world like this, into a tiny conscious focal point and an unconscious hinterland, is known as dissociation – the English equivalent of Janet's *disaggregation*. Dissociation is used as an umbrella term to cover all sorts of states which involve the separation of various mental processes. It is usually discussed in the context of dissociative *disorders* – dysfunctional states (such as amnesia and MPD) which, given the problems they cause, are rightly treated as psychiatric illnesses. But dissociation itself is not an illness, or even abnormal. We all filter out of consciousness many or most of the thoughts, feelings and sensations that are being registered at any moment by our brain. Whenever we put something 'out of mind' such as a nagging worry, an unwelcome emotion or the noise of a road drill when we are trying to work, we are dissociating.

Usually we keep out only those experiences which fall roughly into the category of 'background interference' – the irritating buzz and hum of city traffic or the meaningless faces of the crowd as we move towards the one familiar one we are seeking. Far from being unhealthy, this sort of everyday dissociation is essential because if our brains did not edit out most of the barrage of information competing for consciousness we would simply be overwhelmed.

Hypnotic induction is a way of producing dissociation on cue. The ease with which a person can be hypnotised generally corresponds to their ability to dissociate spontaneously. Indeed, spontaneous dissociation could be seen as unwitting self-hypnosis.

Hypnotisability is often measured on a scale from 0–5. Grade-5s, those who are most susceptible, make up about 4 per cent of the general population, and the vast majority of people with MPD/DID. A slightly larger proportion of people are Grade 0 – they do not respond at all to hypnotic suggestion. Most people are somewhere between the extremes.

A simple way to get a rough idea of a person's hypnotisability is to see if they can roll their eyes backwards into their head. To perform the eye roll test, tell the subject to:

1   Keep his (or her) head steady and look straight ahead.
2   Without moving your head, look upward with your eyes towards your eyebrows, then higher, toward the top of your head.
3   With your eyes held in this upward gaze, slowly close your eyelids.
4   Open your eyelids and let your eyes return to normal focus.

Hypnotisability corresponds to how much of the iris is visible during the upward gaze. Grade 0s continue to look quite normal, while Grade 5s show barely any iris at all. The eye-roll test was developed by Manhattan psychiatrist Dr Herbert Spiegel in the 1970s and has been found to be almost as good at predicting hypnotisability as the long and complex testing methods used to determine it in a formal psychiatric setting.

Adaptive dissociation

While in ordinary situations we dissociate 'background noise' in order not to be overwhelmed, in extraordinary situations it is often the experiences which are potentially the most intense that get cut out of consciousness. This is a natural consequence of the way our experiences are associated – anything which has nothing in common with those already stored in the web will inevitably be out on a limb. The effect, in traumatic situations, is that of a ferociously efficient doorkeeper. It bars the way to experiences – present and past – which are likely to be too much for us to cope with. Whenever you hear someone saying 'All I could think of . . .' or 'All I can remember . . .' as they recall an event you can be pretty sure you are hearing someone talking of a dissociative experience.

Even severe pain can be cut out of consciousness by dissociation. Hilgard (page 12) discovered that almost everyone can dissociate pain under hypnosis, but it can also happen when a person is shocked or distracted by more urgent business. Colin, for example, recalls the time his car skidded out of control and hit a tree, bursting the petrol tank. 'I thought, I must get out in case it explodes,' he recalls, 'but when I tried to move I found my legs were trapped. It turned out that both of them were broken, but at the time I didn't feel a thing.'

Like pain, intense emotion can also be cut out. A rape victim, for example, telling her story after the conviction of her attacker, recalls: 'I was dreading giving evidence, but when it came to it I answered the questions as though I was reciting a laundry list. Only it didn't seem to be me in the witness box – it felt as though there was a puppet there, and I was watching from the sidelines.'

The woman who spoke to me about this particular ordeal was astonished by her own calmness in court. But she recalled then that she had also been calm during and after the rape itself: 'Once I realised there was nothing I could do I just went slack and divorced myself from it all. So in court I was doubly divorced from what I was describing, it was very odd.'

Failure to be consciously aware of a potentially excruciating injury or intense emotion is, of course, abnormal. But abnormal does not necessarily mean *unhealthy*. In situations like the one Colin found himself in dissociation is both a blessing and a direct aid to survival because it allows a person's conscious mind to concentrate on thinking how best to cope. In Colin's case, for example, it gave him time to wriggle out of his car and crawl off the road before succumbing to pain. And the woman who was raped could probably not have got through the ordeal and come out as emotionally intact as she has had it not been for the merciful numbness that came over her.

You can trace the origin of adaptive dissociation to the 'freeze' response that you see in scared animals. If an animal feels threatened the first thing its brain does is to tell its body to run away. If it can't do that, the brain comes up with plan number two: fight. And if it can't do that, or it perceives that the threat is too big to take on, it goes into a third mode: switch-off. Parts of the brain responsible for responding consciously to what is happening close down. In small animals this is particularly obvious – the creature goes limp or becomes paralysed. A rabbit that is caught petrified in headlights, for example, is displaying the classic signs of adaptive dissociation. If the headlights were the gaze of a predatory fox, the rabbit's utter stillness would increase its chances of being overlooked.

Like rabbits, our own ability to distance our selves from terrible events may once have saved human lives in a very direct way. In the face of a physical threat that was impossible to run from or fight off the best thing our ancestors could do would have been to keep very quiet and very still, like rabbits caught in headlights, in the hope that the threat would pass by. Those whose brains pulled the 'play dead' trick were thus more likely to live to pass on their genes, including the ones that made them behave like that. A person who jumped to the last-ditch 'play dead' tactic too soon, however, would fail to make best use of the less extreme measures: flight and fight. So natural selection would have resulted in the majority of people being somewhere between very dissociative and not dissociative at all – which is, in fact, exactly what seems to be the case.

Defending the self

In today's world a threat is as likely to be to a person's pride or mental comfort as to their body, so the defence mechanisms mammals evolved to cope with physical danger have adapted in humans to kick in when a person feels psychologically as well as physically threatened. Hence we may dissociate in situations where we are exposed to ridicule or when we are bereaved or heartbroken, embarrassed or insecure.

Lucy, for example, is pretty hazy about the period immediately before her parents' divorce. 'My brother says that our parents used to bellow at each other "till the walls shook",' she tells me. 'But I can only remember hearing them arguing once.'

Looking back, Lucy pinpoints that event as the moment when she learned, as she puts it, 'to go away in my mind':

> I was flipping through this kiddies' book and there was this picture of a pretty country garden sort of place, with a little grassy path winding away towards a cottage in the distance. On the path, with their backs to you, there was this little girl and a little boy. They were holding hands and walking towards the cottage.
>
> I was looking at this when I heard them start up at each other – my mum's voice sounding like nails on a blackboard, Dad roaring. I felt my stomach flip over. And then this odd thing happened – suddenly, instead of just looking at the picture I was actually *in* it! I *was* the little girl, walking home.

It was such a nice experience that I tore out the picture and kept it. Then at night when I was in bed, I would get it out and practise 'becoming' the girl in it. It got easier and easier until eventually I didn't even need the picture. I would just think of that garden and I'd be there.

Lucy's escape into her garden is what most of us would call daydreaming but, technically, it is a form of dissociation – she was separating the sound of her parents' voices, and her other current sensations, thoughts and emotions from the picture of the children in the garden and the fantasy she wrapped around it. The fearful Lucy in her bedroom was temporarily put to sleep while another Lucy – a little girl in a garden – was created in her stead.

Lucy no longer needs to escape her parents rows, but she still dissociates. Nowadays she uses the skill she learned as a child to cut out the tedious 'here and now' of a dead-end job: 'I'm on the assembly line,' she says. 'It is all mechanised so you don't even have to use your hands – just watch a needle on a meter and twiddle buttons to keep it in the right range. The other girls yatter on about their boyfriends and stuff but I prefer to go off on my own. I make up stories and live them out, have conversations with the people I invent, do romantic things, go to places I've only read about. The others often tell me I'm talking to myself, but I don't care.'

Lucy is an example of someone whose natural tendency towards dissociation was nurtured by childhood events and thus became habitual. The end result is that she has developed at least one minor personality to do the tedious stuff she can't be bothered with. Meter-minder spends most of its life unconscious, but it registers every flicker of the needle and guides her fingers, becoming daily more expert in its own tiny domain. The other people she works with barely know of its existence, but if the needle ever goes out of range it springs into consciousness in an instant. Anyone watching Lucy at such a time would see her dreamy, vacant expression and relaxed stance replaced by a sharp-eyed, quick-acting, highly focused technician who – in contrast to the other Lucys – is absolutely wedded to its job.

The dissociative spectrum

The best way to view dissociation, then, is as a spectrum. At one end there is the everyday, entirely normal neglect of background distractions. Then there are states such as daydreaming and fantasy. The teenager who doesn't hear the call to dinner because they are concentrating on a computer game, the film-goer who weeps at a sentimental ending, the child who doesn't hear the teacher because she is lost in a daydream . . . these people are all dissociating. Far from being unhealthy, though, they are in some ways engaging more fully and completely in the world than if a single integrated personality was obliged to be present at all times.

Edging along the spectrum there is adaptive dissociation – an abnormal state such as physical or emotional distancing or numbness which occurs in frightening or otherwise traumatic situations. Similar states can be deliberately induced by various types of ritual and drugs.

NORMAL	ADAPTIVE	DISORDERED
Absorption/Daydreaming	Detachment in traumatic situations	Chronic detachment
Trance/OBE		Compartmentalisation

Beyond here on the spectrum dissociation becomes pathological. This is the realm of the Dissociative Disorders, which include MPD. This book is not about these conditions, but there is a thin and moving line between adaptive dissociation – a healthy and useful trick of the brain that gives us mental flexibility and maintains a degree of separation between our personalities – and the disorders. There is therefore a danger of sliding from one to the other.

Dissociative disorders can be divided into two categories: chronic detachment and compartmentalisation. Chronic detachment is a state in which, even in normal circumstances, a person feels distanced from, or has some strange perception, either of themselves or the rest of the world. When they are detached from themselves it is known as depersonalisation and when the detachment is from the rest of the world it is called derealisation.

Depersonalisation is often described by those who have experienced it as feeling like a puppet or a robot. 'The first time it happened was when I was walking home after visiting my mother in hospital,' reports Cherie. 'She was really poorly that day and I think I had finally realised that she was going to die. As I turned into our road I realised I couldn't feel my feet touching the ground. It was as though I faded out somewhere around the knees.

'And I had this odd sensation – I have had it in dreams but never before while I was awake – that I was watching myself from outside. I met some neighbours as I got to my door and when I spoke to them it seemed as though my voice was coming from somewhere to the side of me.'

If Cherie's odd sense of detachment had limited itself to the period around her mother's death it would merely have signalled adaptive dissociation kicking in to protect her from the full impact of her loss. The trouble is that Cherie has gone on feeling distanced from herself, sometimes for days at a time, even though it is now years since her mother's death and her life is objectively secure and pleasant. Dissociation has become a sort of default mode – a habit so deeply ingrained that she is no longer able to snap back into the here and now or reactivate her normal sense of self. She has slipped beyond the crucial point on the dissociative spectrum where detachment ceases to be a survival mechanism and becomes dysfunctional.

'I feel as though I'm living behind a sort of screen, watching the world move by, but not really part of it,' she says. 'I can't engage with people on the other side – it seems sometimes as though they are mouthing things at me and I can work out what they are, but they don't mean anything. And sometimes I am not sure whether things really happened or not. It is like living in a waking nightmare, except that I can't even feel the fear. If I'm in a situation where I know I ought to feel something I sort of work out what it should be and then act out feeling it. But inside I feel nothing.'

Derealisation is different from depersonalisation in that the person usually feels fairly normal in themselves but perceives the outside world as distant, or crushingly close, or in some other way distorted and weird. Geoffrey, for instance, started to experience derealisation during his final few months at university, when he was working through the night on a cocktail of caffeine, amphetamines and internally generated adrenalin. It culminated in an alarming experience during one of his final exams:

I looked up and suddenly felt the ceiling was on top of me. Then the room expanded again, and all the people in it seemed tiny, like little ants toiling away over their desks. I felt enormous, though. I looked down at my hand, with the pen in it, and it seemed to swell until I thought it would just take over the room. I must have made a noise, or looked funny, because the invigilator stood up and started walking towards me. That kind of snapped me out of it. I tried not to look at the other people and just kept writing. When I looked up next the people had gone back to normal size, but the feeling of unreality hung about for several hours.

Like depersonalisation, isolated episodes of derealisation – especially when they have an obvious cause like Geoffrey's pre-exam drugs regime – do not signify a disorder; it is when derealisation becomes *habitual* that there is room for concern.

Compartmentalisation is generally regarded as more extreme than detachment, and it also produces different symptoms. This is the term used to describe the complete separation of personalities seen in MPD, and also the kind of amnesia where a person 'forgets' entirely who they are. 'Hysterical' blindness and paralysis – now called 'conversion disorders' – are also a form of compartmentalisation. So are the 'flashback' memories seen in Post Traumatic Stress Disorders. What all these states have in common is that particular bags of memories are completely cut off from all the other memories, so when they are triggered, they are experienced in isolation.

Abnormal dissociation – the danger signs

- Deliberately picking up a book or turning on the TV when an unpleasant but necessary task needs doing.
- Constantly imagining a future scenario instead of living the present.
- Suddenly 'coming to' and realising you have not heard what someone has been saying because you have been day-dreaming.
- Forgetting important appointments because you have been too 'absorbed in something else'.
- Acting out daydreams (e.g. speaking fantasy dialogue aloud) in public.
- Finding yourself somewhere with no idea how you got there.
- Finding things among your belongings that you don't recognise.
- Seeing yourself as though from the outside.
- Failing to recognise friends and family who should be familiar.
- Feeling that the world around, or people or objects in it, are not real.
- Feeling that your body does not belong to you.
- Hearing voices that give you instructions or comment on your actions.

Extreme dissociation is generally rather disturbing when it happens unbidden – it is the sort of experience that can make a person feel they are going mad. Yet it can also be pleasurable or even ecstatic, and a vast recreational drug industry has grown up largely to provide dissociation on demand.

What seems to make the difference between pleasure and discomfort is the intention or assumptions that a person has in their mind when they dissociate. People who take drugs for reasons other than to get high (morphine, for example, for pain relief) often describe the psychological side-effects as unpleasant, even though very similar effects (that is, effects on brain function) are described by experienced drug users as euphoric. Similarly, the dreamlike effect of detachment may be very pleasant if you are having a long lie-in on a Sunday morning and can allow yourself to drift along the top edge of a dream. If you have overslept, however, and find yourself unable to pull out of the dream despite being aware of the need to, the half-waking, half-dreaming state may be quite nightmarish.

The very pleasantness of dissociation in some situations is what sets many people off on the road to a dissociative disorder. The younger a person is when they learn to dissociate the more likely they are to develop a dissociative disorder in later life. Some people are naturally more inclined to get hooked on dissociation than others. These are probably the people who are genetically inclined towards it in the first place – studies of twins who have been brought up apart show that they tend to be more alike in this respect than would be expected if their shared genes had nothing to do with it.[3]

Sliding into disorder

Very little research has been done on normal dissociation but what there is suggests that the vast majority of people are well within the normal part of our spectrum.[4] There is evidence, though, to suggest that there is a general shift, at least in some cultures, towards the end of the spectrum that ends in chronic detachment and compartmentalisation.

It is impossible to get firm figures for dissociative disorders because milder cases tend to be categorised – if they come to the attention of doctors at all – simply as anxiety, stress or depression. Severe cases are frequently misdiagnosed as schizophrenia or some type of personality disorder.

However, one estimate – gleaned from several separate surveys – is that some thirty million people in the US (seven million in the UK) regularly experience symptoms of depersonalisation and derealisation, and seven million in the US (1.5 million UK) fulfil the diagnostic criteria for Multiple Personality Disorder.[5] These figures are based on 'normal' population studies. In other words, these are not people who are already considered mentally ill.

Dissociative symptoms and disorders are far more prevalent in the general population than previously recognised. According to Marlene Steinberg, Associate Professor of Psychiatry at Massachusetts University Medical Center: 'Research has shown that these symptoms are as common as those of depression and anxiety,' 'but the person who is unfamiliar with them may not regard them as significant. If someone doesn't know that "not feeling like a real person" or feeling "apart from who I am" is a dissociative symptom that might indicate a problem, why would that person report it?'[6]

Professor Steven Gold, a former president of the International Society for the Study of Dissociation, thinks that depersonalisation and dereal-isation are now so common that they can be considered 'a normative characteristic of modern life'. Gold cites the best-selling novel (written by Chuck Palahniuk) and feature film *Fight Club* as an example of how the frantic, disjointed, dizzying nature of contemporary life promotes what Gold calls 'normative' dissociation. *Fight Club* features an 'everyman' character and the forceful and charismatic Tyler. At the start of the film the Narrator describes, in voice-over, his experience of the frequent travelling that, as with millions of others, has become a core part of his life: 'You wake up at Seatac, SFO, LAX. You wake up at O'Hare, Dallas, Fort Worth. Pacific . . . Mountain . . . Central. Lose an hour, gain an hour. If you wake up at a different time in a different place, could you wake up as a different person?'

Which is, in fact, exactly what happens to the Narrator. As we discover at the very end, he and Tyler are two different personalities sharing the same body.

If it was a real life story *Fight Club* would feature a clear case of MPD/DID. But, as Gold points out, the plot device of multiplicity is not used here as it usually is, to illustrate some extreme of individual human experience. Rather it is meant to show what is happening, in a less dramatic way, to us all. 'The central message of both the written and cinematic versions of *Fight Club* is that the structure of contemporary society promotes a dissociative mode of existence,' he says. 'In this sense dissociation is not an exotic diagnostic entity . . . [it] is a normative characteristic of modern life.'[7]

You'd be forgiven for thinking that modern life must be pretty catastrophic if our brains are forced into emergency mode to cope with it. But that is to assume that dissociation is necessarily dysfunctional and/or unpleasant which, as we've seen, it is not. The totally focussed 'in the moment' state known as 'flow', for example, is associated with heightened performance and intense pleasure.

Perhaps, then, a 'dissociative mode of existence' is simply a demonstration of our staggering ability to remodel our inner landscapes to fit the terrain in which we find ourselves. As Bob Dylan noted nearly half a century ago:

> You better start swimmin'
> Or you'll sink like a stone
> For the times they are a-changin'*

---

*Dylan is a self-ascribed multiple; by his own description 'a different person every day'. *I'm Not There*, the 2007 biopic about his life, features six different actors, each playing a different Dylan. 'The thing about Dylan that's so fascinating is that he has completely and utterly changed his identity time and time again,' said movie producer Christine Vachon. 'This movie is a play on that – I think it's kind of the only way to look at him.'

CHAPTER 4

Changing Times, Changing Selves

The rise of the pick 'n' mix culture

Last night I caught up with a pile of newspapers and magazines which I had put aside over the past couple of weeks to read when I had enough time. There is never enough time, of course, so I skim-read selected bits, threw out the rest, then turned on the TV to catch up with the latest news.

In that single, brief, dip into contemporary media I came across:

- A TV advertisement for a credit card featuring a holiday-maker who had lost her money in a foreign country where – we are led to imagine – she was seeking spiritual awakening rather than sun, sea and sand. In quick succession she alternated between shrieking with hysteria about her plight and then smiling serenely, as she flipped between being a stressed-out Western tourist and a serenely fatalistic traveller.

- A magazine article about a Korean man who runs a hamburger stall by day and lords it over an elaborate fantasy kingdom in cyberspace by night. In cyberspace his twenty-seven million 'subjects' are hunters, sorcerers, wizards, warriors and warlocks. In 'earthworld' they are bankers, architects, clerks and shopkeepers.

- An interview with author Jonathan Safran Foer in which he spoke of his nervousness about public speaking and how, as he puts it, 'I just go away . . . dissociate until it's over'.

- A review of a TV thriller about a CIA investigation into the disappearance of a 'perfect wife and mother' who turns out to be living a second life as a hooker.
- A promotional item illustrating (again!) the 'many faces' of the singer Madonna.
- A fashion piece entitled: 'Virgin to Vamp in Twenty Seconds'.

In addition there were at least a dozen other items which touched on issues of identity, memory and personal transformation. These are very current preoccupations – it is as though we have only just discovered our ability to shift and change; to be two or more 'people' at the same time.

One reason for the burgeoning interest in personal metamorphosis is that until recently most people weren't allowed to do it. Lives were constrained by duty, custom, limited horizons and a culture that feared and suspected change. Now, suddenly, we find ourselves in a world where flexibility, adaptability and personal reinvention are not just acceptable but positively encouraged. We are also open to a much wider range of voices and influences. Compare, for example, a day in the life of a typical middle-class woman in Britain today with that of her mother at the same age.

Rose is one of the rapidly increasing number of people who works mainly from her own home. This does not mean she gets to relax. On a typical day she is up at six a.m. and by six-thirty she has dealt with a dozen or so overnight emails (and forwarded or deleted a dozen others), checked online for news relevant to the industry in which she works and is flicking through the online editions of two daily newspapers and four trade newsletters. As she reads, the morning TV news show flickers in the corner of the room and every so often she glances at the ticker-tape update running along the bottom of the screen to check she's not missing anything.

On one particular day Rose noted, for me, the number of distant interactions she had, one way or another, with other people. By the time she had dressed, grabbed some toast and got back to her computer, she had eighteen emails in addition to the overnights and her answering service had taken three calls. Seven hours later, when she packed up work for the day, she had communicated, by phone or email, with eighty-three different people, across three continents. She had also absorbed news reports, including thousands of live images, from all over the world. And this was all before her social life had even begun for the day.

Thirty-five years ago Rose's mother, Jeanette, almost certainly spent the day at home too. She was then about the same age as Rose is now and photographs of her show that if you could cheat time and put them side by side they would look surprisingly similar, in their faded jeans and T-shirts, even if you discount the family resemblance.

Jeanette, however, was in many ways a very different being. She can say with some confidence that she spent that day at home because she spent nearly every day at home during that period. She had lived in the city for a while, then moved back to the small town where she was brought up in order to get help with her young children from her own mother, who had never moved away at all. Back home, she picked up many friendships which dated back to her days at school and which are still intact today.

Jeanette was (and still is) a chatty and engaged person, but compared to Rose her social interactions were very limited. In the course of a typical day she would probably have talked face to face to her husband, her children, a couple of neighbours, her mother, a shop assistant or trades-man and perhaps a visiting friend. She would have made and received a handful of telephone calls, all of them from people who lived within ten miles of her. Long distance calls – especially abroad – were reserved for special occasions, rather as telegrams were for her mother. In the entire course of the day she might not have interacted with a single person who had been born in another country.

Until recently the relatively insulated existence lived by Rose's mother was common to the vast majority of people in the Western world. It was not unusual for a person to live in the same place, among the same neighbours, married to the same partner and doing the same job, for their entire adult life. Even those people who lived in cities kept mainly to a village-style community life within the metropolis.

Such an existence, in the developed world, is almost unthinkable today. People who would once have followed their parents, and possibly their grandparents, into predictable familial furrows now pursue their individual ambitions as a matter of course, not rebellion. Families are often scattered across the world and absorbed into cultures that they probably would not even have visited a generation ago. Jobs are hardly ever for life and the notion of lifelong marriage has in some places become a slightly cultish lifestyle choice alongside an increasingly normal pattern of sequential monogamy. If present trends continue, in twenty-five years' time half the middle-aged people in the UK will be single, compared to less than 30 per cent today.[1]

This new way of living presents each of us with a phenomenally wide array of viewpoints and ways of being. Newspapers, magazines, TV and radio carry an almost infinite range of opinions and beliefs. Interviews and documentaries probe the thoughts, feelings and activities of celebrities and warts 'n' all biographies dissect the private lives of public figures. Reality programmes – currently 60 per cent of the entire global output of TV[2] – display the most intimate behaviour of everyone from members of royal families to vacuous wannabes.

Much reality TV focuses on personal transformation, and change is seen as good *in itself*. The message is that whatever comes along it must be better simply because it is new. The public platform no longer displays a 'normal' or 'right' way to be but a help-yourself buffet of lifestyles to pick 'n' mix as you please.

At the same time our patterns of social interaction have changed enormously. For many of us, like Rose, it is an everyday event to talk to and swap opinions with dozens of different citizens of the world, each one of which is likely to come from a different culture, hold different political views and religious beliefs and engage in different family and sexual relationships. Wider but looser friendship networks have evolved thanks to the ease of communication made possible by email, texting and low-cost international transport.

One effect of this is to make friendships seem very intimate while actually making them more superficial. Courtesy titles, for instance, have largely been abandoned, so we are instantly on first name terms with every otherwise-anonymous telephone salesperson. Not so long ago, to start calling someone (other than a child) by their first name was an important milestone in the gradual development of a friendship, but now using a forename is more or less meaningless. It might not even be the person's name at all. In the course of a recent conversation with a woman who worked on a technical helpline I asked for her name so that I could call her – specifically – back. 'I'm Jane,' she said. And then: 'Oh – no, sorry – I mean Karen.' She explained that the workers were not allowed to reveal their real names, but that each was given a name for the day, according to which work station they happened to be sitting at. So today she was Karen, while yesterday, when she was in the booth next door, she had been Jane.

How multiplicity can protect your health

Instant intimacy at first meeting – the sharing of personal information such as what you earn or your religious beliefs – is now quite normal, whereas once such things would have been known only to your nearest and dearest. Many bloggers (online diarists) and newspaper columnists go much further and happily share the most intimate details of their lives – or seem to.

Over the last few months I have been reading, fascinated, a regular column written by a journalist with whom I happen to share some friends. Her writing would lead you to believe that she is revealing every tiny detail of her life: each spat with her partner, every bitchy thought about her mother-in-law, every episode of chaotic child-rearing. Nothing seems to be left out. She writes amusingly, and the picture that emerges is of a blessedly privileged woman whose worst miseries can easily be turned into entertainment. Yet I know that she is actually coping with an ongoing health problem in the family that is so severe you would expect it to entirely eclipse the day-to-day tribulations she writes about. She seems to be telling us everything, but the biggest thing of all in her life is never referred to at all.

It is easy to leap to the conclusion that this woman is putting on a mask when she writes, hiding her sadness and fear behind a 'false' personality. Last time I met this woman, however, I asked her: wasn't it a strain, making out that the small irritations of her life are so central to her when they clearly aren't?

'Oh but they *are*,' she replied. 'When I write the column those things are my only concerns. That is why I do it, and love doing it. For a while each week I am a woman with nothing more to worry about than my husband using my silk knickers as a baby's bib. I'm not pretending to find it maddening – at the time it really is the biggest thing in my life because the other me, the one with real problems, just isn't there!'

Not so long ago such a response would be seen as evidence of 'shallowness' or duplicity, but in this woman's case it just indicated her ability to switch in to a different mode – to *become* the frivolous, not-a-care-in-the-world columnist that her readers have come to expect.

It is tempting simply to bemoan all this and get sentimental about the days of fixed identities, enduring relationships, unchanging habits and constant values. But in doing that we forget that in many ways those days were, for many, cruelly restrictive.

Anyway, to look back to such times is simply pointless. Unless there is some catastrophic social upheaval on a global scale it is unlikely that the pace of technological change and social expansion will slow down. If we are to swim in a disjointed and ever-changing world we need more than ever to pull on our ability to see things from multiple viewpoints and to adopt different behaviours in different situations. As we hurtle from one encounter to another, the 'self' that we project has to be altered, if ever so slightly, for each one.

A trend towards multiplicity, like the shift toward greater dissociation generally suggested by Steven Gold, can be seen, then, as an adaptive response to a changing environment. The wider the experiences we are offered the greater number and varieties of personalities a person is likely to develop. Far from being unhealthy it is a natural consequence of the astonishing flexibility of the human brain.

Recognising the many inner 'yous' may even protect you from illness. A research project conducted by psychologist Patricia Linville, now of Duke University (previously Yale) suggests that the more of what she calls 'personality tributaries' or 'self-aspects' a person can identify, the better equipped they are to weather stressful events.

Linville asked a hundred college students to select characteristics such as 'outgoing', 'lazy' and 'affectionate' which they thought described themselves. She found that the more of these qualities that a student selected and – importantly – the more distinctive they were from each other, the less likely they were to suffer backaches, headaches, infections and menstrual cramps when they were under stress. They also reported fewer symptoms of depression.

Linville concluded that this was because a stressful event has less impact on a person who is aware of their multiplicity because it affects only one, or some, of their group. As she puts it: 'a tennis player who has just lost an important match is likely to feel dejected, and these negative feelings are likely to become associated with this person's "tennis-player" self-aspect. But it won't spill over and color the individual's other self-aspects if they are both numerous and distinct from one another. You have these uncontaminated areas of your life that act as buffers.'[3]

Problem families

Useful though it potentially is, multiplicity does not always make our lives easier. Like any group of people who are bound together our various personalities may not always work as a team. Sometimes they withhold information from one another, fight for control or refuse to step forward when needed.

Have you, for example, ever *really* wanted something – then thrown it away just as it is within your grasp? Or sabotaged a relationship for no reason you understand? Have you blurted out the thing that you least wanted someone to know, or exploded with anger at the very moment you most needed to stay calm? Can you recall flunking out of an important event you spent weeks preparing for, or turning over in bed and going back to sleep on a morning when it was vital you rose early? Do you ever, in the small hours of the morning, *groan* with embarrassment at some stupid thing you have done?

Perhaps you never experience any of these things. But if so you are unusual, to say the least. Practically all of us do and feel contrary things from time to time. Afterwards we talk of 'not being ourselves'. We berate ourselves for our stupidity or self-destructiveness, or agonise over what's wrong with our lives. Should we divorce? Resign? Downsize? Change continents? Change sex?

To be in two, or more 'minds' about what to do is generally considered to be bad because it tends to produce the discomfort of uncertainty and inner conflict. Most of us therefore try to quash all but one of our personalities. Invariably it is the quieter, less assertive minors that are made to shut up, even when they might be talking better sense than the major who vanquishes them. The problem, in other words, is not that we are multi-minded but that we refuse to acknowledge our multiplicity and so use it to advantage.

Feeling as if we are just one has its uses, as we'll see. Paradoxically, though, a strong conviction of unity can actually create inner conflict. A thought experiment might help to explain why.

The early-riser and the alarm-clock saboteur

Imagine you are due to start a new job next morning, so you go to bed determined to get up bright and early. During the night, however, the personality who commanded 'Bright and early' is ousted by one who couldn't care less about work but really likes the comfort of their bed. When the alarm clock goes off at some unearthly hour this new 'you' sensibly says 'to hell with it', turns off the alarm, and goes right back to sleep.

Now imagine that during this lie-in the old you is reinstated. When it wakes up and finds the alarm clock switched off and the new job already in jeopardy it is, of course, very annoyed.

If the two personalities were completely separate – as in a person with MPD – the up-with-the-lark personality would just be baffled because it would have no memory of the earlier, brief, awakening. But we are not talking about entirely separate personalities – rather the sort that exist in most of us: different in many ways but able to peer into each other's memory bags and thus recall, at least vaguely, what they did and why they did it.

So the lark personality recalls the earlier awakening, the irritation with the alarm and the decision to go back to sleep. Indeed, it recalls it *as though it made that decision itself*. So, rather than just be baffled by the earlier act, it is irritated about it. And because it does not realise it was done by a different personality it is angry with *itself*. The shared memory gives it the illusion that it is responsible for its neighbour's behaviour, which it perceives as a fault – a weakness – in itself. So it blames itself. Feels guilty. Thinks itself unreliable, flawed and 'neurotic'.

Meanwhile, of course, the alarm-clock saboteur has exercised its will and got clean away with it! The early riser takes the rap for both of them, so, although it knows the consequences of its actions, the alarm-clock saboteur doesn't care. As this pattern repeats itself over years and decades, the alarm-clock saboteur becomes more and more irresponsible, while the early riser becomes guilt-ridden, undermined, increasingly convinced that it is 'bad'. To others, the 'individual' who comprises these personalities seems inconsistent, moody and unreliable.

Renegades

Minors that have thoughts, emotions and behaviour that are directly at odds with a person's major grow so far apart that they cut off from it completely. This is especially likely when a person is under unusual external pressure. In some cases a perfectly normal person can experience the sort of memory black-outs that plague those with MPD.

An old friend of mine, Sara, recently told me about something she did when her daughter (now twelve) was a toddler. Sara has always seemed to me to be an exceptionally conscientious mother (which is probably why she never mentioned this until I spoke to her about this book) and in my experience she is about as steady and reliable as it is possible to be. Both the uncharacteristic nature of the act, and her subsequent haziness of memory suggest it was done by a character who is very different from her major personality:

Emma was going through that awful tantrummy stage and one day we were in a crowded store when she lay down on the floor and simply squalled. I think it happened because I wouldn't let her have a packet of crisps. Normally I would have tried to reason with her, or I'd have ignored her for a bit, or physically picked her up and taken her out of the shop. But this time I did none of those things. I walked out. Just left her there.

Looking back – which, of course I have done endlessly – I honestly don't know what I was thinking when I did it. I remember looking at Emma kicking her legs on the floor and seeing her little face scrunched up with such fury. Then the next thing I remember is being in a shoe shop surrounded by sandals. I must have walked out of the super-market, crossed the road, walked into the shoe shop and asked the assistant to get me the shoes. It must have taken ten minutes at least.

When I got back to the supermarket Emma was being walked up and down the aisles by a member of staff, looking for me. I made up some story about turning my back for a moment and losing her . . . said I had panicked and run outside to see if she had wandered off. I got away with it – no harm done. But it was a very frightening thing to happen – not for Emma, as it turned out, but for me.

Until she left Emma squalling, Sara didn't know that she – literally – 'had it in her' to do such a thing. The personality that took her off to buy shoes was just not visible to the good mother who was usually so firmly in charge. It was only by looking back on what happened – viewing it as though from outside, that Sara realised she is not quite the wholly inte-grated person she imagined. In her attempt to be a perfect mother she had locked away the personality in her that – before Emma came along – had indulged a passion for fashionable clothes, fun outings and inde-pendence. Just for a moment, in that supermarket, it flared back into life, eclipsing the mother for just as long as it took to get Sara to the shoe shop.

Taking responsibility

One reason, perhaps, why people are reluctant to acknowledge human multiplicity is the fear that to do so would be to undermine the principle of personal responsibility. If everyone started blaming their less acceptable behaviour on someone else there would be chaos, so it is safer to hang on to the illusion of singularity. Indeed, our brains may even have evolved to generate the illusion because, in our socially interdependent species, it aided peaceful co-existence by forcing us to hold ourselves responsible for all our actions.

In fact the notion of personal responsibility is a frail one even without introducing the notion of multiplicity. This is why: responsibility is generally taken to mean *conscious* responsibility. I'm not likely to hold you responsible for treading on my toe if you are pushed on to it by the lurch of a train we are travelling on. And sleepwalkers who commit crimes without apparent conscious intention or knowledge are generally not held to be criminally responsible (providing they can persuade a court or other accuser that they really were asleep!). It is conscious intent that matters – the *decision* to do the act.

When you look closely at decisions, however, you find a funny thing. A decision to do something seems, quite obviously, to be made *before* the action is started. Indeed, it is difficult to see, at first, how it could possibly be any other way. But this apparent timing – the very thing that makes a decision a decision – turns out to be another illusion.

If you were to look at your brain activity in the second or so before you move your hand to do something – reaching for a cup, say, you would find that the bits of it which produce the action (the part that works out exactly which muscle fibres need to contract in order to carry it out and so on) become active before you 'decide' to make the movement. By the time you think, I'll take a sip of coffee, your body is already prepared to reach for the mug.

In other words, it is not the conscious 'you' – not *any* of them – who dictates the action. It is the dancing neurons in your brain, responding to cues of which the currently conscious personality may be entirely unaware. We know this because of a remarkable series of experiments carried out by the US neuroscientist Benjamin Libet nearly a quarter of a century ago. What he did was to rig up volunteers with brain sensors and then, while monitoring the activity in their cortex, invite them to make a hand movement in their own time while noting very precisely when they decided to do it. Libet then compared three things: the time when the neural activity associated with the movement began; the time when the volunteers said they decided to move, and the time when their hands actually moved.

What he found – to his own surprise – was that the brain activity that would lead to the hand movement started more than a quarter of a second before the volunteers made the decision to move. And the actual movement occurred a fraction of a second after that. The brain, it seemed, was way ahead of the conscious 'self' that thought it was controlling the event.

What feels like a decision, then, is really only the conscious recognition of a decision your brain has already made without any help from a conscious personality. The conscious thought seems to dictate the action because it occurs in the split second between your body being prepared for it and the muscle fibres actually contracting and carrying it out.

Given that we experience this thousands of times a day – we think of an action, then we see it happen – it is not surprising that we learn to feel as though we are controllers, rather than mere observers, of our behaviour. The illusion of self-determination is such a good one that to all intents and purposes it really doesn't matter that it is illusory. We *feel* as though we are in control, we talk as though we are in control, and we assume everyone else is in control. The question of whether we really are seems pretty academic – an updated version of how many angels can dance on a pin head.

Intruders and gate-crashers

The question of responsibility becomes very difficult to ignore, however, when we consider multiplicity because it acts as the leading edge in what philosopher Daniel Dennett has called 'creeping exculpation'. Increasingly people have denied responsibility for their acts by claiming it wasn't them who did it but – variously – their upbringing, their education, their genes, or their brain. Multiplicity could be seen as an encouragement to go one step further still – to claim they weren't even there at the time! Indeed this has already happened. There have been several instances of killers claiming the deed was done by an alter, and in one case a person tried to get off on the basis that the personality who committed a crime was below the age of consent, even though the body they inhabited was well past it.

Furthermore, as we discover more about precisely which bits of the brain produce which responses it is going to get easier and easier to alter behaviour and consciousness – in other words, to create and trigger different personalities – through drugs and surgery.

There is nothing new about this, of course. We have known for at least a century that changes to the brain, particularly to the frontal lobes, can produce quite dramatic alterations in a person's behaviour. In the early twentieth century some doctors and psychiatrists tried to turn this observation to good use by altering the frontal lobes surgically. The idea was to improve the inner life (and behaviour) of the hordes of mentally distressed people who were languishing miserably in asylums or failing to be helped by the only 'talking' therapy then available, psychoanalysis. Tens of thousands of these people were thus given lobotomies – a procedure that involved inserting a small ice pick into the front of their brains and swishing it about to cut various connections.

Contrary to received wisdom, the personality changes wrought by this crude operation were a godsend to a large proportion of those who had them. But it was horrendously crude, based on only the vaguest understanding of frontal lobe function, and it was used too often, on the wrong people, for the wrong reasons. The ensuing scandal that resulted from this was one reason why psychosurgery for mood and personality fell out of fashion and has since come to be widely regarded with fear and loathing.

A sophisticated form of lobotomy remains, though, a last-ditch option for the treatment of severe and otherwise intractable mood disorders. Its ability to silence one personality and create or revive another is clear in this account of the aftermath of one such operation.

British doctor Cathy Wield suffered eight years of horrendously severe depression. During that time she was plagued by a self-destructive personality that constantly urged her to self-harm. One week after the surgery a defiant, protecting personality suddenly became active and successfully challenged the one that had been active for so long.

Cathy describes the moment her personalities first switched like this: 'I was sitting in the TV room with a nurse beside me quite late in the evening. L., the patient who had shared the room with me before the operation, came in. She had returned from home leave and was clearly fed up. She slumped into a chair saying, "All I want is to be at home with my husband and children." I was thinking, I wish she would just be quiet, when all of a sudden a light switched on in my head! It was as if a power cable had been connected and the generator had gone on: this tremendous sensation of light blazing through my innermost being happened in an instant. I was amazed, startled, almost bewildered. I started to cry, realising that the darkness had gone, the depression was over! Now I was like her – all I wanted was to be at home with my husband and children.'

At this point Cathy asked the nurse for permission to leave the room to assimilate things (she was under twenty-four-hour observation because of her habit of cutting herself.) 'As I left the room,' she recalls, 'I experienced a very clear internal voice. It did not seem to come from me at all. "What about the self-harm?" I answered it defiantly: "I do not want it any more. I want to be at home with my family." It left me alone. After three days it left, never to return again.'[4]

Apart from its maligned reputation, another reason why lobotomies became, and remain, very rare is because drugs have been developed which can do a similar job without the stomach-turning business of cutting flesh. Whereas the lobotomists' ice-pick physically severed the 'wires' that carried messages from one part of the brain to another, drugs work by altering the effect of neurotransmitters – chemicals which transmit messages from cell to cell and 'instruct' brain areas to spark up or shut down. The effects of a drug, like those of the ice-pick, are not entirely predictable and sometimes they do nothing at all. While they are working, though, they can they can produce a new personality as effectively as a lobotomy.

Millions of people have discovered this for themselves through the use of mood-altering drugs such as antidepressants. The drugs not only alter the way people feel, they also seem to switch the bag of memories a person holds. If you ask a person with depression to recall happy memories they will typically be hard-pressed to find any. Negative recollections, by contrast, come to mind only too easily.[5]

As you might expect, if the drugs are actually creating a switch in personality, the mood and memory changes are accompanied by a change, too, in the way people see the world. 'It wasn't just that I felt happier when the antidepressants kicked in,' recalls my friend Isobel. 'I saw things differently. This really came home to me once when I was falling about with laughter at a film on TV and J [her husband] said: "You didn't laugh once when we saw this in the cinema." Only then I remembered that, yes, I had seen it before. And I hadn't found it funny at all. So who was this person clutching her ribs? I liked being her – but she felt like a stranger.'

It is easy to understand why a drug-induced personality may seem like an interloper, or even an alien. Most of our personalities have developed slowly, growing up within our environment like local flora and fauna. Their characteristics don't just spring up from nowhere – they have been moulded, usually quite slowly, by repeated experience and often we can see (or think we see) why we developed that particular response to that particular situation.

Personalities which are produced by direct physiological changes in the brain bypass this developmental process. The functional and anatomical changes that usually happen slowly are produced instead in a matter of days or weeks. Older personalities – if they are still active at all – may well feel the new one is not 'one of them'. So it is perhaps not surprising that our increasing awareness of multiplicity is producing more and more situations in which major personalities are refusing to take the rap for minors who fail to comply with group values.

The 'gate-crashing' quality of some drug-induced personalities makes them an easy target for this sort of rejection, especially if the previous personality (or personalities) never asked to be relieved from duty in the first place.

At the time of writing US lawyers are preparing to sue the producers of a type of drug used for Parkinson's disease. The suit is being brought on behalf of dozens of people who claim the medicine turned them into sex-mad and gambling-addicted obsessives. The drugs in question enhance the effect of a neurotransmitter called dopamine, the neurotransmitter which is depleted in Parkinson's patients. The chemical is responsible for keeping us moving steadily, which is why Parkinson's patients develop a jerky gait and sometimes come to a halt altogether. Dopamine also motivates us in a more general way, and when we are motivated the direction we go in is to seek things which will give us a pleasurable kick. In some people, it seems, upping the effect of dopamine produces such a strong push for pleasure that they cannot walk away from situations which seem to promise kicks, even when they know them to be ultimately bad for them.

One woman litigant claims, for example, that after twenty-nine years of faithful marriage, starting the drug caused her to quit her religion and embark on a torrid extramarital love affair. Another woman became addicted to gambling. It started, she says, on a weekend visit to Las Vegas with her sister when she surprised herself by playing the tables in the casinos until dawn – and then went right back in next day. When she got home she began gambling over the internet and soon she had exhausted her credit cards, emptied her retirement accounts and sold jewellery to fuel her habit.

'I won huge amounts of money,' she said. 'I stood in front of a machine and won $62,000 and $28,000 in single spins.' Yet, with one exception, she never walked out of a casino with money because the gambler in her could never walk away. 'You always put it back in,' she says, 'because no amount of money is enough.'[6]

Although this woman's new, apparently drug-created personality clearly had a strong grip by now, her previous major was still active enough to make the occasional attempt to control it. First it put a filter on her computer to block the gambling websites, but the new personality responded by driving her to casinos. Her major then got her voluntarily banned from the casinos in her home state of Illinois, but the new minor started driving to play in Indiana. Now her major (presumably) is seeking compensation for being so rudely usurped.

Acknowledging we are not alone does not itself create responsibility where there was none. Once our personalities realise there are others sharing their mind, however, they can start to get to know each other, explore their strengths and weaknesses, discover what situations bring each of them to life, and allow each its moment in the sun. Majors can learn to give way on occasions to those who are more retiring, imaginative or patient. Fearful, pessimistic and distrustful personalities might learn to come out only when they are really useful. Over-conscientious majors can agree to give ne'er do wells and shopping queens their lie-ins and indulgences.

The sections of this book that show how to engage inner personalities in conversation with one another should also help them to sort out their various responsibilities. But before that, let's look at where our personalities come from – the raw material, if you like, from which we construct the people we are.

CHAPTER 5

The People You Are

Every personality within us is unique because no two share an identical personal history. They tend, however, to fall into types: naughty or fearful or playful children, controllers and subordinates, censorious or protective adults, pacifists and troublemakers. As we have seen, the stuff from which they are constructed are experiences which click together, like building bricks, because they share some common (usually emotional) factor. I have already explained how they are linked together into the clusters which form our personalities. This chapter looks at the various ways that our brains select this raw material, and the different types of personalities that result.

Inner parents

Babies are natural mimics, and they are also both literally and metaphorically short-sighted. So the first building blocks of our personalities – the fragmentary responses I am calling micros – inevitably come from the people closest to them. Some of these may stick as isolated quirks, but others form the cornerstones of minors which may stick around for a lifetime, or the kernel of what may in time become the child's major.

'My granny had this odd expression that she came out with sometimes,' remembers Maureen:

'Oo-er!' she'd go. 'Oo-eeer!' I was only ten when she died, but I can remember her making this sound, just these two vowels. I suppose it made a particular impression on me because she only said it when something kind of frightening was happening; something she didn't understand. Even as a child I remember finding it irritating, because it conveyed the sort of child-like fear of the unknown that I thought was silly even then.

I had forgotten all about it until the other day, when I walked into my bedroom and saw my drawers had been tipped out and the things scattered. And what do I say? Not '**** it! I've been burgled!' No, I say – clearly as anything – 'Oo-er!' I hadn't heard that sound for forty years and suddenly there it was – coming out of my own mouth!

Although Maureen's 'Oo-er' might not seem to mean much, it carried a whole clutch of nervous, superstitious beliefs, born of ignorance. This wisp of a personality lay dormant for decades, but given an appropriate trigger it emerged with all the strength and clarity it had when it was part of her grandmother.

Micros derived from our parents and other early carers inevitably creep into our repertoire of learned responses. But as children grow up they tend to seek out new ways of being, and actively resist copying their parents. Indeed, by the teenage years the influence of a child's parents has been largely eclipsed by that of their peers.[1]

When a child rejects those bits of themselves which they have absorbed from their parents, though, it doesn't necessarily kill them off. Habits of mind that are picked up in the first few years of life often just go underground, like Maureen's 'Oo-er'. And although some may remain dormant for a person's entire lifetime, others may babble away constantly just beneath the level of consciousness. Such semi-buried minors may be useful sources of comfort, wisdom or creativity – our parents' most valuable legacy to us. But some seem intent on waging guerrilla warfare with the dominant major.

Eleanor, for example, hosts an almost continual skirmish between a part of her mother that she took in as a child and her own major. The first is a clutch of harsh and judgemental ideas with which her mother was inculcated during her constrained Scottish Presbyterian upbringing and which she, in turn, passed on to her daughter. Eleanor's major, on the other hand, was created largely during the 1970s, when she lived in an urban commune which embraced a set of values almost entirely at odds with her mother's. She says:

> I think of 'me' as liking people who are unconventional and carefree. But when I actually meet people like that I often find that, even as I'm smiling at them and thinking how nice they are, little words or thoughts pop into my head like 'Wastrel!' or 'Lazy!' or 'Selfish!' For instance, several years ago my son brought home a girlfriend. This girl had a ring in her tummy button and a tattoo below it, disappearing into her jeans. When I saw this girl a voice piped up in my head saying, 'Common tart!'
>
> It really quite surprised me because I wasn't thinking that. I mean, I didn't THINK I was thinking that! I went over it in my head afterwards – kind of replaying it. And I realised that not only were the words my mother's (she was always calling girls 'tarts') but I actually heard them in my mother's voice.

Parentally derived minors often come to the fore when a person has children of their own. 'My mum wrapped me up in cotton wool when I was little,' says Suzanne:

> She would keep me back from school if there was any sort of illness going round and she wouldn't let me go horse-riding because she had once read about a girl who got dragged along the road with her foot caught in a stirrup. Once she stopped me going on a rock-climbing holiday with the school because she thought I'd fall off and break all my precious little bones.
>
> After I left home she turned her worry on the world in general. She used to cut out stories of peculiar accidents from the newspapers – people who got struck by lightning or got their limbs bitten off by crocodiles. She'd show them to people when they came round to the house – it got really embarrassing.

I thought I had escaped all of that. I made a point of not being scared of danger. I took up hang-gliding and water-skiing and even tried drag-car racing, just to prove to myself that I could. But when I had Jamie everything changed. Of course you expect to be changed by having a baby but what I never expected was to be changed into my mum. I found myself reading about cot deaths all the time, and rare baby diseases. And when he started toddling the whole planet seemed to be made of objects put there just to kill him.

One day, a couple of years ago, my partner came home and found Jamie squalling with anger and me trying to explain to him that he couldn't go swimming because the pool was probably polluted. John [Suzanne's partner] was usually really tolerant about my obsessions, but for some reason on this occasion he went ballistic. That was when he pointed out that I was turning into my mother.

Another event that often jogs internalised parents into action is when a person's real parent dies. Immediately after the death of his father, neuroscientist Robert Sapolski found himself spouting the older man's sayings, and taking on his mannerisms.

'I found myself arranging the utensils as he had, or humming his favourite Yiddish tune,' he recalls. 'Soon I had forsaken my own blue flannel shirts and put on his. I developed an interest in his profession, architecture, absentmindedly drawing floor plans of my apartment.'

About a month after his bereavement, the father inside Sapolski 'broke through' while he was lecturing to his students. He says:

I thought to tell them about what a spectacular lecturer my father had been, to pass on some of what I had learned from his teaching. I intended a eulogy, but something became confused, and soon, wearing his shirt, I was lecturing for him, offering the frail advice of an octogenarian.

I warned them to expect setbacks amid their ambitious plans, because every commitment would entail turning their backs on many others. I told them that though they wanted to change the world, they should prepare for the inconceivable – someday they would become tired. This was not me speaking, still with a sheltered optimism, but him with his weathered disappointments.[2]

Inner children

Young children, as we have seen, are natural multiples. The illusion of unity doesn't kick in until they learn to see themselves as though from the outside – in other words, to be self-reflective. Until then there is only the 'I' of the here and now, quite unconnected with the 'I' of yesterday or the 'I' that will be around tomorrow. Hence the child generates countless 'I's – each one a distinct state of mind.

In late infancy children develop the ability to think in symbolic terms. This releases them from the here and now and allows them to imagine things existing in the past and the future. With that, children begin to join their multiple 'I's together. The toddler realises that the 'I' that chucked the pretty yellow paint on the pink carpet a minute ago is connected with the 'I' that is now being sent quite unreasonably early to bed. The child may not yet feel a sense of responsibility for the experiment in interior décor, but he does remember it as though it was his own action. And with this the notion of a continuing, single self takes root.

Children get better at weaving together their 'I's as they get older, but the juvenile network of self is generally much patchier than that of adults. Most of the little I's that children generate just fade away, like wispy clouds in a summer sky. But some are too intensely experienced to disappear. If the experiences in which they are incorporated are also very different from anything the child has previously experienced these small characters may not merge with others and will remain isolated from the rest of the previous and future 'I's and frozen in time.

Most of us do not have terrified child minors like those so often seen in MPD, and the existence of child minors certainly does not mean that a person was abused. But many of us have a nervous child, or a shy child, or a needy, jealous or insecure child. This is because the intense experiences that create unforgettable infant personalities are often highly charged with pain or shame or embarrassment.

When we experience these emotions as adults the child that first experienced them may be shaken back into life, even if the particular experiences which brought it into being may be lost. Not for nothing do we speak of feeling 'small' when we are humiliated or ashamed.

'Recently I was at a party, feeling like a wallflower,' says Hazel:

I didn't know anyone there and no one was taking any notice of me, but I still felt very self-conscious. And suddenly I had this memory of being in the playground at my first school. All the other children were playing with each other and shrieking and laughing and I had no one to play with and I was sort of slinking along what seemed to be a massive redbrick wall and wanting it to kind of – absorb me, I suppose. I was trying to make myself disappear.

Just for a moment, at that party, I was that child. I mean I really felt that small, and I found myself leaning against the wall of the room wanting it to swallow me up just like I did that day at school. Thankfully a friend came and rescued me and I sort of snapped back to being grown-up.

Another woman I interviewed for this book, Gail, also described the emergence of an angry and hurt child. In her case it appeared when she entered shops:

For years I loathed shopping because I always felt I was being watched with suspicion. I would constantly survey the other customers and wonder if they were store detectives. If I picked something up to take to the till I would hold it aloft in order to make it quite clear that I was not about to slip it into some concealed pocket. If I saw something else that I was interested in on my way to the pay desk, rather than lingering with the unpaid for item in my hand, I would go and pay for it, then come back to the second thing. If I decided to buy that, too, I would have to make two separate transactions. All the time I was doing this absurd thing, I would feel angry. As though I was suspected of shoplifting, and was feeling the fury of the false accusation.

The child responsible for this came to light when Gail saw a book jacket in a store which featured a partly demolished sandcastle:

> Quite suddenly I was transported into a memory of a particular day at the beach. I must have been about two and a half or three. In my mind my mother is sitting in a deckchair, dozing, while I make a sandcastle. There is another little girl playing in much the same way just a few yards away. I see her putting a little flag in the top of her sandcastle. I want it. Badly.
>
> Now I know I can't just take it. I know that you have to have permission for that sort of thing. So I crawl up to my mother and ask her if I may have the little girl's flag. My mother doesn't respond at first, and I realise she has dropped off. So I pluck a bit at her skirt and ask again. And this time she stirs and says, 'Mmmmmm . . . yes, dear.' Or something like that. Certainly not 'No'.
>
> So, confident with parental approval, I crawl over to the other child's sandcastle and take the flag off the top. Next thing is that the child's mother is grabbing my hand and removing the flag, and then leaning in towards me and saying something with an ugly expression on her face. It is scary, so I open my mouth and scream.
>
> Somewhere in the midst of this my mother arrives, but instead of comforting me she picks me up and carries me away quite roughly. And then – to my astonishment – she gives me a slap on the leg. I don't remember feeling the slap, but I remember howling louder after it – not with pain but with outrage!

As she recalled this incident Gail realised the emotions she felt when she shopped were identical in quality (though obviously less intense) to those that were generated in her then. Her fear of store detectives belonged to the mistakenly accused three-year-old.

Child personalities are not always angry or scared. Qualities such as playfulness, curiosity, wonder, trustfulness, naivety, creativity and sheer fun are quite often held by child minors because the adult self (or selves) did not incorporate them. This is most likely to occur in a person who is thrust suddenly into a grown-up world and feel obliged to 'put away childish things'.

Jim's childhood was abruptly ended at fifteen when his father died and he was forced to go out to work to earn money to help support his mother and four siblings. His wife, Ellen, believed that early introduction to the responsibilities of adulthood prevented Jim from enjoying his own children. 'He was a "good" father, but distant,' she says. 'He never played games with [our son] or made model airplanes with him, or even took him to football matches. All that was left to me.'

As a grandfather, though, Jim is entirely different. Because he does not feel responsible for his grandchildren in the way he did for his own children, they seem to release in him a child that was invisible for six decades. Unlike children that have merged with adult personalities, though, Jim's juvenile personality is *purely* childlike. 'When our two grandchildren are here Jim gives them a wonderful time,' says Ellen. 'But it is awful for me because I find myself dealing with *three* children. And however much I warn him not to overdo it physically (he is nearly seventy) he always does. So next day he is back to his dour old self and complaining about a stiff back!'

Roles and stereotypes

Mimicry and, ultimately, empathy, depends on special brain cells called mirror neurons. These are cells that are activated both when we do something and when we see another person doing that same thing. If I see you, say, picking up a cup, my mirror neurons give me a faint cup-picking-up experience myself. I don't have to work out what you, the picker-upper, is experiencing because I have a shadowy, but first-hand echo of it. I might not actually move my hand to grasp the handle, as you do, but the neurons which make the grasping muscles contract will prod me to just that. This is why people copy one another's body language so faithfully – you cross your legs and I, seeing it, get prompted by my mirror neurons to do the same even if I am not conscious of it.

At an unconscious level mirror neurons continually simmer away, bringing us in line with the behaviour we see going on around us. Riding a commuter train, for example, most people tend to adopt typical 'commuter behaviour', avoiding eye and – if possible – body contact with fellow commuters, moving determinedly through the concourse, hurried, distracted. For the duration of the journey a person becomes just that insular, single-minded 'commuter' – a minor personality that comes out for this single daily activity.

Stereotypical minors like this exist in nearly all of us, created by the demands of a situation or the pressure of others' expectations. Certain jobs encourage their development. A nurse is expected to be efficient, kindly, calm, organised. A doctor is meant to be confident, all-knowing. A mother nurturing, a teenager rebellious, a gang leader aggressive.

Of course, the stereotypical commuter, doctor, mother and so on does not get created in every person who travels to work, practises medicine, is a mother and so on. Some people do not adopt these roles at all. The tendency to do so, though, is great because stereotypical behaviour is often useful. A doctor who fails to create a professionally detached personality to deal with suffering patients may become emotionally overwhelmed or exhausted by her work. A gang leader who does not behave aggressively will not lead the gang for long.

Over and above the specific demands of day-to-day life, most societies also impose more general expectations. In some cultures, for instance, girls are still meant to be shy and submissive, while men are meant to be assertive. Individuals growing up in such a society almost inevitably develop personalities which incorporate these characteristics. Frequently, though, these are minors which are shed as soon as societal pressure is lifted. Hence people who are brought up in two (or more) distinctly different cultures often have a different personality in each one. Such differences tend to be amplified in people who speak more than one language.

The Turkish writer and commentator Elif Shafak was brought up in what she describes as 'a life of discontinuities', constantly moving from a fairly conservative culture in Turkey to a far more liberal world in England. She subsequently forged a career in Turkey, but then moved to the USA, where she discovered that switching back to writing in English brought out 'voices that were already inside me'. She sees this happen all the time in her multicultural friends: 'In every language a person is different,' she says. 'It is not just the voice that changes – the whole mindset changes too. I know many girls who find they can't swear in Turkish, for example, because the culture prohibits it so strongly. But when they speak in English they have no inhibitions about it.'[3]

Bilinguals have even been shown to have different profiles on standard personality tests, depending on which language they are speaking. Researchers at the University of Texas tested individuals who were bilingual in English and Spanish for various personality traits and found that the subjects answered the questions differently according to the language they did the tests in. In English they came out as more extroverted, agreeable and conscientious. Another study found that Chinese–American bilingual managers came over as more ambitious and egotistical when they were quizzed in English than in Chinese.[4]

The ease with which stereotypes can be created and subsequently activated by other people's expectations has been demonstrated in several intriguing studies. In one, researchers took a group of both black and white college students who had previously gained similar grades in school. The students were split into two groups, then asked to fill in a form which involved giving verbal answers to some tricky questions. At that time (and still to some extent today) there was a widespread notion that black people are less good at verbal reasoning than whites. Before the test the students in one of the two groups were subtly reminded of this prejudice by being asked to declare their racial origin before being informed, pointedly, that the quiz was a verbal reasoning test. The other group was simply told that they would be filling in an unimportant 'research tool' with no hint that there was anything competitive about it. Under these circumstances the black students in the first group performed notably less well than the white students in their group. Those in the second group, however, did just as well as their fellow whites.

What seems to have happened is that in the context of a competitive word test, the forced reminder of their colour triggered in the black students a minor personality that dutifully fulfilled what was expected of it. As Julius Caesar is said to have observed: 'In the end it is impossible not to be what others think you are.'

Similar effects of stereotyping have been found in several other groups. Some of the most telling experiments have involved Asian–American women. These people are subject to two contradictory stereotypes. One is that, as Asians, they are good at numbers, but bad at anything involving use of the English language; two is that, as women, they are good at verbal tasks but bad at numbers. One study found that when the women were subtly 'primed' to think of themselves primarily as Asians, their performance on a maths test improved while their performance on a verbal test became worse. When they were primed to think of themselves as primarily female the opposite happened: their maths performance declined while their language ability improved.

Other studies confirmed that the stereotypical minors triggered in the Asian women didn't just *behave* according to what was expected of them – they also felt more Asian or more female according to the situation. Asked to recall memories which were primarily about their ethnicity – a visit to the country from which their ancestors came, say, or taking part in a ritual or celebration that was traditional to that country – they proved better at retrieving such memories when they were asked to do it after a number test rather than the language test. They also rated the memories as happier. The opposite was true of their female identity. Memories of their first date, for example, came more quickly and were remembered more happily after the women did the language test.[5]

Another cunning experiment showed how women will produce a stereotypical 'weak' personality when they were reminded of the perceived shortcomings of their sex. A group of female students were asked to put up with having their hands squeezed for as long as they could as a measure, they were told, of their self-control and tenacity. Half of them were warned, before the hand-grip test, that they would subsequently be taking part in a test of mathematical ability. This acted as a reminder that women are meant to be bad at maths and the effect of it was to undermine the women's performance not just in the maths test but in the hand-squeezing exercise, too. The women who had been told about the forthcoming test begged to be released significantly sooner than the women who had not had the warning. It seemed that the reminder of one anti-female prejudice (lousy at sums) jogged another (weak-handed and weak-willed) and hence brought out a stereotypically girly personality in the women.[6]

Opposites, shadows and renegades

One effect of the extraordinary expansion of opportunities and challenges that has occurred for many of us in the last twenty years or so is that more and more people are developing personalities which differ quite dramatically from one another. In some people two or more may be so unalike that they effectively live separate lives, sometimes even under separate names. Each one may dress differently, have different friends, different interests and different habits. One may binge and another starve; one may pursue a hermetic existence and the other a wild social life; one may be heterosexual and another gay. One or more may even appear to be the opposite sex to the others.

Take, for example, Grayson Perry, the English potter who won the prestigious Turner Prize in 2003. Perry collected his award wearing a frilly pink frock and a hair-bow. Claire, the personality that came out for the occasion, co-exists perfectly happily with Grayson the man, a devoted husband and father and proud possessor of a Harley-Davidson motorbike.

Perry does not have MPD – he and Claire are well aware of one another and she only comes out when he wants her to. Indeed, Claire was quite consciously created by Perry's male major during his adolescence. 'Claire is to be looked at and treasured because that's what I want,' says Grayson. 'That is why I dress up: to externalise my need for attention; almost like a child, to be doted upon. So I'm doted on, hopefully, while I'm Claire.'[7]

Personalities like Grayson and Claire complement each other, but others may live in perpetual conflict. The most obvious examples are the increasing number of people who alternate between being very self-restrictive in their consumption of food, drugs or alcohol and bingeing. In 2001 some four million Americans were estimated to fulfil the diagnosis of binge-eating disorder.[8] Five years later the number had risen to nearly nine million – more than those with bulimia and anorexia nervosa combined.[9] Bingeing on alcohol and drugs, meanwhile, is rapidly becoming normal behaviour among the young. A recent study of American college students found that nearly half of them admitted to bingeing on drugs and/or alcohol.[10]

Addicts and Bingers may be held in check very successfully, but they are rarely vanquished altogether. One study, on rats' brains (which, like those of students, have much in common with normal adults) showed very clearly how reward-related habits can flicker back to life after they seem to be extinguished.

Neuroscientists at Massachusetts Institute of Technology used tiny electrodes to record the electrical activity in a part of the rats' brains where habits are known to be encoded. The animals then learned to associate certain sounds with a rewarding piece of chocolate – a classic bit of Pavlovian conditioning. As the rats learned the researchers noted the electrical patterns in their brains. Then they played the sounds without the chocolate, repeating them until the rats took no notice of them. Later, long after the rats had given up on their chocolate habit, the researchers put the reward back and again played the sounds. Almost instantly the old pattern popped up again. As one of the researchers, Ann Graybiel noted: 'It's like all that time they spent trying to break the habit doesn't count.'[11]

Addict personalities may emerge only in very particular situations. Juliana, for instance, has smoked for most of her adult life and was smoking when she met her current lover. Recently she gave up the habit and has successfully overcome it for several months. But when she is with her lover the desire to smoke returns. 'It's only with him that it happens,' she says. 'I think the reason is that our smoking helped bring us together because we were the only two people at work who did it and at some level I think our relationship was to do with being "the naughty ones" in the office. Now, when he is smoking and I'm not, I feel a bit as though I'm aligning myself with the others.'

At their simplest Addicts and their opposites, Self-Deniers, are just opposing drives – one composed of the urge to eat and the other of the desire to be slim; the urge to get pleasurably high and the urge to stay in control. But Addicts can turn into very complex personalities.

Ego-state therapist Marcia Degun-Mather reports a patient whose destructive eating binges were instigated by a child personality who was terrified of starvation. The patient, Mrs Z, was aware of some 'other' personality besides her major, but it was only under hypnosis that the child articulated what it was about. The personality confessed:

> I am not really powerful but Mrs Z thinks I am. In fact I am more pathetic than she is. I won't let her have a life. I need her more than she needs me. I want to keep her helpless, it's best. I can fool her and manip-ulate her. She makes me feel powerful, and I don't want her to know that I am not brave enough to be on my own. I have to teach her a lesson when she tries to get rid of me, but I don't actually help her at all. I feed her things and she stays stuck, and I don't have to move. I am smug, but not happy. I pull strings and make her do what she does – like bingeing. I am not her friend. I am just a manipulator and keep her scared.[12]

Encouraging troublesome personalities to explain themselves can be useful and bringing them to consciousness can help to engage them in dialogue with their neighbours. Such conversations may need to be carried on over a long period however. The co-conscious 'Alexes' I described in Chapter Two, for example, have been working for years on curbing the activities of a renegade personality in their otherwise exemplary household. About twice a year this particular Alex risks his life, and the others', by driving at breakneck speed through the streets of London. There is a particular spot near his home where the road curves around a couple of gentle S-bends and then twists sharply around a blind corner. Alex can take the bends at 85mph providing he brakes sharply at the oak tree just before the final turn. If he leaves the braking for another twenty yards the car skids off the road. The night he discov-ered that was one of several he has spent in a police cell.

The officer who scooped Alex out of his wrecked vehicle and arrested him for drunken driving encountered a rude and obstreperous personality, but the officer who brought him a cup of tea next day met one who was polite and apologetic. As the drink wore off, the reckless, criminal Alex slid into the background, leaving one of the responsible members of this co-conscious household to clear up the mess.

'It's like we have this stupid teenage thug living with us,' explains the estate agent Alex later. He goes on:

> Most of the time he sleeps but once in a while – if the rest of us are off our guard and there's drink about – he just takes over. Hijacking the car is his favourite thing. It's particularly terrifying because when he's driving the rest of us are in there with him – in the back seat, if you like – but unable to control our body. It used to happen all the time, but in the last few years we've started to get control of him. After the rest of us have apologised and done whatever has to be done to min-imise the damage we force him out and confront him. We've made a deal: if you want to come out you can – but wait until after we drive home. Then you can put on your CDs and annoy the neighbours if you must, make a mess, do whatever you like, but no driving! It's starting to work – he hasn't got loose for over a year now. But we have to watch him the whole time.

Identikits and celebrities – personalities from pieces

While some personalities construct themselves out of desires or needs which are denied by the other inhabitants, others are deliberately put together to achieve something which an existing personality may feel is missing from themselves. A major, for example, will pluck little bits of behaviour from their images of other people and then try to make them its own. If they do not fit easily with the major, however, they may form a separate personality.

So, for instance, we might take a particular way of walking from a film star, a certain tone of voice from a friend, a way of dressing from a temporary peer group. In doing so the personality who wants these attributes might succeed in changing itself, or it may create a new personality altogether.

Once we would have had to find our personality fragments from people in our own community or by embellishing in our heads the people we heard or read about in stories. But when photos and then movies came along, people started to cast their net wider.

The crazed celebrity culture that has developed in the last two decades has expanded the range and vastly multiplied the number of living icons to ape. We are surrounded by walking, talking, full-colour and ever more revelatory images of a huge cast of characters which have become the primary reference point for people searching for a new personality. Why model a Self on your mum or dad when you can make yourself into Johnny Depp or Nicole Kidman?

Although the gossip columns and fan magazines peddle endless 'intimate' details about these people's lives they are presented primarily as visual objects and those who seek to become them go first and foremost for the look. Two out of three women admit to spending money on deliberately copying some aspect of a celebrity's appearance – a hairstyle, way of dressing and so on and many go much further.[13] A TV programme called *I want a Famous Face*, for example, helps people to transform themselves into their idols through plastic surgery. In one episode, two twenty-year-old males from Arizona had nose jobs, chin implants and major dentistry designed to make them look like their idol, Brad Pitt. Following the surgery, Mike and Matt were ebullient about these changes. Other episodes of *I Want a Famous Face* allowed contestants to look more like their favourite stars: Kate Winslet, Pamela Anderson, Jennifer Lopez and Elvis Presley.

Copying another person's look is only the start of what can become a profound, *internal* transformation, triggered by other people's responses to the new image. If people see a Kate Winslet lookalike in front of them they are inclined to treat that person a little as they would treat the real Kate. As we have seen, other people's reactions to us are 'situations' which trigger or create different personalities in us, so if people treat you like a film star the wannabe film star personality in you will be fleshed out and encouraged to express itself.

Just seeing yourself in the mirror will begin the process. An acquaintance of mine who had a nose job found, when the swelling diminished, that it had lent her something of the look of a young Julie Christie. 'I had never felt glamorous before,' she told me. 'In fact I had always thought of myself as ugly. But once I had seen that likeness I started to think of myself as a beauty and it altered my behaviour in ways that I hadn't expected. I started to wear clothes that drew attention to me rather than disguised me, and that in turn made people look at me, especially men. And I found I looked back instead of scuttling past. I started flirting, I suppose, for the first time in my life. So what started as taking a tiny bit of bone out of my nose ended up completely changing me.'

You do not have to go under the knife of course to kick off the process that can end in the creation of a new personality – simply altering your expression or hairstyle can have a profound effect on how you feel. Mimicking the external features of another person – their physical features, their walk, their voice, their gestures, expression – is well recognised as a quick way to get the sense of being them. It is what actors call 'getting into character', though it might be more accurate to say that the character gets into *them*. Those who are particularly good at it are known in the profession as 'shape changers'. In the film *Aviator*, for example, Leonardo DiCaprio adopted the walk and manner of the film's subject, Howard Hughes, so completely that his director Martin Scorsese said the crew would sometimes fail to recognise the actor as he walked on set. 'He *was* Howard,' said Scorsese. 'Each time he came on it gave us a jolt of surprise.'

Similar stories are told of Dame Helen Mirren. When she was making the film in which she played Queen Elizabeth II she started rehearsals 'just being Helen in a wig', according to the film's writer, Peter Morgan. But a few days later 'she suddenly became this rather squat, piggy woman with enormous presence. She would walk onto the set and you would find yourself stiffening slightly. You minded your Ps and Qs and started saying things like, "Goodness gracious".'[14]

Some actors wear their roles externally, but others absorb them to the extent that the adopted character ousts the actors' other personalities, even beyond the duration of the performance. The British actor David Suchet, for example, had a long stage run in *Timon of Athens* during which he found it increasingly difficult to flip back into his own major when the nightly performance ended. One evening a psychiatrist friend visited him backstage and observed that he seemed still to be acting like Timon. Suchet dismissed his concern, at which point the psychiatrist shot at him a number of questions such as: ages of your children? Phone number? Date of birth? To his own consternation, Suchet found he had to work hard to retrieve the answers – the 'Timon' personality he had created was so firmly in charge that his major's memories were temporarily irretrievable.[15]

It is not just actors who deliberately use our powers of mimicry to create new personalities for specific purposes. This is how the trainer of a large sales force instructs his representatives to improve their pitch:

> I get them to think of someone they really admire – someone they think projects confidence and success, someone they would like to be. It could be an actor, Brad Pitt or Pierce Brosnan, or a corporate head or a world leader – it doesn't matter who so long as it is someone they really admire. Then I tell them to go and get some video clips or a DVD of that person and watch it and watch it, and look for particular gestures, or a characteristic posture, or maybe some tone of voice that is absolutely distinctive. Then I tell them to mimic it. Get in front of a mirror and walk the walk, or make the gesture. I tell them to keep right on doing it until if they just caught a glimpse of the mirror they could – anyone could – for a moment mistake them for the person they are imitating. Eventually it becomes second nature, and by imitation a little bit of that person will get into them, and make them feel better about themselves. Eventually they will forget it was ever NOT a part of them, and when that happens it will be a part of them.

Something as simple as mimicking the way a person speaks may be enough to produce a new minor in yourself. An English friend of mine says:

> A few years ago my children started to talk in a way that I associate with Australians. Every sentence ended on an upswing, as though it

was a question. At first I was irritated and told them it sounded affected. But my elder daughter said: 'And YOU sound like you are giving orders all the time – it's like you're so sure of yourself no one dares answer back.'

So when I was with them, or other people who spoke that way, I started mimicking them – deliberately making statements sound like questions. And I found when I did it that I became less domineering, less sure of myself and more open to others' view-points. Now, if I hear myself getting into some sort of altercation with another person, or sense that I am intimidating someone, I deliberately slip into 'upswing' and suddenly I find I am hearing more of what the other person is saying. I become a more tolerant person.

Deliberate mimicry can also be used in psychotherapy. Therapists are well aware that some clients tend to 'dump' negative personalities on other people, including the therapists themselves. And good therapists are alert to the converse – the danger of dumping on their clients. But some deliberately mimic the visible expressions of their clients' problems in order better to understand them.

'I first recognised the physical force of empathy as a college student, with the help of my friend, Nancy, who was studying to be a physical therapist,' says Babette Rothschild, a Los Angeles psychotherapist who has worked extensively with traumatised clients:

As we walked down a street together, she would follow total strangers and subtly mimic their walking style. Copying a stranger's gait, and feeling it in her own body, gave her practice in identifying where one of her patients might be stiff, or in locating the source of a limp. Intrigued by this mysterious way of 'knowing' someone, I asked her to teach me to do it, too. What startled me was that not only did 'walking in someone else's shoes' change the way I felt in my body, but it often altered my mood, as well. When I copied the swaggering gait of a cocky young man, for example, I would momentarily feel more confident – even happier – than before.[16]

Virtual personalities

The personalities we make are strengthened by being acknowledged in the real world, so externalised minors that get to be read about or seen by the public tend to be more robust and enduring than those which are known only to their creators. Plus of course, there is much more incentive to create external minors if there is a chance that they will be seen and get to interact with others.

Until quite recently it was difficult to send your minor out into the world; to publish or act you needed to be exceptionally good, lucky or rich. But today anyone can put their creations into the public domain via the internet. Minors in cyberspace take many forms. Some of the most elaborate are packaged as avatars – cartoon or graphic symbols of their maker. Avatars come to life in online multi-user fantasy games, many of which are played by millions of people.

Some avatars are effectively replications of the creator's own major. 'I change my avatar every couple of weeks so that it could represent more truly how I look and dress and what I do these days,' says one multi-user games player. 'My current avatar is indoors with a pile of book beside it. This represents me at the moment – I'm studying hard for the upcoming exams and I practically don't leave my room, just like my avatar.' Others are deliberately designed to go and live a very different life from that lived the rest of the time by their inventor.

As cyberworld becomes more and more realistic and challenging, the avatars that work and play in it inevitably become more complex personalities. In doing so they often diverge quite sharply from the original intentions of their creators. One player describes how he was completely taken by surprise by his avatar's furious reaction to having its virtual homestead trespassed upon in a game which involves, among other things, territorial colonisation: 'At first, I wonder why I (or my avatar) has such a visceral reaction to this perceived intrusion. Then a flush of parental pride washes over me: my avatar, which so far has acted much like me, hanging back from crowds and minding his punctuation in text chats, suddenly is taking on a life of his own. Who will my alter ego turn out to be? I don't know yet.'[17]

You do not have to create an avatar, of course, to send a personality out into cyberspace. You can simply wander into a chat room or sign up on a networking or dating site. These intimate but distanced meeting places seem to serve as a rehearsal room for people who want to try out new personalities in relative safety. A massive survey of teenage girls, carried out by a US Government department as part of an attempt to assess the risks to children of online communication, found that practically all of them project an online personality that differs substantially from the one that they would describe as their own.

'You can be absolutely *anyone* you want to be,' explained one girl, 'which is why a lot of people do things that they would not normally do. In real life, people everywhere judge you based on your looks, actions, and who knows what else, but online, all that really matters is your attitude and personality.'

Not surprisingly, the relative anonymity of internet communication leads people to be less restrained – the personality that gets to be exercised online is likely to be more extrovert, flirtatious and provocative. 'I am much more bold online than in real life,' said one. And another: 'I am *very* shy and I say things on the internet that I normally wouldn't say in public.'

Teenagers in particular use the net explicitly to 'try out' new personalities: ' I changed myself to be someone I wasn't because I wanted to get a different reaction from people,' said one girl. 'It gave me a way to see myself as who I wanted to be. You pretend to be older or you pretend to be a guy or you just pretend to be whoever you wanna be.' One of them summed up: 'We've *all* pretended to be older or have a different name or something. Who doesn't? It's part of the fun about being online. You can be whoever you want to be for a little while.'

These, then, are some of the psychological mechanisms that we use to manufacture the personalities who come to be part of our inner – and sometimes extended – families. The next section of this book describes how you can recognise your personalities and get to know who they are, where they come from and what triggers them into action. Like the

Alexes, you may discover characters in you that you do not approve of. You may also discover some that have strengths and virtues you never dreamed you had because the personalities who encompass them have been pushed so far off the stage. You may rediscover people you thought you had left behind decades ago, along with ones who come out only on rare occasions or with certain people. You can't be sure who you will find, but you can be sure that the encounters will be interesting – a little like meeting up with a whole crowd of people you once knew but have since lost touch with. Enjoy the party!

PART II

Introduction

This part of the book is made up of practical exercises supplemented with illustrative case histories. The first section will help you to get an overall view of the 'landscape' of your mind: whether you are composed of many disparate minor personalities or a more integrated cluster – perhaps so integrated that they have become a single 'major'. To make this easier I have devised a tool, the Personality Wheel, which allows you to chart your minors in graphic form, so you can see at a glance their main attributes and how they differ, complement or oppose one another.

For those who are reading this section first it is important that you do not assume that 'integrated' is necessarily better than multiple. Multiplicity is an adaptive response – the brain's clever way of coping with a complex and rapidly changing world. Today, when practically all of us have to deal with a dizzying rate of cultural change and contradiction, those who have developed a multiple 'mindscape' have an advantage over those who have a one-size-fits-all way of reacting to the world.

Multiplicity can, however, go too far. If your personalities are so separated that they no longer communicate (a state which manifests at its extreme as Multiple Personality/Dissociative Identity Disorder) you will be unable to cope in the ordinary world, where at least some degree of continuity and consistency are essential.

The second set of exercises is designed to help you recognise your minors and find out who they are and what they are like. The Personality Wheel is one of several techniques which will help with this – others include visualisation and forms of what might loosely be called psychodrama.

The final exercises are to help you to work with and on your minors – encouraging them to communicate together, to become active when they are needed and hold back when they are not, to strengthen the ones that are beneficial to you and curb those that threaten to get out of hand.

Before you start – a word of warning. These exercises are not intended for people who have, or have reason to think they have, Multiple Personality Disorder/MPD (or, as it is more commonly known today, Dissociative Identity Disorder/DID). Indeed, this section is unlikely to be helpful to anyone who has been pushed into the 'disordered' range of the dissociation spectrum (see page 67). It could even be harmful.

The reason for this is that minors are not the same as the totally compartmentalised personalities, commonly known as 'alters', that exist in people with MPD/DID. Practically all of us have minors, but few have alters. Unlike the latter, minors are linked together in the memory 'web' (page 52), like conjoined siblings rather than entirely separate beings. Hence they each know, hazily at least, of each other's existence and they are accessible to one another without resort to techniques such as hypnosis, which rely on inducing an abnormal (though not unhealthy) form of dissociation in order to work (see Chapter Three).

The exercises here therefore use ordinary introspection, imagination and observation to make minors more visible to one another and to promote greater understanding and co-operation between them. The idea is not to bring out anything that has hitherto been entirely buried, but to throw more light on minors that are currently lurking in the shadows.

These exercises should not, therefore, 'trigger' any dramatic switches of personality of the sort seen in dramas and documentaries about people with MPD. Even if they are done by someone who, unknowingly, harbours an entirely compartmentalised personality, it is very unlikely that such an entity will suddenly leap out of the closet, quaking with terror or demanding revenge for childhood traumas.

Having said that, triggering alters, should they exist, is always a possibility when a person is encouraged to probe their memory in the way that these exercises demand. Before embarking on them, therefore, please take time to answer the questions below. They refer to some of the more common signs of MPD. This is not a diagnostic test, but if you answer yes to any of them you should not continue with the exercises. You may like to turn instead to page 254 where I have listed some sources of information, support and professional help for people with dissociative disorders (including MPD).

- Do you have an entirely blank memory for certain periods or events in your life? For example, do you have no recollection of your teenage years, or do you sometimes find it hard to recall being on holiday, or on a course, even if it was within the last year?
- When you go from one place to another – from home to work, perhaps, or from the street into a store – do you have a hard time recalling where you were immediately before?
- Do people ever accuse you of saying things, just a moment earlier, which you could swear you did not say?
- Or do they mention things you are meant to have done recently which you can't remember?
- Do you ever find yourself 'a day behind', or look at the clock and see that hours have passed and you have no idea what you were doing during them?
- Do people you don't recognise regularly come up to you and claim to know you?
- Do you own things that you don't remember buying?

Preparation

Most of the exercises depend on your ability to place yourself into another state of mind – to create, if you like, a virtual reality and then put yourself in it and report back. For them to work properly you need to get yourself into a relaxed, neutral frame of mind, so that you can roam your memory and exercise your imagination.

Do not attempt to do them, therefore, when you are very caught up in another project, or when you are particularly excited about something, or in a particularly intense mood – depression or elation or irritation, say. Such states 'lock you in' to a particular personality and make it difficult to see others. If you are very sad, for example, you will find it very difficult to reconstitute your happier minors (see pages 48–51 on state-dependent memory).

Most of these exercises can be done with a friend, or friends, or a partner. There are benefits to doing them this way because companions may point out personalities you were not aware of and may be able to help you with identifying situations that bring certain minors out.

There are potential drawbacks to the communal approach, though, which you should bear in mind. One is that even those who are closest to you are unlikely to know all your minors. Other people are the most powerful situations we encounter and you may find that just being with a particular person makes it impossible for you to access certain personalities. You may even find that you get stuck in a particular minor so long as you are with them. Furthermore, it may be socially or emotionally risky for another person to see all the minors within you, and the minors themselves might not want to be seen by certain people! Ideally, then, you need to do the exercises with *and* without other people, and with different people at different times.

Some personalities like well-defined, clear-cut tasks while others favour an intuitive, 'feely' method of exploration. The exercises here allow for both approaches. The Personality Wheel, for instance, relies primarily on you remembering how you behave in certain roles. If you can also reconstitute your feelings and thoughts in the role – *become* the personality you are considering rather than just observe it – it will be a huge bonus, but the exercise can be done relatively objectively. Other exercises, however, depend on your getting right into the personality you are working with. Some use visualisation and will therefore come more easily to those who are able to conjure up very vivid images in their mind's eye.

It is likely that some of your personalities are good at some of the exercises and others good at others – but to find and activate the right personality for each exercise requires first that you *do* the exercises, so there is an element of trial and error here. On the other hand, situations bring out the minors best suited to them, so you might find that the image-maker in you naturally comes out when you get to the visualisation task and so on. This is great, except that it means that you might find a different minor is doing each exercise, with the result that you get seemingly conflicting results. The image-maker in you, for instance, may have a clearer (and kinder) view of the sensual or artistic minors in the family, whereas the character who does the Personality Wheel may be closer to the one who likes to keep things cut and dried and logical. Recognising these biases makes it all very complicated, but that is all part and parcel of getting to know your selves.

However you do the exercises, alone or in company, in the order they are presented or in one of your own choosing, it will be very helpful for you to keep an ongoing record. This can be a written or visual journal using painting or drawing, or a combination of both. If you are more of a verbal person, then perhaps a pocket tape recorder would be a better tool. Some people supplement their journal or scrapbook with pictures or objects they find that seem to symbolise your personalities. This can be very useful as a 'touchstone' to take you into that personality on cue. Keep your Personality Wheel too, because you will almost certainly find that you can add to it as you become more familiar with your selves. You might find it useful to redraw it at regular intervals, to see how you are changing. You may find, for instance, that some of your minors are merging with your major as you get a better working relationship with them, or that troublesome minors are shrinking.

The following general pointers may help you to get the best out of the exercises:

- Find time. It is important not to rush work requiring introspection and self-analysis. You need time to prepare and, afterwards, to reflect on what you have done. Setting aside time at weekends or at holiday times may work well or you might like to ring-fence an hour for it at the beginning or end of the day. If necessary, book the time in your diary to ensure you will not be interrupted.
- Create a peaceful atmosphere. Turn off your computer and mobile phone and set the answerphone to pick up your calls silently. At the end of the exercise, do not rush back into your routine; take some time to reflect on what has happened.

- Stay with the process. Do not expect instant revelations. You may need several sessions before you have even named your personalities, let alone explored them. This kind of introspection may not come easily to you, but the more you practise the better you will get at it. As well as providing specific insights, the exercises should also equip you with a whole new way of seeing people – a sort of lens through which people's behaviour, including your own, will in future look quite different. Such a change of perspective is very unlikely to happen overnight.

- Stay open. People are complicated. No two are the same. Indeed, no two *personalities* are the same, let alone any two people. As far as possible I have tried to present tick-the-box questions, but don't necessarily expect tick-the-box results. You will have to work at this to get anything out of it. Sorry. That's just the way it is.

CHAPTER 6

How Multiple Are You?

Like dissociation (Chapter Three) to which it is closely allied, multiplicity can be seen as a spectrum. At one end lie people whose inner landscape is completely smooth and continuous – every part of it attached to every other part. At the other end there are those whose personal geography is ragged and discontinuous. The following exercise is designed to find out where you lie on it. That is, it will help determine the *degree of separation* between your personalities, not the number you have, or what they are like. These you will discover later.

Most of us lie somewhere in the middle of the multiplicity spectrum. We may not manifest entirely different characters with their own names, ages and histories, but our moods fluctuate, our desires alter and our behaviour varies. We might refer to our 'reckless side' or 'obsessive streak' or the 'food addict' in us. At work we may make major decisions with ease, then, on the way home, find ourselves dithering over what to have for dinner. A man may be a devoted husband and father at home, and a faithless womaniser when he is away on business. A woman may be a compliant, exploited daughter and a domineering, bitchy wife.

It is possible to complete this questionnaire on your own, but the result will probably be better if you do it with the help of someone who knows you. Ideally your helper will be someone who has seen you in many different situations over a long period of time, rather than someone who knows you very well in one sphere of your life only.

The reason for this is that, without an external observer to check with the personality that is active at the time you complete the questionnaire may discount or neglect the feelings and behaviour of your other personalities and answer just for itself. Normal multiplicity does not involve complete ignorance of our other personalities but it does mean that whichever personality is active at any time gives more weight to its own concerns, and has better access to its own memories than to its neighbours'.

If you do answer the questions on your own try to do it from the point of view of a detached outsider looking back at your own thoughts and behaviour over a period rather than as an insider monitoring your current state of mind.

Take your time. Unlike most personality tests, which instruct you to give a quick answer without thinking about it too much, you will get a better result from this if you give careful consideration to each of your answers. Some of the questions also lend themselves to being checked objectively. Before answering question two, for example, try to find some examples of your handwriting – things that were written at different times and for different purposes. Compare the handwriting in a shopping list, say, with that in a recipe you once took down, or an application form. Look at the written appointments in your diary and see how they differ in appearance according to when and in what circumstances you entered them. Before answering the question about nicknames, run through your friends' emails to you and see how they address you. Go and look at your clothes before answering question fourteen.

Where are you on the spectrum?

Score 0 for 'never' 1 for 'sometimes' and 2 for 'absolutely, all the time'.

1   Do you find your mental skills, including memory for facts, vary from time to time for no obvious reason (e.g. not connected with tiredness or drinking). For example, are you aware that sometimes you can romp through a crossword puzzle while at other times, given a similar puzzle, you cannot get a single clue?   ☐

2	Does your handwriting change noticeably at different times?	☐
3	Do you ever refer to yourself as 'we'?	☐
4	Do your personal memories sometimes feel like a film you have seen, rather than something that actually happened to you?	☐
5	Are you called by a number of different names or nicknames and/or do you think of yourself by different names?	☐
6	Are you ever gripped with enthusiasm for a while by a hobby or pastime (DIY, gymnastics, gardening) that you find utterly boring at other times?	☐
7	Do you ever find yourself uttering the phrase 'What on earth made me do that [or words to that effect]?'	☐
8	Do you talk to yourself?	☐
9	Do you have 'binges' – of food, cigarettes, or alcohol?	☐
10	Is your behaviour chamelion-like, e.g. do you find yourself adopting the accent or intonation of the person you are talking to, or putting on a 'telephone voice'?	☐
11	Do you swing suddenly from one mood to another for no apparent reason?	☐
12	Do certain circumstances trigger skills or knowledge that is not usually available to you? E.g. in a foreign country do you find yourself speaking the language better than you thought possible?	☐
13	Do your tastes – in food, music, films, literature – differ widely from time to time?	☐
14	When you look in your wardrobe do you see clothes that you cannot imagine wearing and wonder why you bought them?	☐
15	Do vague acquaintances treat you as though they know you far better than you would expect?	☐

16 Do friends and acquaintances refer to events they claim to have shared with you which you cannot recall? □

17 Do people you would regard as trustworthy claim you have told them things which you cannot believe you would have said? □

18 If you come across something you wrote a while ago – an unposted letter from you to a friend, perhaps, or an old diary or notebook, do you sometimes fail to realise at first that the author is you? □

19 Do you find yourself laughing or crying, to your own surprise, for no reason you can think of? □

20 Does your level of self-esteem/self-love go up and down regardless of others' expressed opinion of you? □

Now add up your total score. ▭

Scoring

Basically, the lower your score the nearer you are towards the singlet end of the spectrum. Most people score between 10 and 30. A very low score (less than 8) can mean one of two things: either you are exceptionally unified, or it means that the personality who completed this questionnaire is unable to see the others and is answering just for itself.

To distinguish between these two, come back to these questions at another time – ideally when you are in a different place, doing a different thing, with different people and at a different time of day. If your score is similar and your answers to each question are more or less the same it is likely that you really are fairly unitary. If the score is different, it suggests that you have at least one more personality than you might at first think.

A high score (over 30) puts you well up towards the multiple end. There is nothing wrong with this in itself – it can even be advantageous.

But if you are disturbed by any of the things you have scored 1 or 2 on – laughing or crying unpredictably, say, or things that seem like memory glitches (failing to remember events your friends claim to have shared with you) – you may like to re-check yourself on the MPD-marker questions (page 117) and also read the section on dissociative disorders (pages 71–3).

The Personality Wheel

The very nature of multiplicity makes it difficult simply to look inside yourself and see who is there. Whichever personality is doing the looking – the one that is the 'I' of the moment – may have only a hazy view of the others, depending on how dominant it is, or how alien the situation is to the others. However, as we saw in Chapter Two, background personalities can be ushered to the fore by inviting them into their own 'frame of reference', as psychologists call it. For this exercise the frames we are going to employ are 'roles' – sets of behaviours that are clearly linked to the demands of particular situations.

Personalities grow into their roles like jelly taking the shape of a mould. You begin with one personality *behaving* in a way that fits a particular situation and go through a period of 'playing' that part. Sometimes the role is so alien to your existing personalities that you abandon it. A person with a strongly pessimistic major may find it just too difficult to act like a Pollyanna-style optimist, for instance. Or it might be a role that you need to play for a short time only. In these cases the act may remain just an act and soon be forgotten. But if you repeat a piece of role-playing enough you end up *learning* the part. As we have seen (Chapter Three) learning involves a physical change to the neural structure of the brain and once those changes have consolidated it is difficult to reverse them. In learning a role, then, you effectively create a new personality – one that is 'semi-detached' from the one that originally acted it out. Thereafter, when you slip into that way of behaving you are no longer acting – you *are* the role.

So although roles and personalities are not, strictly speaking, one and the same, by imagining yourself in a role (i.e. getting into the frame) you can often activate the personality that has come to inhabit it. That, essentially, is what this exercise is about. It depends on recalling, or even activating, the minor who plays a particular role by imagining yourself in the situation that usually prompts it to come out.

To start you need to spend a little time in advance relaxing and trying to attain a fairly neutral state of mind – one which allows you to range freely in thought and memory. If you are unable to activate the minor – get 'into it' – don't worry. This exercise can be done from the outside, so to speak, provided you can recall enough details of the behaviour that the target minor displays when it is active. This is where other people can come in useful – reminding you of things you do or have done in the role. You can also jog your own memory by, for example, looking at photographs of you taken when you were in that role. If one of your minors is a character you have dubbed 'off-duty', say, it might be helpful to browse through the holiday snaps. If one is 'mother', get out the pictures taken of you with the children. Identifying clothes that you wear in the target role may also serve as a useful reminder. You might even put them on to make the effect more powerful. If you are trying to pin down a minor which comes out only when you are with a particular friend or friends, try phoning them and having a chat immediately before you do the exercise. If you have a minor noted for sentimentality, get your favourite weepie movie on and watch half of it. If you have a very angry minor, recall or seek out something that really, really gets you going.

Once you have a clear view of the minor you will be invited to rate it on a trait-type personality test, similar to the Big Five, or OCEAN model, discussed in Chapter Two.

If you have already read Part I you will remember that the Big Five are character dimensions: open-mindedness, conscientiousness, extroversion, agreeableness and neuroticism, each with an implied opposite: closed-mindedness, carelessness, introversion, disagreeableness and emotional stability. Psychologists arrived at these dimensions by analysing all the words that describe personality – some eighteen thousand of them. They found that almost every one of them could be considered to fit somewhere into the five 'Big' descriptors. Words like 'chattiness', 'outgoing', 'fun-loving' and 'gregarious', for example, were all indications of extroversion that would place a person further along that dimension, while words like 'shyness', 'retreating' and 'bashful' would push them in the opposite direction.

If you gather together all the information on a personality, therefore, you can place it on just these five dimensions and be confident that very little is left out. Economical though the end description may be, you still have to find some way of deciding *where* a personality lies on each dimension and to do that you really need to do a lot of questioning.

To get over this psychologists have come up with what they call 'mini-markers' for each of the dimensions. These are sets of a hundred or even just forty words which a personality can be rated on and which give results very nearly as good as an entire assessment session which could take many hours.

I have used a similar – though simplified – system to arrive at a graphic way of describing minors. The spokes on the Personality Wheel represent character dimensions that are very similar to the Big Five and should therefore allow practically all the characteristics of a personality to be mapped on to them. To decide where the personality lies on each dimension I have given a set of mini-markers, each of which requires a simple yes/no answer.

To begin work with the Personality Wheel you first need to identify some roles you play in life in which you know you have a distinct set of behaviours which differ from the way you behave at other times. Most of us have at least two fairly clearly defined roles in life such as mother/worker; son/employee; business person/neighbour. It is easy to identify them because they have publicly visible 'markers'. The mother role, for example, applies when the person is actually dealing with her children in some way, or acting on their behalf. The business person role is marked by being at a place of work, or travelling, and, of course, actually working. It might be marked also by wearing particular clothes (a suit rather than sweater and jeans, perhaps).

The roles adopted by a person need not be stereotypes. Your 'worker' may be a very different character from my 'worker' and neither of them might be the standard idea of how a worker should be. Nor does the personality that is bound into a role necessarily pop up as soon as you step into the situation associated with it. For instance, a woman may have a very distinct 'mother' personality which usually fills the public mother role. On a weekday, however, she may already have become 'worker', or 'commuter' by breakfast time. So although she may still carry out actions associated with the public 'mother' role (giving children food, getting them ready for school) her personality is out of synch with the external situation. Instead of coming out in response to the events that are happening in the outside world, it is triggered by the woman's interpretation of the situation – others see it as a domestic scene, but she sees it as 'preparation for work'. Hence, in imagining yourself 'in the frame', you need to ensure that you are stepping into the *right* frame – in this case the 'mother' frame rather than the 'commuter' frame.

At this stage the idea is not to examine the personalities as individuals. Rather it is to survey the general layout of your inner landscape, especially the extent to which your personalities overlap or are separated. The entire exercise will take at least an hour to complete but you can split it into parts and do each one at a different time. In some ways this may be better than doing it all in one session. Like the previous questionnaire, you can do it alone, but you will get a better result if you do it as well with another person or even a group of friends. You will need at least three different coloured pens or pencils.

The dimensions on which you will be rating each personality are very similar to the Big Five (see Chapter Two), but whereas Big Five personality tests are designed to produce a single, coherent character reading, the Personality Wheel detects and amplifies the inconsistencies that reveal our different personalities.

To start, identify the major roles that you regularly play in life. For example, if you have children you will have a 'mother' or 'father' personality; if you work outside the home you will have a 'worker' and if you play an active part in the community you may have a role as, say, 'charity fundraiser' or 'drama club secretary' or 'council member'. If you are a keen sportsperson or a serious hobbyist, that might be a 'mountaineer' or 'poker player'. You will probably find that you have at least two such roles, although you may have half a dozen or so. For the purposes of this exercise you are probably best to limit it to the main two or three or perhaps four.

You may also be aware of roles which do not have standard labels but which nevertheless are clearly delineated in your own mind. You may have noticed, for instance, that you behave and feel in a very particular way when you are on holiday, or when you are with one set of friends as opposed to another, or when you are with neighbours rather than co-workers. Give role-titles to these such as 'townie', 'off-duty', 'shopper' and include them in your list.

Try to place the roles in the order that they are most commonly 'on stage'. So if you spend more time being 'mother' than, say, being 'student' or 'painter', think of 'mother' as role number one. Next, look at the lists of qualities on page 132. As you will see, each eight-term list comes under a general heading. These include four of the 'Big Five' discussed in Chapter Two – openness, conscientiousness, extroversion and agreeableness – plus their opposites: conservativeness, carelessness, introversion and disagreeableness. There is also a dimension which I have called 'uptight' and 'laid-back', which is similar to neuroticism on the Big Five, with its attendant opposite: stability. The qualities listed under each of these headings are aspects of the more general term. Under extroversion, for example, the characteristics include talkative, assertive and cheerful. An extremely extrovert personality would probably exhibit all of these qualities, but a moderately extrovert personality might just be positive for, say, five of them.

Now concentrate on one of your chosen roles. Think back to when you were last 'in' it and try to remember as much as you can about how you felt and thought and behaved at that time. You will probably find it helpful to recall particular events or incidents and then try to pin down what was in your head at that time. Let's say you have nominated a role which you have called 'rebel', which is a personality that constantly seems to be breaking the rules or challenging figures of authority. Think back to the last time rebel was actually in action – an altercation with a senior colleague, say, or an incident in which you broke a rule in a demonstrable way. Close your eyes and conjure up the scene visually, then try to remember exactly which words you said, or which thoughts went through your mind and how you felt emotionally.

If you can't get inside the role it does not mean that the personality is in some way unreal. Make a note of your difficulty, however, and, if possible, repeat this exercise on that personality when you are next aware of it emerging, or when you come across something that jogs your memory of it.

Once you have a clear sense of yourself as the personality that you are charting, look at each eight-term group and tick the qualities which you feel to be true of you in that state. Only tick the ones that you certainly feel or display – leave blank any that you are unsure about.

Ideally, in scoring each personality you should ask the opinion of someone who knows you well in that role. Your partner, for example, might know you extremely well in a domestic situation but have absolutely no clue what you are like at work. If you can't or don't want to canvass others' opinion, try to do the scoring for each role *while you are in that role*. And if you can't do that, then try very hard to score it objectively.

If you want to do this exercise really thoroughly, the way to improve your results is to take each characteristic and put it into the form of a specific question relating to a real event. If you are trying to determine how you should score 'dutiful' in the worker role, ask yourself: 'Did I finish the report I was working on before I left the office today or did I put it aside when X came in and suggested I knock off and go for a drink?' Apart from giving you an objective benchmark against which to score, recalling specific situations in which you were in a role will help to make that personality more active.

Don't worry if you do not have any characteristics in an entire eight-term set – it is practically impossible to have a high score in two opposite sets because they are opposing characteristics! And don't be concerned if

you have no ticks in a set and none in its opposite either. Minor personalities, by definition, are not wholly rounded characters so they are quite
likely to score zero on at least one dimension and its converse. There
may be no reason to expect the 'neighbour' to have any place on the
conservative/open-minded dimension, say, or for the 'painter' to rate on
'agreeable/disagreeable'. Some minors, indeed, are so narrow that they
may score on one or two dimensions only.

When you have completed the scores for Role 1, count up the ticks in
each box and record them in the score chart on page 133. Now take a
coloured pen and turn to the Personality Wheel on page 134. Look at
how many ticks you made in, say, the Extrovert box, then find the 'spoke'
marked 'extrovert' on the wheel. Put a mark on the spoke according to
how many ticks you have. For example, if you have one tick, place the
mark between the innermost and the circle marked two. If you have
three, mark it between circles two and four. If you have no ticks, mark
it on the innermost circle. Move on to the next section and do the same
thing, until each spoke has a mark on it. Then join up the dots to make
a shape.

You may break the exercise here and come back to repeat it with each
of the other roles at another time. Make sure that you use a different
colour pen or pencil to mark up the wheel for each personality.

Keep your completed Personality Wheel. The personalities distinguished in it so far are only those which are associated with your main
public roles so the picture may not be anything like complete. Later, as
you learn more about minor personalities, you may discover some in
yourself that are not linked to specific roles. By adding these to the wheel,
as you find them, you will gradually build up a complete picture of your
inner family.

Before completing this exercise you may like to look at the example
that follows on page 134.

OPEN-MINDED	EXTROVERT	STABLE	AGREEABLE	CONSCIENTIOUS
Creative	Talkative	Even-tempered	Warm	Organised
Questioning	Bold (socially)	Satisfied/content	Kind	Efficient
Artistic interests	Energetic	Relaxed	Cooperative	Methodical
Emotionally open	Gregarious	Optimistic	Trusting	Dutiful
Adventurous	Assertive	Self-accepting	Friendly	Tenacious
Liberal	Thrill-seeking	Tolerant	Open	Dependable
Romantic	Cheerful	Laid-back	Forgiving	Hard working
Playful	Enthusiastic	Self-sufficient	Teamworker	Responsible

CONSERVATIVE	INTROVERT	UPTIGHT	DISAGREEABLE	CARELESS
Uncreative	Shy	Moody	Unsympathetic	Disorganised
Dogmatic	Quiet	Jealous	Rude	Sloppy
Cautious	Bashful	Envious	Stubborn	Inefficient
Habit-driven	Withdrawn	Touchy	Critical	Reckless
Routine-bound	Reserved	Anxious	Quarrelsome	Immature
Unromantic	Polite	Angry	Distant	Extravagant
Unquestioning	Timid	Depressed	Distrustful	Rebellious
Conventional	Reclusive	Self-obsessed	Obstructive	Exhibitionist

Score chart

Name:

	Role 1	Role 2	Role 3	Role 4
Open-minded				
Conservative				
Extrovert				
Introvert				
Stable				
Uptight				
Agreeable				
Disagreeable				
Conscientious				
Careless				

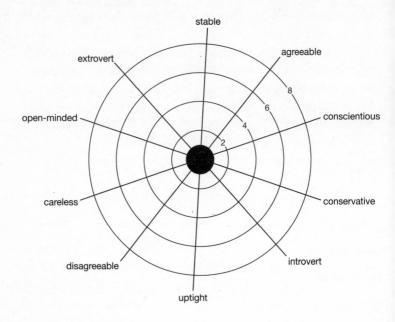

The Personality Wheel

Example

Stephanie is a twenty-eight-year-old nurse-turned-air stewardess. She left nursing because she wanted to travel widely and enjoy a more exciting life than nursing seemed to offer. Most of the time she is very competent at her job, diligent and hard-working. Her work is extremely important to her, and therefore Stephanie selects 'air steward' as her number-one role.

Stephanie's parents had a rocky marriage to start with, and as a child she often worried that they would split up. However, the marriage got stronger and by the time Stephanie left university they acted as though they were, and always had been, a devoted couple. When her mother died two years ago her father was bereft. Stephanie is an only child and now feels obliged to spend more time with her father than she would ordinarily choose. She finds this boring, but works hard to be consistently cheerful and affectionate. Given the time she spends caring for him, Stephanie's second role is 'daughter'.

The only time Stephanie really lets herself go is when she is on a stopover in a foreign city. Given the chance, and with a like-minded colleague, she will seek out the wildest night club in town and dance the night away, fuelled by whatever mood-manipulating substances are on offer. A couple of times she has failed to report back from duty and once she was disciplined for turning up for a flight still drunk. Stephanie privately refers to these occasions as her 'away-days'. She chooses this title for her third role.

Her scorecard therefore might look like this:

OPEN-MINDED	Air steward	Daughter	Awayday
Creative			
Questioning			■
Artistic interests			
Emotionally open			■
Adventurous			■
Liberal	■		■
Romantic			
Playful	■		■
Total	2	0	5

CONSERVATIVE	Air steward	Daughter	Awayday
Uncreative		■	
Dogmatic			
Cautious		■	
Habit driven		■	
Routine bound		■	
Unromantic		■	
Unquestioning	■	■	
Conventional			
Total	1	6	0

EXTROVERT	Air steward	Daughter	Awayday
Talkative		■	■
Bold (socially)	■		■
Energetic	■	■	■
Gregarious	■		■
Assertive	■		■
Thrill-seeking			■
Cheerful	■	■	■
Enthusiastic	■	■	■
Total	6	4	8

INTROVERT	Air steward	Daughter	Awayday
Shy			
Quiet			
Bashful			
Withdrawn			
Reserved			
Polite	■		
Timid			
Reclusive			
Total	1	0	0

STABLE	Air steward	Daughter	Awayday
Even-tempered	■	■	
Satisfied/Content	■		
Relaxed	■	■	
Optimistic		■	
Self-accepting	■		
Tolerant	■	■	
Laid-back	■	■	
Self-sufficient			■
Total	6	5	1

UPTIGHT	Air steward	Daughter	Awayday
Moody			
Jealous			
Envious			
Touchy			■
Anxious	■		
Angry			■
Depressed			
Self-obsessed			
Total	1	0	2

AGREEABLE	Air steward	Daughter	Awayday
Warm			■
Kind	■	■	■
Cooperative	■		
Trusting	■	■	
Friendly	■		■
Open			■
Forgiving	■	■	■
Teamworker	■	■	
Total	**6**	**4**	**5**

DISAGREEABLE	Air steward	Daughter	Awayday
Unsympathetic			■
Rude			
Stubborn			■
Critical			■
Quarrelsome			■
Distant			■
Distrustful			■
Obstructive			■
Total	**0**	**0**	**7**

CONSCIENTIOUS	Air steward	Daughter	Awayday
Organised	■	■	
Efficient	■	■	
Methodical	■	■	
Dutiful	■	■	
Tenacious		■	
Dependable	■	■	
Hardworking	■	■	
Responsible	■	■	
Total	**7**	**8**	**0**

CARELESS	Air steward	Daughter	Awayday
Disorganised			■
Sloppy			■
Inefficient			■
Reckless			■
Immature			■
Extravagant			■
Rebellious			■
Exhibitionist			■
Total	**0**	**0**	**8**

and her Personality Wheel would therefore look like this:

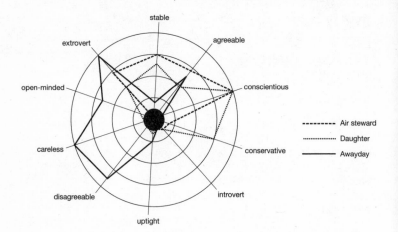

Reading the Personality Wheel

To start, look at your completed Personality Wheel as a whole. Do your personalities overlap or are they separated from each other? Is the general outline spiky, or solid? Do they cluster in one half of the circle, or spread to both? In other words, what is the bird's eye view of your mental landscape – a solid continent, a jagged coastline, or a scattering of loosely connected islands? Although no two mental landscapes are ever identical, there are basic types of formations, just as there are types of personalities. Look at the Personality Wheels below and see which one most closely resembles your own, then read the matching description of each type on the following pages.

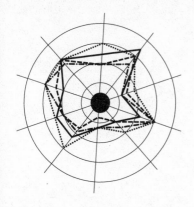

Single Major

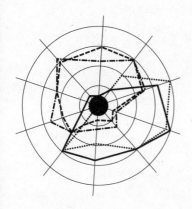

Double Major

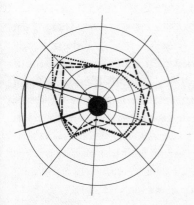

Major–Minor

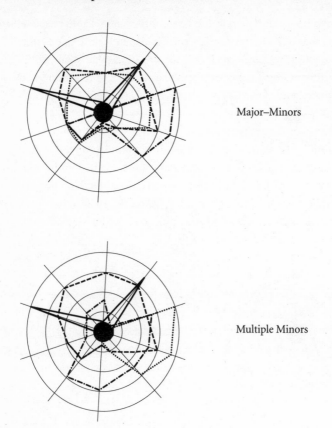

Major–Minors

Multiple Minors

Single Major

If your personality outlines closely overlap each other you may be one of the rare people who effectively has just the one, entirely integrated personality – a 'Single Major'. This is what we are all meant to be – a 'whole', integrated personality, with every bit closely connected to every other bit. No loose bits, no conflicts, no inconsistencies. The characteristics that identify Single Majors are always apparent, so if one of their traits is impatience a Single Major will be impatient whether they are peeling potatoes or running a multinational corporation.

Single Majors tend to be reliable – even if they are reliably unstable! But overall they tend to be inflexible and unadaptable. If Single Majors are thrown into a situation which calls for a response that is not within their repertoire – anger or aggression, perhaps – they either flounder or they are forced to invent a new personality on the spot to deal with whatever is happening.

This is easy for children; they are, anyway, 'making up' themselves as they go along. But as people get older their ability to create a new response from scratch diminishes. Meanwhile little-used minor personalities, created in earlier days but never exercised enough to become active members of the family, tend to fade away. People who live fairly stable, unchanging lives therefore tend towards a Single Major formation, especially as they get older.

Sarah

Sarah was born into a comfortably off and loving family. She had one sister, four years younger, whom she adored and adopted from birth. One of her first memories was being called 'mother's little helper': 'I remember positively glowing with pride,' she says. 'Looking back, this was in the mid-sixties and that term was used then – ironically – to refer to the tranquillisers all the housewives were getting addicted to. Even then I must have been a soothing influence.'

After graduating from university in the 1970s, Sarah took a civil service job in the Department of Education. She rose steadily through the ranks, without making waves, and had in prospect an extremely solid career in government bureaucracy. Then Sarah married a local businessman and fairly quickly gave birth to two sons. After the birth of the second she resigned and dedicated herself to her home and family.

For all her efforts, however, Sarah's home life did not run smoothly. Her husband went bankrupt, they lost their house and Sarah took a modest job in a local office to support the family. In the subsequent inquiry into her husband's business dealings he was accused of financial impropriety and had to defend himself in a complex civil lawsuit that lasted eight months. Throughout this time Sarah supported him stoically, turning up to the hearing with him each day, comforting him each night, shielding the children from the effects and turning their now-modest home into a refuge. Then one of her husband's creditors – a former family friend – informed Sarah that her husband had been having an affair for the past five years.

'I thought of leaving him. Yes, of course. Everyone said I should. It wasn't even as though the children would have suffered because by then J—— was no sort of father to them, he was too busy trying to get himself out of trouble. But I didn't.'

However, Sarah's constancy wasn't appreciated by her husband and a couple of years later he left her.

'I suppose I should have been angry, yes,' she says now. 'But mainly I was relieved. Friends of mine tried to persuade me to get revenge. But I found I couldn't do it. We are still friends, actually. He has broken up with his girlfriend and I think he would like us to get back together. But I am happy now, on my own. The children are both away at university and it is time for me to start a new life. I am thinking of becoming a landscape gardener.'

Five signs of a Single Major

- Friends who go back a long way and all know (and generally like) one another.
- Established habits, such as always going on holiday to the same place, loyalty to product brands, always reading the same sort of book.
- Long-standing relationships, e.g. lifelong marriage, lengthy business partnerships, close family ties.
- Consistent physical appearance – people rarely say, 'Oh! I didn't recognise you!'
- Coherent and unchanging views/attitudes. For example, likely to vote for the same political party every election.

The False Single Major

In some cases a Single Major formation may simply mean that your minor personalities play no part in your main roles. Your major personality deals with all the situations you encounter on a regular basis – work, home, social life. The minors may be triggered only in quite exceptional situations.

The fact that minors do not get triggered in any of your main roles suggests that they are cut off from the personality who is reading this book at the moment. It may be that they are redundant personalities – younger 'you's that have outlived their purpose and are now quietly expiring in a mental backroom. There is absolutely no point in reawakening one of these entities if it really has no use. You may well have an angry, terrified or uptight person somewhere in you, whose only possible contribution to your life is to cause havoc. So long as they are completely inactive they are best, like sleeping dogs, left to lie.

However, if a 'hidden' personality is causing trouble, by 'waking up' occasionally and intruding disturbing thoughts and emotions, it is worth finding out who they are and what they are about.

So if you have a Single Major formation, be alert for moments when you find yourself acting or thinking or feeling in a way that is not reflected by the shape on the wheel. If possible, make a note of the way you are feeling and acting in these moments, and describe the situation that provoked it.

Remember the situation you see may not be quite what it seems to outsiders. For example, you might find that you go uncharacteristically quiet at some social events and become extremely talkative at others even when the events from outside, seem very similar. If you can't immediately see what is special about the event at which you display uncharacteristic behaviour, examine your interpretation of what is happening. Are you unusually tired, so that you see this party as a social duty while normally you would see it as a treat? Are you feeling cool towards your partner because of some disagreement between you that occurred before you came out? And is this now colouring your perception of the people at the party? In which case, did the other personality actually take over in that earlier situation and is now simply refusing the give way to the party-goer in you?

After a while you may find a link between a particular situation and the emergence of behaviour or thoughts or feelings which do not fit in to the shape you have drawn for the major roles. You will have made contact with a minor personality who might need some attention.

Double Major

Major–Majors are 'balanced' people. Balanced, that is, between two (often entirely opposing) personalities. It is always a precarious balance because if one personality 'gets the better' of the other it will grow while the other will shrink and the person will turn into the more common Major–Minor. So Major–Majors stay that way only in the – quite rare – case that the two different people they are get equal time 'out'.

This is most likely to occur in people who are equally invested in their home and work life, each of which requires an entirely different set of talents and responses. Unlike Multiple Minors, the different personalities in a Double Major are 'weighty' and distinct, so they tend not to switch chaotically but only in the particular situation where each is called for. When a major is active it is not easily ousted by the other (in the way that Andrew's 'clubber' is pushed aside by the police officer; see Major–Minor below) so the person is generally stable and reliable, switching only when the situation (work to home, say) changes.

Clare/Clareta
Clare is known as two quite different women to two sets of entirely different people. They are even known by different names. If the two groups ever got mixed this could be a problem, and one of Clare's personalities would have to take charge. As it is, it is easy for Clare to

maintain the separation because one lot of friends
live in Suffolk and the other is in Peru. Even if there was no
geographical divide, however, it is unlikely that Clare would invite
Clareta's friends to mix with hers, or vice versa. They wouldn't get on.

One person who does see the two of them, though, is Angela,
Clare's younger sister. It is through her that I came to know about
Clareta. The two girls were born in Lima to English parents who
were members of the diplomatic community there. They spoke
English at home and their early education was at an English school.
But all their 'fun' times were spent with local Spanish-speaking staff
and their children.

'All our English speaking was done either at school or at family
meals. Both of them were pretty formal and boring. It was difficult
to make friends at the school because we all got whipped back
home in chauffeur-driven cars after lessons, and there wasn't much
chance to get to know the other children. And meals at home were
excruciating. My parents didn't like children much, I don't think.
So the people we really relaxed with, and the children we played
with, were local – Spanish speakers all of them.'

Clare and Angela's parents retired when Clare was sixteen and
Angela was thirteen. The family moved back to England and the
girls were sent to a local private school. 'It was a frosty old place, but
I quite liked it,' says Angela. 'Clare hated it, though. I didn't take that
much notice – we weren't very close then – but I think she became
anorexic for a bit. She certainly got very thin. She was always
terrifically well-behaved, and spoke in this formal way like
something out of a Victorian novel. I just thought of her as some
weird relative – Little Miss Goodie Two-Shoes. Nothing to do with
me really.

'I went a bit mad when I was sixteen, seventeen. I got in with a bad
crowd and had trouble with the law and drugs. Clare happened to be
back in Peru – my parents had kept a little house there for holidays
and we treated it like a second home. So the parents sent me off there
to get me away from 'bad influences'. And I think they hoped Clare
would straighten me out.

'But when I got there Clare was someone else altogether. She was hanging out with these local lads, drinking, smoking, doing drugs and sleeping around. It was a much wilder scene than I'd been into. And I realised that this was what she did whenever she was out there. The uptight Victorian Miss got left in the departure lounge at Heathrow.

'There's no point in talking to her about this because I really don't think she recognises the change that comes over her. I've often tried to find Clareta – that's what she calls herself in Peru – in Clare but she makes out she doesn't know what I'm talking about.'

Five signs of a Double Major

- Two distinct sets of friends who do not mix.
- Commitment to two roles which demand different qualities, e.g. child-rearing and a taxing career.
- Rarely talks about the life s/he leads outside the one s/he is currently in, e.g. talks work at work, domestic matters at home.
- Two very different types of clothes, e.g. a woman may have a collection of stern business suits and a number of girly frocks, but little in between.
- (If in a committed relationship) a long-time mistress or lover in addition to the partner.

Major–Minor

Major–Minors often appear to be Single Majors: predictable and consistent. Every so often, however, when triggered by a particular situation they become someone else altogether. The behaviour of their minor may be entirely inconsequential – a hobby or interest that simply gives the major personality a rest. Or it may be an intensely emotional personality created out of desires, urges and beliefs that have been rejected by the major personality, either because they clash with the rest of its beliefs and attitudes, or because the major is locked into a role which prevents it from exercising this particular personality.

Although a minor may be very different from the major, it doesn't necessarily give any trouble. Indeed, a minor may exist explicitly to give the major personality 'time out'. This works particularly well if the two personalities have completely separate external domains – home and work, say – so they never need to compete. If they are forced to meet on common ground, though, there may be a conflict. In such a situation the minor invariably gives way to the major.

Andrew

Andrew is a policeman – an extremely dedicated and good policeman, not least because he has never wanted to be anything else. If asked, he laughingly attributes this vocation to a fascination with TV cop shows in his childhood (and he is probably right).

'I was right on target for this job – I got in just when there was a push to get more ethnic faces on show in the Force, and I'm half Jamaican. They wanted to keep me on the beat, but I wanted to do CI [criminal investigation] work so I went for promotion early and got put to steer a desk. It's not like it was in the Sweeney any more – you have to follow procedures now, and I suppose that goes against the grain sometimes. When you've spent the best part of a month nailing some villain and then they walk free on account of some technicality, you need something to take your mind off it.'

The process is simple. Andrew gets home to his comfortable flat, takes off his working suit and puts on casual wear. The change of clothes releases the new personality: Andrew is a clubber. There is nothing immediately obvious about the transformation. He remains law-abiding, avoids the drugs that circulate freely at most of the venues and always takes a cab home if he drinks. But this Andrew happily turns a blind eye to the activities of others. He avoids noticing certain people he knows to be drug dealers, even a couple that his policeman personality has in the past pursued. If he sees a drunk getting in a car, he ignores it. If he sees a fight he walks by.

'It was a girlfriend I had who brought it home to me that I'm a different person when I'm out. I was with her in the street and we passed this bloke who was pushing this girl up against the wall and threatening her. I didn't see it. I mean I didn't *see* it! I can only tell you what happened because she made me stop and intervene. "You've got to," she kept saying. "That's what you're for!" And I realised she was right.'

In forcing Andrew's attention to the incident that the clubber did not see, the policeman in him – the major personality – was brought back to consciousness and took over from the minor. The effect was to reduce the clubber a little – nowadays a situation in which a clear breach of law is taking place is likely to call out the cop in Andrew, a change that he reluctantly admits might be for the better.

Five Signs of a Major–Minor

- Their partners recognise there is a part of them that can't be shared or is 'out of bounds'.
- Poor memory for certain events.
- Occasional acts that are 'out of character'.
- Ability to give up quite deeply ingrained habits for short periods, e.g. stopping drinking for Lent.
- A small collection of clothes that are entirely different from the rest.

Major–Minors

Major–Minors are probably the most common type of characterscape: the sort of people who have a well-recognisable major personality, but also a number of others that come out in different circumstances. (Major–Minors differ from the Major–Minor in that they have several minors rather than just one.) Providing their personalities complement each other this is rather a good formation: stable enough to allow the person to sustain long-term plans and relationships, but flexible enough to adapt to change.

Jonathan

Jonathan started his working life as a builder's apprentice and
worked his way up to establish his own small construction company.
Even Martha, his wife, jokes that Jonathan's first love is his company.
That may or may not be true, but his business is certainly what
sociologists would describe as Jonathan's defining role. It is how
most of the rest of the world that knows him, sees him – as a
straight-arrow, hands-on contractor, a man who plays fair
financially, who gets jobs done on time, and who consequently is
rarely without customers.

But while Jonathan is dedicated to his business he is also a good,
if frequently absent, husband and father, who tries to make up for
his periods away from Martha and the children with occasional
intense spells of excessive generosity and attention.

His employees would not altogether recognise this Jonathan, the
doting family man, and even Martha is surprised when it appears. His
foreman, who has worked for Jonathan for more than twenty years,
was astonished when he first met this 'other' personality.

'It's a strictly working relationship between Jon and me. We
don't get together socially and I like it that way. He treats me well
enough, but he's a tough customer and sometimes he asks too
much of the men . . . And he's tight with the money – straight
enough, but he doesn't exactly throw it about. So I have to stand up
for the lads, squeeze a bonus out of him if they've done particularly
well – that sort of thing. I couldn't do that if we were best mates,
could I?

'Last year, though, his wife asked mine if we would go round for a
celebration party – his oldest daughter was getting engaged. Bit of a
surprise actually and I wasn't too keen, but my wife insisted so we
went along.

'Well, we walked in, and there among his family he was a different
man. I mean, really different. He was welcoming and talkative and
joking. And it turned out that for an engagement present he had
bought his daughter a house – no kidding! It cost him more than the

company had made him in the whole year. Now, how do you square that up with a man who won't even buy his men a crate of beer at Christmas?'

The petty criminals in Jonathan's neighbourhood see another Jonathan again. He is also a local magistrate and has spent a good deal of time studying both criminology and civil and criminal law. On the bench neither the quick-tempered, tight-fisted Jonathan nor the excessively generous one is to be seen. Instead he comes across as careful, considered, measured and reasonable.

And none of his male friends see much of any of these Jonathans. He used to play in a local football team and some of his former team-mates keep their sporting links in middle age by taking occasional golfing and fishing breaks. These 'weekends out', as he calls them, consist of boisterous days and lively, alcohol-fuelled nights. He makes sure they take place a long way from home.

Five signs of a Major–Minors

- Difficult to get to know: just when you think you are getting some-where they become someone else.
- Wide interests and knowledge of surprising areas.
- Reliable enough in general dealings, but you can never be sure of them . . .
- Interesting and varied CV.
- Wardrobe may contain many different styles.

Multiple Minors

Multiple Minors are butterflies, flitting from one thing to another. No major ever gets to develop because they don't stay with one habitual set of responses for long enough to establish it as a 'default'.

The personalities in Multiple Minors tend to be very distinct, for it is the difference between them that keeps them all separate. In some cases, though, the personalities in their complicated system may be quite similar to one another, in which case the person will seem quite consistent and may even be confused, by those who don't know them well, with a Single Major.

Multiple Minors may be bewildering and irritating, but they can be amusing and stimulating too. Indeed, Multiple Minors are usually very creative and often burst with ideas and plans. The problem is that they rarely carry them out because the personality that conceives them is not around long enough to get them under way. Even if one of the personalities is the sort that concentrates obsessively, it never gets to be 'out' for long enough to get very far. Other, less committed, personalities interrupt and when the obsessive one gets back it may feel furious that its plans have been thwarted by – it feels – itself!

Typically, Multiple Minors start one task then break off and start another, often without being able to give a sensible reason for doing so. They pick up interests, hobbies and enthusiasms then drop them almost immediately, only to come back to them perhaps weeks later and carry on as though they had never lost interest. They are the same with friends, and have a disconcerting habit of being intimate with you one time then distant when you meet them again.

With no major to steer them, Multiple Minors are like sailing boats without rudders – entirely at the mercy of the wind. Usually they have been in windy weather all their lives, which is why they developed their multiple characterscape. If their life subsequently stabilises, one of their personalities – the one most suited to the current life – may grow into a major. But if they continue to live a life of constant change (which they are inclined to contrive) they may continue to host a large and increasing number of diverse personalities. If these characters are aware of one another and can control when one comes out and another goes away this very diversity can make them spectacularly successful, especially in today's world. But if the personalities fail to know each other the person's life is likely to fall into chaos.

Amy

Looked at from the outside Amy had a perfectly normal childhood. She was born, the eldest of four children, into a working class family in the north of England and brought up in a fairly conventional way. You have to look quite closely at her background – and perhaps take into account her genetic inheritance – to see why she developed as she has.

'My mum was moody. Well, that's what we called it then. Today she would probably be called manic-depressive [bipolar disorder] but then it was just "moody". When she went into a dip she was kind of cold – not horrible, just not caring. So I invented all sorts of ways of comforting myself: I'd pretend I had another mum altogether – model them on other kids' mums or people off the telly. I was lonely a lot of the time, so I made up little friends, too. I used to pretend to have this big sister, Sheila, who shared my room and I would talk to her at night.

'Because I was the oldest I had to look after my little sister and brothers when Mum was down, and behave sort of grown-up. I'd look after the others all evening, then go to bed and dream of being looked after by someone else. I switched in my head from being "little looker-afterer" to "little me". Then Mum would brighten up, and instead of having to be quiet and sweet and caring I was suddenly allowed to be noisy and childish, and I learned to make the best of it because you never knew how long it would last.'

Amy's practice at 'switching in her head' came in useful later in life when she became involved with an alcoholic who was a fervent protector of Amy while he was on the wagon and hopelessly dependent on her when he wasn't. 'I could do "little-miss-helpless" to a tee,' she recalls. 'It wasn't that I needed him to look after me – I didn't. But I could see it made him feel good, and that helped him keep off the booze. And it felt good. You can really get into it. One day I forgot how to turn on the video and I needed to tape something. So I called him at work and he came home and did it for me. If I heard of someone doing that now I'd say "spoilt dumb bitch". But it seemed normal at the time.'

Around this time Amy signed up with a rather grand domestic help agency and soon she was besieged by rich families offering her well-remunerated full-time work. She had a knack of becoming an instant 'treasure'. 'They were offering me my own cottage, holidays in the Caribbean with them, other staff to lord it over, all that,' she recalls. 'And I took up the offers a couple of times but – I don't know.' Amy pauses. Then:

'OK, this is what I know about myself. I can't be tied down. It's not that I don't want to be – it's just that it doesn't work. I'm a freelance. People say I don't take anything seriously but that's not true. I do take things seriously – it's just that, however seriously you take something there's always something else, isn't there?'

Five Signs of a Multiple Minor

- Erratic career path.
- Talents and abilities come and go – one day a brilliant cook, the next day can't boil an egg, and so on.
- Sudden mood swings: down one moment, up the next.
- Wide range of acquaintances, but few really close or long-term friends.
- Attitudes, opinions, beliefs change rapidly.

How do your minors relate?

The previous exercises will, I hope, have given you an idea of the sort of pattern, or landscape, that is formed by your personalities. That is, how connected or separate they are. They should also have brought at least some of your minors out into the open so that you can see them directly, rather than just sensing they are there because of their influence on your behaviour.

This exercise is designed to show how your minors relate to one another – whether they are all 'good guys' or 'bad guys'; complementary to one another or opposed. Then there is a guide to some of the more common minors. Of course, the cast of characters I present here are only a few of the countless personalities that a human brain can create. They are stripped down as much as possible to their essential characteristics, and in reality even the most skeletal minor will have idiosyncrasies which distinguish it from these stereotypes. Certainly your own are bound to be far more complex and intriguing. It would be surprising, however, if you did not consider at least some of these examples recognisably similar to one of your own 'inner family'.

Each profile shows what a particular minor does and why it does it. You might choose to read just those that you recognise as your own, but if you look at them all you may spot some that you have missed, or identify some that are within other people that you know. Even if none of the minors here apply to you, the descriptions of them should help you to analyse the functions and intentions of those minors that you *do* discover in yourself.

The case studies illustrate how each minor may manifest in a real life situation. Many of them are cautionary tales – showing what happens when a minor becomes too dominant or, conversely, when it is neglected or eclipsed by other personalities.

The descriptions below also touch on the way that the minor is likely to have originated. A minor's origins can be useful to ascertain because it can throw light on its present function and purpose. However, the idea is not to encourage you to probe your ancient history or 'get to the bottom' of your personalities' behaviour – it is to discover what they do *now*.

To begin, look again at the overall pattern that your personalities make on the wheel and decide which of the formations below best describes the general layout.

Clustered at the top

Each of the five dimensions on the Personality Wheel is independent of one another, so if you score high on one there is no reason why you should score high on the one next to it. You are as likely to be highly extrovert and highly disagreeable, for example, as highly extrovert and highly agreeable.

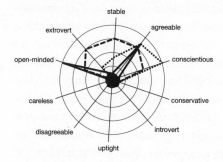

However, the Personality Wheel is constructed so that the characteristics which are most highly valued in our culture are those in the top quadrant of the circle: extroversion, stability, agreeableness. Those which are valued less are at the bottom. At first sight, therefore, it might be pleasing to find that all your personalities cluster in the top half of the circle. It suggests that even your minor personalities are pretty regular guys.

However, there are few human characteristics that have no purpose at all – even those we may prefer to keep quiet about. Any quality that consistently worked against us as a species would probably have disappeared by now because natural selection ensures that attributes which reduce our chances of passing on our genes are slowly eradicated. So although we tend to value certain characteristics over others – extroversion is commonly thought to be 'better' than introversion, for example, and laid-back people are generally believed to be healthier than those who are uptight – there are situations when being shy, bashful and even moody, angry and jealous are *useful*. Bashfulness may bring out the protector in a person who might otherwise crush you; moodiness allows you to swing with events, adapting your physiological responses in a quickly changing environment; anger gives you the energy to right wrongs; and jealousy is a crude but very effective way of telling you that someone else may be getting what you would like to have for yourself.

For these reasons our brains are fulsomely equipped to produce the entire range of responses and it would take a very unusual mixture of genetic inheritance and upbringing to produce an adult who did not just sometimes feel disagreeable, anti-social or anxious. So if all your personalities are up there in the sunlight, ask yourself if you are really so bereft of the characteristics in the rest of the circle. Is there never a time when you feel uptight or behave in a disagreeable way? Could this be a case of one personality (the one who has done this exercise) refusing to acknowledge the existence of those s/he doesn't approve of? Is this situation – being asked to examine and report on yourself – one that brings out a personality you *like* to be rather than one that you usually *are*? Are you telling yourself what you think other people want to hear, and switching into that personality in the process, like the students in Chapter Two who matched their self-descriptions to the people they thought they were going to be working with?

This is a case where it may be very useful to ask others – those you can trust to be honest with you – to say whether they have ever detected in you any of the characteristics that your shapes do not cover.

Clustered at the bottom

Always disagreeable? Always shrinking from other people? Constantly moody, anxious, self-obsessed? I hardly need to tell you that you have problems, whether it is with one personality or several.

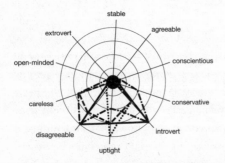

But are you sure there are not personalities in you who lie in the empty spaces of the circle? Could it be that the self-admittedly uptight personality who has done this exercise just can't remember the agreeable, enthusiastic you? As we saw in Chapter Three, when you are down it is extremely difficult to remember or even to imagine feeling and behaving differently. Could you be a victim of particularly strong state-dependent memory, edging towards compartmentalisation?

Here again you need someone else to tell you honestly whether the characters you have identified are really the only ones you manifest. Don't just ask the person you are with now, though. It might be that they are the very situation that brings out the self-deprecating personality who has just filled in the wheel. Try instead to ask a range of people how they see you. You might be surprised.

Suggestion: if you really do not discover a more positive personality lurking somewhere inside you, consider creating one from scratch. Various ways of doing this are explored in Chapter Three.

Extending into every section

1 Your personalities between them get a mark on every spoke

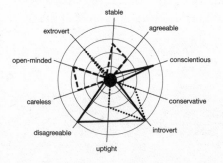

This is potentially good – between you all you have the entire range of responses which in theory allows you to adapt to more or less anything that life throws at you.

The question is: are the personalities coming out at the right time? For example, there are very few roles that would ideally extend very far up the 'disagreeable' or 'uptight' spokes, while there are a large number that would usefully eat into the conscientious and agreeable segments.

Suggestion: look at each role and see whether the attributes it scores highest on are appropriate for the situation in which it tends to emerge. You may, for example, have a personality that rates high on careless and extrovert, which is great if the role it is associated with is, say, 'holiday-maker' or 'party-goer'. It may not be so good if the role in which it is activated is 'librarian' or 'operating theatre nurse'. If you find such a mismatch between the role and the characteristics of the personality it brings out you may want to think about what it is particularly in each situation that triggers the 'wrong' personality.

Say you really are a librarian and in that role you manifest a high level of carelessness. Ask yourself why you should react so perversely to a situation that clearly calls for care. The very fact that you are careful in other roles (you must be to get this particular pattern) means that one of your personalities has that quality, so why is it not coming to life in the library? Could it be that the personality who does come to the fore *wants* to be fired?

2 Individual personalities extend into opposite segments

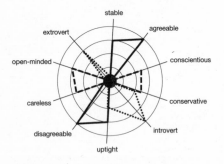

If you have a personality that registers a significant score on two opposing spokes, e.g. 5 on agreeable and 5 on disagreeable, it strongly suggests that the role you have distinguished contains two personalities, each of which comes out in subtly different situations. If under 'worker', for instance, you tick not only talkative, bold, energetic, gregarious, assertive, cheerful and enthusiastic, but also shy, quiet, bashful, withdrawn, reserved, polite and timid, you should examine the particular work situations that trigger each type of response. You may find an obvious division, e.g. you may be extrovert in your own department or when you are with your peers, but introverted with your superiors. The roles then would be split into 'worker' and 'employee'.

By this stage in the excercises you should have a fairly clear 'head count' of your personalities and some idea of how they relate to one another. Contradictory characteristics and behavoiurs which you have previously observed in yourself with some puzzlement should now be starting to make sense as manifestations of different psychological entities. The next section examines how these personalities came to be created and what purpose they play in your life.

CHAPTER 7

Meet the Family

Every 'family' of personalities is unique, but they are created in brains that are put together in much the same way and from experiences and needs that are pretty much common to us all. Hence each of us tends to have an inner family which has a broadly similar structure. For example, we all have personalities whose main purpose is to protect us. Others can be regarded as 'controllers' – there to drive and steer our behaviour. Then there are minors who monitor our progress, others whose job it is to keep up our morale and yet others who are compelled to undermine it. We make personalities to deal with particular roles: school, dating, work, parenthood. And most of us carry around old versions of ourselves which once had a use but are now redundant.

This section is designed to help you identify your particular personalities and understand what they do, how they do it, and what can happen if they get neglected or over-dominant. It presents profiles of some of the most common minors grouped into functional categories:

- **Defenders**   Protect and guard us against threats, both real and imagined.
- **Controllers**   Drive and steer our behaviour.
- **Punishers**   Controllers or defenders whose energy has become misdirected.
- **Role players**   Personalities created for a particular situation or purpose.

- **Relics**   Old minors which no longer have a useful function.
- **Creatives**   Originate new ideas, aims, visions.

You may well have some personalities which do not fall into any of these categories at all, but most people will find they have one or two personalities from each group. To help you identify them I have provided a Wheel outline for each one which shows that personality's essential characteristics – a high level of agreeableness for the Pleaser, for example, and a high degree of disagreeableness for the Bully. The position on the wheel – which quadrant it falls in – is also significant. However, these shapes are intended only as a very rough guide to what such personalities might look like. Your own 'artist', say, will almost certainly not look like the typical example because it will have more characteristics – extroversion or agreeableness, perhaps – which are not part of its essential 'artist' nature, but happen to be attached to your particular artist and therefore show up on the wheel. So if you do not recognise the form made by a typical personality in the table, it does not mean that you do not have the equivalent.

For this reason you should not depend on the wheel alone to recognise your personalities. Look also at the phrases next to each shape. Are these things you find yourself saying or thinking at particular times but not at others? Ideally, ask someone else if they have noticed you using words or expressing sentiments like this and if so, in what circumstances. Try not to depend on your own memory because the wise words of the Guardian, say, will seem quite alien to you if the Clown is currently to the fore.

The likelihood is that you will find echoes of your own personalities in these rather than perfect descriptions – the thing to look out for is the recognition that even if your minor might not behave in the same way as the stereotype, it is there to do that particular job.

DEFENDERS

Defenders are absolutely essential. If they are too weak we might be indifferent to the dangers of walking down a dark unfamiliar street late at night, or of taking on a physical challenge that is too much for us. The problem with Defenders, though, is that they are often quick to overdo their remit. They exaggerate dangers, or even invent them, so that instead of preserving us from danger or injury they cocoon us, hold us back and prevent us from experiencing and enjoying a full life.

The Guardian

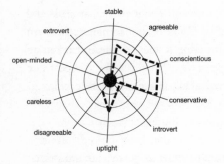

What it says:
'Be careful!'
'It's not worth the risk.'
'Better safe than sorry.'
'There's something lurking in the bushes!'

What it does
The job of the Guardian is to watch out and alert us to danger. It steers us away from doing straightforwardly reckless things and makes us shy of new situations and challenges. The Guardian's origins lie in the alarm system that is hard-wired into every animal, including humans. At its

most basic level this system produces fear – not the conscious feeling of being frightened, but the physical changes which prepare us to run away or fight in threatening situations.

Running away or lashing out is not always the best way to cope with a situation, however. Certainly it is rarely helpful in social situations. Humans have therefore evolved a capacity to inhibit primitive urges such as these, while the more sophisticated, conscious parts of their brain assess the situation and work out a better strategy than simple fight or flight. The Guardian is part of this rational fear-assessment mechanism. It is able to describe and explain dangers rather than just reacting to them. That doesn't mean, though, that the fears are necessarily realistic. The Guardian always errs on the side of caution. It is basically a *stopper:* endlessly calling out, 'Don't take the risk!'

Strengths

Obvious. Without some form of active internal 'protector', most of us would lead extremely short and miserable lives. We would repeat our mistakes and walk carelessly and repeatedly into physical and emotional harm.

Weaknesses

As the most powerful and significant member of the defence group, our Guardian's voice is usually strong and urgent, which is why most of you are here right now with all of your faculties intact, able to read this book. It is a voice that commands. But its self-appointed task is cautionary and preventative. So that loud, urgent voice can often insist upon unnecessary and even unwise caution. One bad relationship does not mean – as the Guardian may insist – that we should avoid all future relationships. Few really satisfying things are achievable without taking some sort of risk, so the Guardian should not be allowed to rule as much as it would like to.

Recognise/expect it

In risky or unfamiliar situations.

Questions to ask it
'Are you overreacting?'
'Do I need you at all at this point in time?'
'Are you aware that I am no longer three years old?'
'Do you equate all fresh experiences with danger?'

The Guardian's voice is generally strong and insistent. But other, more reckless personalities may drown it out at precisely the time you should be most aware of it:

I'm a fireman and when I started in the job I remember that when the bell went off I couldn't wait to get to the scene; no nerves at all. I got this reputation for being a real gung-ho character.

I'd had the training, of course, and a lot of that is about self-protection – you're worse than useless if you get yourself hurt because then some other b—— has to come in and rescue you. So heroics are not encouraged. But if we were in the middle of an incident it would be me who'd go that one step further than what the rule-book said – I'd take the proper precautions but, say the call came to withdraw from a building where there was still some slight chance of there being someone inside, I would just hang on that big longer, do a last look round before I pulled out. Nothing that an outsider would see, but my mates noticed. Like I said, they didn't approve, but I liked the sense of, well, heroism, I suppose.

And that was how I got injured. We were in the top floor of this sweatshop down in east London. It was an ancient old building – all rotten timbers, like a tinder box – and very soon after we got in my superior officer gave me the signal to pull out. And on this occasion, unusually, I was pleased to get it. Something – I don't know what – must have warned me that this time I really shouldn't hang about. But then I thought, No, I always give it a few seconds more – one last look! And that's what did it. A beam came down behind me, blocking my exit.

The rest is history. And I'm OK now, thanks to my mates. But the thing about it is this: as a firefighter, any sort of professional I suppose, you get a feel for things. On top of, or as well as all the stuff you know from the book, and all the stuff you can tell from your own experience, there is this other sense that you develop. And you either listen to it or you don't. On that occasion I didn't listen. I heard it loud and clear, and I ignored it. And lived – just – to regret it. I teach new men now, and I sometimes try to explain it to them. Follow the rules, yes. Do it by the book. But over and above that – listen to your gut.

– Colin

The Worrier

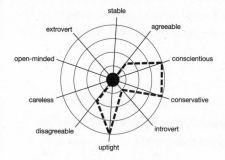

What it says:
'Why isn't Mary home yet? She must have had an accident.'
'My boss definitely gave me a funny look – he must be planning to fire me.'
'It's definitely cancer.'

What it does
The Worrier differs from the Guardian in that it generates fear whether or not there is real cause to be afraid. Whereas the Guardian grasps what is happening and then thinks up all the things that can go wrong, the

Worrier never even bothers to look out. Instead it hides away in its little dungeon thinking up all the bad things that could ever go wrong and telling everyone else about it without actually checking to see if any of them are *likely* to happen. It thinks the world is a dark, dangerous place and that unless we spend much of our time thinking and fretting about perils we will walk right into them. It does not trust the Guardian to give adequate warning of danger, but when the Guardian does speak the Worrier amplifies it a thousand times. Although it seems to be highly sensitive to everything, it is actually more cut off from reality than almost anyone else.

Strengths

Few. In truly risky circumstances, if it works with another personality – one with a practical bent, say, who will devise a way out of the situation – it has some use. It is also useful as a curb on a reckless minor who is hell bent on self-destruction. The Guardian may sound the alarm against some reckless course of action, but the Worrier is the one that will go on and on warning, long into the night.

Weaknesses

The Worrier's wildly over-imaginative, negative interpretation of the world can prevent you from acting in it, let alone enjoying what you do. If it is allowed free rein it can even make you ill.

Recognise/expect it

In the early hours, when its insistent whisperings prevent you from sleeping.

Questions to ask it

'What evidence is there that you're going to get the sack?'
'What are the odds on a burglar knocking at your door after eight p.m.?'
'Hasn't Mary – like everyone else you know – often got home a little later than she expected?'

Given half a chance the Worrier amplifies small risks into major perils:

I've always enjoyed our holidays. When we first got married we used to go to local resorts for a week or two. Have fun on the big dipper and at the fairground, walk along the pier, eat fish and chips, sit in deckchairs on the beach if the weather was fine, go to the cinema or a show at night. I really looked forward to those holidays.

Then as we started to get more money, and as foreign holidays became cheaper and more popular, like other people we began to go abroad. It was my husband's idea really, but I quite liked the idea at first. So we took a fortnight in a big hotel in Spain. And the year after that we went back. And then we had a fortnight in a resort in Turkey.

And I just wasn't enjoying it all because I worried about everything. I suppose it all came from when I was young and people used to say that the water abroad wasn't fit to drink – and sure enough, when you got there you found that instead of drinking water from the tap people were selling bottled water.

Then one of the first times in Spain I had one of the local meals at a restaurant. It was rice and prawns and tomatoes and things, but spicy, which I didn't really like. That night and all the next day I was laid up with a really bad stomach. I'd never been that ill at home from something I'd eaten.

Then my purse was stolen – or at least it went missing. I'll never be sure. But I'd put it down somewhere and when I went to look for it again, it wasn't there. It was no great loss, there wasn't much in it. But we reported it to the police and they were terrible. None of us could really understand each other, but when we made it clear to them how little money had been in it, and that I couldn't even be sure whether I'd mislaid it or it had been stolen, they just lost all interest. They didn't seem to care. They more or less told us to forget about it.

My husband wasn't bothered and told me to relax. And he insisted on continuing to go abroad. But from then on, all I could do was worry. You'd see these reports on television about big tourist hotels abroad collapsing because they'd been put up too quickly and too cheaply – and I'd get a cold shiver down my spine and think, We could have been in one of those.

Of course, I'd never have the local food or drink again. I'd find an English pub and get fish and chips or pie and peas there. But even then I wasn't really happy. You couldn't trust the ingredients. And I was always worried about having things stolen. Some of the hotels didn't have a safe to keep your money and things in and the rooms never seemed very secure. So before we went I'd spend lots of time and money on taking out all sorts of insurance, from sickness to injury to theft. But it never stopped me worrying. I'd worry before we left, all the time we were there, and then when we got back I'd start worrying about having to go through the same thing again next year.

– Marion

The Pleaser

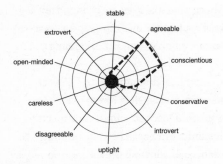

What it says

'Smile!'

'Sorry!'

'There's no sense in arguing.'

'If I just keep quiet she will soon relax and we can go back to having a normal time together.'

'I know I'm being taken advantage of but it keeps the peace.'

What it does

The Pleaser's job is to ensure that we are always on the 'good side' of other people and thus safe from their anger or dislike.

The Pleaser believes, often wrongly, that anything is better than conflict. It is happy to abandon arguments in favour of 'agreeing to differ', and may be quite prepared to say and do things that the rest of the family don't believe in order to avoid bad feeling.

This personality is most often born out of fear. It may be the straightforward fear of punishment from someone perceived as being stronger. Or it may be that the person is aware of the potential strength of another personality – a Bully, perhaps, or a Mule – and is scared of getting into a conflict in which it might be unleashed to the detriment of everyone (inside and out). The Pleaser may also be created out of simple laziness. If you live with a very dominant person it may just be easier to constantly appease than to summon the energy to insist on your own rights.

Strengths

It is often very effective. Appeasing a potential aggressor can indeed protect you from harm. And at times – when the aggressor is too powerful and dangerous to tackle in any other way, pleasing and appeasing can be the only course open to you.

Weaknesses

It often does not work. The Pleaser inside us cannot be expected to recognise this fact, but not all hostilities can be talked away or bought off with gifts and soft words. The danger of allowing the Pleaser too much scope is that you can slip into the habit of pleasing and appeasing everyone and everything and become a social hearth-rug.

The Pleaser can make us a soft target for any neighbourhood bully – the kind who might actually back down if confronted rather than appeased. But if we insist on pleasing him he will return with increased hostility and confidence. The Pleaser can also threaten the sense of self-esteem which is carried by other members of the family and is important, ultimately, to everyone. If it triumphs over them too regularly they will become weaker and the sense of our selves as capable and confident personalities will suffer. It may also infuriate other, feistier personalities in the same family, who will then breed resentment and anger because they feel their own needs are not being met.

Recognise/expect it
Whenever you come up against what might be called a 'strong' personality outside your family.

Questions to ask it
'Is this threat really serious?'

'Are you here just because everyone else around here is frightened to come out?'

'Have you considered alternatives to appeasement – such as simply walking away?'

The Pleaser is very often to the fore in relationships where one person is more committed than the other:

I had fallen in love with him at first sight. I knew from that moment onwards that he was the only one for me. I was prepared to do anything to win him, and then to keep him. And at first it seemed to work both ways. Our first months together were deliriously happy. We couldn't do enough for each other. Life was just one happy round of giving and receiving pleasure.

Of course, I thought that could go on for ever. At my young age, so madly in love for the first time, there seemed no reason for it to end. I wasn't looking for any signs of change. So when things began to alter, at first I didn't notice, and then I suppose I chose to ignore them. They were such small signs. We had developed this ritual of giving each other presents, little things, nothing special, after every time we'd been apart for more than a day. Well, David stopped doing that, but I didn't. It hurt a bit, somewhere inside – but I quickly forgot, and he always seemed to appreciate my gift.

I suppose I'd always done more than him around the apartment. But gradually I came to be doing almost everything, from the cooking and cleaning to taking out the rubbish, paying the bills, washing up – everything. But the funny thing is, I didn't really mind. If David was happy with that arrangement then so was I.

One or two of my friends would comment on this, saying things like they'd never let a man get away with that! I suppose I saw what they meant, but felt that it wasn't really their business – what made David and me happy together was our concern, no one else's.

But I adored him, you see. Even when I discovered that he was having an affair with a woman from work I couldn't contemplate losing him – and the crazy thing is, as I now see it, I thought the affair must be my fault! I obviously wasn't pleasing him enough. So I cried when I was alone and put on make-up and sexy clothes and redoubled my efforts when he was at home.

I don't need to say that it didn't work. In fact, it seemed to have the opposite effect to the one I intended. Every extra effort that I made to rediscover my old David, to turn back the clock, seemed just to distance him further from me. He told me as much, on the day he walked out. He couldn't bear my smothering, needy attentions, he said. He said he thought I deserved someone else – someone better! – who would appreciate what I had to offer. Then he left. And I have to say, I haven't found that 'someone else' yet.

– Christine

The Fighter

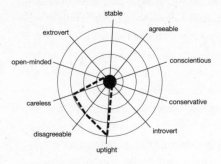

What it says

'Tackle trouble head-on.'

'Never give an inch.'

'I'm going to get my blow in first.'

'Stand your ground.'

'Don't show your weakness.'

What it does

The Fighter hits out against threats; takes the battle to the enemy and gets her retaliation in first. Fighters are convinced that aggression can only be countered by aggression, and that aggression is quite a good policy even when there isn't any obvious aggression to counter. Fighters are not necessarily physical combatants, of course. They are much more likely, today, to fight with words. The fact that the aggression is usually fairly well removed from actual bodily interaction may disguise the Fighter: a clever one can wield verbal weapons with devastating effect and never be recognised for what she is.

The Fighter may often develop into a Bully, but actually her main purpose is not to put others down but to keep them *away*. Seen as an individual s/he may seem absolutely selfish but in the context of the inner family she is often behaving in a misguided, but well-meaning way. By getting her blows in first she believes she is protecting the other members from attack.

Strengths

Fighters frequently get what they want. The best and most energetic fighting personalities are, and probably always have, featured largely in the majors of effective politicians, for example, and successful business people.

Weaknesses

Unless it is kept in place by other, more amenable personalities the Fighter is likely to be destructive to others and to its own family. By definition, it does not know or care when it is time to stop – or when it is time not to fight at all, but to adopt an alternative strategy. Somebody who spends their life in search of arguments, however successful they may be in winning those arguments, is likely very soon to run out of both friends and adversaries. The Fighter's armoury has always been useful to us, and for that reason will probably always stay with us. But it must not be allowed to delude itself that it is the only, or the most popular, or the least fallible card in our pack.

Recognise/expect it

Whenever you are in a situation where there is the possibility of confrontation, or a whiff of threat.

Questions to ask it

'What are you doing here?'

'Are you really required and were you actually called for, or did you just muscle your way to the front?'

'What do you hope to achieve?'

The less often the Fighter is deployed the greater effect it will have when it emerges:

The first ten years of my schooldays were pretty happy. I was at local primary and secondary schools, with boys and girls that I had known all my life. I did OK in lessons. I was a pretty cheerful teenager. Then when I was sixteen my family moved to the other end of the country. I went to a new school where I just didn't fit in. I didn't know anybody and my accent was all wrong. Then they started bullying me.

It was just comments at first, on the street and stuff. Then the text messages started. At first it was just one or two of them – really horrible messages about being a peasant and stuff. Or just something like 'Oink oink', making out I'm a pig. But they got more horrible, and they came more and more often, so my mobile would be bleeping all the time, and it was just this big stream of horrible texts – all day, last thing at night, and I'd wake up to them first thing in the morning.

It was really horrible and I just didn't know what to do. I couldn't tell my parents, they wouldn't have understood and anyway couldn't have done anything about it. I couldn't tell any of the teachers, partly because I didn't know them and was scared of most of them – and anyway they never do anything. They're meant to, but you know if you tell it will just make things worse.

Then two of my old friends came to visit and I told them. They were great. We talked about it, and they reminded me of that time when we were a lot younger and there was a bully in our class and I got mad with her one day and slammed a desktop down on her fingers – and she never bothered us ever again.

So we made this plan. We just made a note of all the numbers that texted in those messages. Then one night we sat down in my room and the other two started calling them on their phones, so they didn't think it was from me. It was amazing how many of them answered and then stayed on the line as we called them everything under the sun.

Then I did it myself. I got up early one morning and began calling them. I told them that they would really suffer if they didn't stop – because I wouldn't stop. Those that cut me off, I texted them saying the same thing. Then I rang, or texted, to ask if they'd got the message!

It was astonishing because most of them stopped. But one or two still came in and I went into overdrive – I really hit back at them, calling them and texting them twenty-four/seven, all hours of the day and night! They didn't like it one bit. But they stopped bothering me. Oddly enough I became pretty good friends later with a couple of that gang. I go out with them at weekends.

– Myra

CONTROLLERS

Controllers want to make the decisions about daily life and dictate how we behave in it. The single huge difference between these characters and Defenders is that the latter are always trying to stop us from doing things whereas Controllers point us in the direction in which they think we should travel, and try to send us there. Controllers are doers. As a result, Controllers may struggle with Defenders (and others) to take charge of our actions, causing conflicts both within the family and with those outside.

The Wise Friend

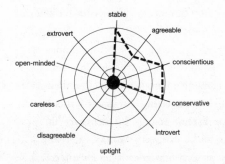

What it says
'Get to know him better before you commit to that deal.'
'Haven't you been this way before?'
'Are you sure you want to do that?'
'Don't expect too much and you won't be disappointed.'

What it does

It is easy to get the Wise Friend confused with the Guardian. Both have grown-up, sensible voices and claim to be acting for the good of everyone. The Wise Friend is also quite quick to spot dangers. It points out things that other personalities often do not want to acknowledge – that the person you are crazy about is less than crazy about you, that the job you want so badly is actually going to drive you mad, that the house you have set your heart on has a leaky roof and the potential to make you bankrupt.

The difference between the Wise Friend and Guardian, however, is that the latter is motivated by 'gut' reactions. The Wise Friend, though, is not an extension of the brain's warning system and its thinking processes are therefore far less coloured by fears. Nor is it a servant of our compulsions and desires. It really is a 'mature' character: it develops later than most and depends on the brain's frontal lobes with their extraordinary ability to weigh up information.

Strengths

The Wise Friend can see the advantages, as well as the perils, of any given action and offers a genuinely balanced view of things. It is more or less the only personality that is free from emotional pressure. You can therefore trust its judgement.

Weaknesses

When it does come through loud and clear the Wise Friend is often assumed, both by itself and others (inside and out of the family), to be our 'real' self. In fact, the Wise Friend does not necessarily have any special claim to superior status and it can, quite simply, be wrong. The Guardian is never wrong because it has only one message (albeit wrapped up in many different packages): 'Don't!' It doesn't *care* if you fail to achieve something that other personalities dearly want – its purpose is to prevent you from taking risks and never mind if you stay just where you are – that suits it fine!

The Wise Friend on the other hand genuinely tries to arrive at the 'best' solution for everyone, and that calls for a complex and delicate computation which is bound, at times, to go wrong. Nobody, not even the Wise Friend, *always* knows best. But the danger with a Wise Friend's mistakes is that the bad advice is likely to be both impeccably well-intentioned and persuasively phrased. The Wise Friend uses the 'Tried and Tested' rule to make many of its judgements, so it is basically conservative by nature. If you always obey it in such situations you may neglect more adventurous options.

Recognise/expect it

Don't bank on the Wise Friend emerging when you need it. This is one you should learn to call on whenever you have a complex decision to make or you are in need of calm reassurance or counselling.

Questions to ask it

'What do you have to say?'
'What are you basing this advice on?'
'What do the others have to say about this?'
'Are you sure you are taking everyone's emotions into account?'

We all have the *potential* for a Wise Friend, but it is one that needs to be encouraged because, without the forceful engine of emotion behind it, its voice is often drowned out:

I had been intending for some time to have a career change. I'd been in my current job for almost ten years, having joined the company straight from school. It wasn't a bad job. It was reasonably well paid – although I'd never get rich there. I liked most of my colleagues. But I was increasingly convinced that I was being taken for granted. I got a small wage increment regularly, every couple of years, but it had been five years since my last promotion and there was no sign of another one on the horizon.

And I was in a rut. I wasn't bored rigid – I still quite looked forward to going in most mornings. But I did have this regular sinking feeling that my life was going nowhere. So I thought that it was time to take the plunge and move on. The trouble was, every time I sat down and thought about it for any length of time, this voice inside me kept throwing up objections – 'Why give up a good thing?', 'Think of the friends and colleagues you'd lose', 'There's no guarantee the grass would be any greener in any other business – in fact, it could be a good deal worse', that kind of thing.

The difficulty was that this was just about the only internal advice I seemed to be getting. It was while I was on holiday that things changed. I was relaxed for the first time in what seemed like years and when I turned my mind to the job thing I seemed to see things in a whole new way. Instead of just worrying about what could go wrong I started thinking about what could go right. It's not that the old worries had gone, but now I was able to balance them with the advantages. By the time I got back home I knew I was going to take the plunge. It still took months of agonising to write a single application. But I was offered a new jobj and I took it.

And it's fine! I couldn't say it made an immense, dramatic overnight improvement to my life, my finances or even my happiness. In fact, once I'd settled in, the new job wasn't all that different to the old one. Which made me occasionally wonder what all the fuss had been about. Fear of the new, I suppose.

– *Raymond*

The Driver

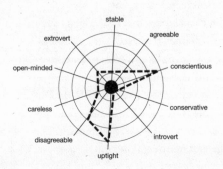

What it says

'Don't stop now.'

'Don't stop now either!'

'Get on with it!'

'You are falling behind – catch up!'

'You've got to do better than this!'

'Now do that too – you can relax later.'

What it does

The Driver is the one who gets us going and keeps us going. It is the character who is too busy to eat properly, is oblivious to tiredness, refuses to recognise defeat. It is the voice that tells us to get up in the morning (earlier!) and to stay up at night (later!). As soon as one task is finished the Driver pushes us to complete the next.

The Driver is rooted in the brain's reward system, a neural circuit that creates the urge to act in order to pursue pleasure. This particular circuit is fuelled by the neurotransmitter dopamine, which gives a sense of pleasurable anticipation. When activity in the circuit is diminished by lack of dopamine, as happens in people with Parkinson's disease, for example, we lose the ability to move forward and sink into lethargy and depression.

Strengths

The Driver gets us up in the morning, forces us to work through the day and stops us collapsing in front of the TV come evening. It tells us to turn our dreams into reality and not to give up on them at the first obstacle. It cracks the whip, gees us along and generally keeps us going.

Weaknesses

It doesn't know when to stop. In fact, it doesn't have the concept of stopping. Left to itself it would drive the entire family into the ground.

Recognise/expect it

When your other personalities start shouting 'Enough'.

Questions to ask it
'When are you planning to stop?'
'Where is this actually getting us?'
'To whose benefit is all this activity?'

If the Driver is not kept under control it can create compulsions which destroy the very ambitions that the Driver originally set out to fulfil:

I set up my internet business in 2000 and worked at it day and night. It was just me then – it was before I was married – so I can't say I was doing it for anyone but myself. The more I worked the more I enjoyed it. I was doing a full-time job by day as well, and building up the business at night. I didn't slack on the day job – actually the more successful I became online the harder I worked during the day.

I suppose you would say that I became a workaholic. There was a definite addictive quality to the way I was behaving. I would work until three or four in the morning some days and I was meant to be at work by eight next morning, so I often only got about three hours sleep.

In the middle of this I got married but it didn't slow me up. In fact it made me work harder because now I reasoned I had someone else to work for. She kept complaining that I was never there for her, though. So I gave up the day job, but then I found I just spent the hours I would have been doing that on the computer, so I still didn't have time for her. I wouldn't even stop for meals. And she left me.

Even that didn't bring me to a stop. I just went at it even more frantically. I think I had some idea that if I became really successful she would come back to me. What happened instead was that the business went belly-up. It wasn't my fault – I did everything I could to save it but the market just wouldn't support it. So suddenly I had nothing to do.

That was when I started trying to get her back. I still say that I was just, well, 'courting her', like I should have found time to do before we were married. But she put it another way: 'stalking'. So now she has an injunction out against me and I'm not allowed near her.

– *Vikram*

The Organiser

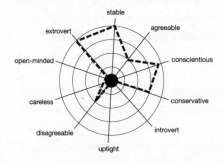

What it says
'Things need sorting out round here.'
'I can't bear this mess.'
'No one else is going to do it so I suppose I will have to.'

What it does
The Organiser compulsively files, grades, shelves, stores and stacks – essentially, puts into manageable order – every animate and inanimate thing that it encounters. It is the part of us that we depend upon to keep as much of our world as possible stable, dependable and organised.

Strengths
Organisation is an essential part of human society. The value and rewards of organisation are usually learned early in life, whether they be the recruitment and ordering of a junior football team or the benefits of properly labelled and shelved CDs, and without organisation (and by extension, organisers) our lives would be confused and unworkable messes. We could not catch trains to work, live in buildings, fly away on holiday, watch television, read books, eat in restaurants, as well as select CDs to play and take part in junior football.

Weaknesses

If allowed too much dominance the Organiser can become obsessive. In making the world too orderly it may remove a lot of fun and creative possibility from life. If every outing is organised down to the last detail, for instance, there is no chance that it might take off in some unexpected – and ultimately more rewarding – direction.

Recognise/expect it

When you find yourself remarking inwardly on the mess in another person's home, or find that you cannot relax in your own home until every item is in its right place.

Questions to ask it

'Are you needed or wanted here?'

'Are you organising this for a particular purpose or because you would be worried if it was out of order?'

'Can't you let someone else manage this particular operation/outing?'

'Will imposing order here actually improve this situation?'

The Organiser is never happy until it has imposed 'order' on its surroundings. Sometimes the effect is literally deadening:

My husband spent his working life building up and running a big travel company. The company was successful because he was such a stickler for detail. He used to make surprise visits to branches whenever he was in a town and if anything was out of place – even a coffee cup left on a desk – he would make sure the branch manager knew about it. And then he'd do another check in a few weeks time to make sure the message had got through.

When he retired we decided to move to the country. He had always said he wanted to garden in his retirement and I didn't want him getting under my feet so I encouraged him to buy a house with a nice big garden. Before then all we'd had was a little square that he'd paved over because he said he didn't have time to see to it.

The new garden had mature borders and some good trees and it really was a picture in spring – full of blooms. But of course, what he had to do was reorganise the whole lot. He didn't like the weeds in the borders so he pulled them out and then other weeds sprung up – even more of them. So he grassed over the borders. He didn't like the way the ivy got hold of the trees, so he poisoned it. Then the two nicest trees fell down because it turned out the ivy had been holding them up! He didn't like the way the lawn grew unevenly where he had extended it, so he turned it into a terrace. Then he didn't like the hedge because he couldn't manage to cut it exactly horizontal. So he replaced it with a brick wall.

Now he's happy with it, but I'm not. We had our tea out there yesterday, and I looked around and realised there wasn't a single flower in the whole garden. We could have been sitting in one of his branch offices. Next spring I'm going to scatter some wild flower seeds in all the little crevices. Just to keep him busy pulling them out.

– Marjorie

PUNISHERS

Punishers are often Controllers or Defenders who have got out of hand. Instead of directing us safely forward, their energy has turned into a corrosive force which manifests as continual criticism, attack or negative evaluation. This may be turned inward or out.

The Critic

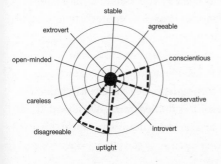

What it says

'You/they are useless.'

'They are not praising you, they are being kind.'

'Why can you/they never get anything right?'

'You/they are letting yourself/themselves down.'

'You're letting everybody else down.'

What it does

The Critic constantly monitors our own or other people's performance – depending on whether it is turned inwards or out – and concludes that it is not up to scratch. When it is turned inwards it tells us that we are not competent, that what we have done is rubbish, that what we will do tomorrow will be just as bad and that we will never be as good as everyone else. When we make a mess it says 'I told you so'. When we do something well it homes in on the one tiny thing we got wrong and ignores everything we got right.

When it is turned outward the Critic monitors the performance of everyone else, pointing out where they are falling short of some impossible ideal. Its voice is harsh and cruel and hurtful, but when challenged it will appeal to facts: 'I am simply pointing out the truth', it will insist.

The Critic thrives in our current world of celebrity, where we are constantly reminded that other people are more beautiful, rich and successful than ourselves.

Strengths

The Critic is fine so long as it knows its place and stays there. It is useful to have a personality that acts as a reality check and monitors our performance. By doing this the Critic can help us to improve. At its best it is a useful teacher.

Weaknesses

If the Critic is unchecked he will undermine and ultimately paralyse the other, more positive personalities in the family. When turned outwards he will drive away friends and colour the world his own jaundiced hue.

Recognise/expect it
Whenever you have reason to compare your own life and achievements with those of anybody else.

Questions to ask it
'Are your criticisms actually useful?'
'Are your comments and suggestions doing more harm than good?'
'Are you simply indulging a spasm of negativity?'

The Critic is not happy just to criticise the person – it often extends its negative view to anything that the person is associated with:

It would be easy to say that I'm never happy with anything. But it's probably truer to say that I'm never happy with anything from the moment it becomes mine! I can't really understand it. On the face of things I've done OK; I've got an OK life – as my friends never stop pointing out. But a good job, house and the rest of it never seem quite OK to me.

I got a new job last year. When I applied for it I thought it looked great. I really wanted it badly and I put everything into my application and interview. And I got it. Then I started it and very quickly I was unhappy with it because it suddenly didn't seem that great a job any more. In fact, it seemed worse than my last one.

Objectively I know that can't be true – but it's not what I *know*, it's what I *feel*. On a completely different level, a good friend of mine bought some great new curtains. At least, they looked great in her place. They looked so great that I just had to get myself an identical set. And they should – objectively, I know they should – have looked just as great in my living room.

But they didn't. They looked ordinary at first. Then very quickly they came to look completely out of place – terrible, in fact. But they are the same curtains that I loved enough to splash out an enormous amount of money on. The only difference is that now they are my curtains, and a really insistent part of me keeps saying that they are just not good enough, I shouldn't have bothered, I should have used my own taste, it's all been a waste of money.

– Peta

The Bully

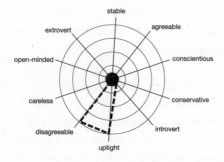

What it says
'If *he* is down, *I* am up!'
'That person is trying to get one over me.'
'You won't get away with that!'
'This person is a threat to me, therefore I must attack him.'
'This person frightens me, therefore I must attack her.'

What it does
The Bully was originally a protector (see Fighter) but now hits out at people who do not constitute a threat. In a blinkered way the Bully still thinks of itself as keeping the other guys safe by preventing others from getting close. The effect is to prevent the development of close or warm relationships with those outside. Essentially the Bully is frightened and by hitting out first it hopes to pre-empt any challenge to its power. If it is confronted its fear may become stronger than its aggression and it will back down.

Strengths
Disappearingly few.

Weaknesses
It is dangerous to those within and outside the family.

Recognise/expect it
The Bully in us tends to be activated by people who frighten or challenge us in some way, yet do not have our status, strength or position. Hence you should watch for it carefully in situations where you are dealing with people over whom you have power.

Questions to ask it
'What are you scared of here?'
'Are you using your power/status/authority correctly?'

Bullies may be created out of the anger 'left over' in a person who feels they once 'lost out' to a weaker person. Their pre-emptive aggression is designed to prevent it happening again:

I've spent a number of years trying to work out what turned me into a bully. Or I suppose I should say what turned me into a 'full-time bully', as I guess most of us do a bit of bullying some of the time. There was one period in particular that I'm not especially proud of, partly because I later became really good friends with the girl I was bullying. She had arrived at our school from somewhere a long way away – somewhere up north.

She was obviously vulnerable. Anybody would have been at that age and in her situation, in a new home and school, with absolutely no friends, not knowing any of the teachers. She was a sitting duck to be picked on. And did we pick on her! We got her mobile phone number and started sending her texts.

They were OK at first, I think, but the whole thing just gathered momentum and got out of control, until a whole gang of us were texting her morning and night, sending her really awful, threatening texts. We stopped when she started sending them back! And I think she phoned us in the night – something like that. Anyway, the fun went out of it. And then we got to know her and she was great!

So all's well that ends well. Not really, because I knew I had done something pretty awful and I didn't really know why. But when I look back, I think I'd probably been bullying other people quite a bit before then and I continued doing it a bit to others even afterwards.

I was an only child. My parents couldn't have another baby, but wanted one, so they adopted a little brother for me. I pretended to be happy, but I was really unhappy about it. I felt threatened. I felt that I'd been pushed aside. At least half of the love and attention that had been mine exclusively was now going to be given to someone else. So I bullied my little brother throughout our childhood. And when this girl from the north arrived at our school, I suppose she might have reminded me of him. She was pretty and outgoing – obviously people were going to be attracted to her. So I stepped in to stop that happening – or to make her feel as miserable as possible. Perhaps I just wanted her to go away.

I have to watch myself even now, years later. I know that I'm prone to bullying, specially to newcomers in my life. So I just have to be careful and keep a close eye on myself, or I wouldn't have a friend left in the world.

– Suzie

The Martyr

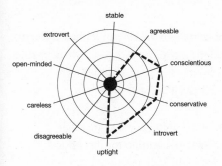

What it says

'Show this person that you will do anything to please them.'

'You are not worthy.'

'Obviously, do not offend – but more than that, prepare to debase yourself in case neutrality is seen as an offence.'

What it does

The Martyr probably started off as a Pleaser, but it went one step further. Pleasing others, it decided, was not enough – it had also to sacrifice its own aims and ambitions, however legitimate, and even demean itself in order to continue pleasing. The effect is that it inhibits other members of the family from pursuing their own needs and therefore generates resentment in them. The Martyr interprets this internal conflict as evidence of her own unworthiness which can only be put right by yet more self-sacrifice.

Strengths

The Martyr may actually lead a person into doing a lot of good work for others.

Weaknesses

In doing good for others it may do positive harm to those within its own family. If it gets the upper hand it may lead the person into warped, one-sided relationships and ultimately to a cheerless, virtually masochistic existence.

Recognise/expect it
Whenever you feel inferior to somebody to whom you are attracted. Whenever you feel urged to offer more pleasure to a friend or partner than you receive in return.

Questions to ask it
'Is your "cause" really worth it?'
'How about giving an equal amount of attention to yourself today?'

Martyrs may encourage other people to walk over them, then feel resentful when they do:

My sister, Elizabeth, was the clever one in the family and we all had high hopes for her when she got into Cambridge. It was there she met Robert. They both got almost identical degrees, but Elizabeth got herself a job while Robert went on to do a postgraduate degree. As far as we could understand the deal was that after three years or so he would be in a position to get a good job and Elizabeth could stop work and have babies – which she desperately wanted to do – and he would support her. Then, when the children were old enough, Elizabeth would take up her career again.

It didn't work out that way at all. Robert decided he didn't want children and Elizabeth went along with it. I remember she was very upset at the time and we all (the rest of the family) thought she should leave him. But she insisted that if that's what Robert wanted that's how it would be. She had this idea that he was some sort of genius that needed nurturing and that children might get in the way of his brilliant career.

Eventually he did make a prestigious career for himself in the university. But there was never any money and Elizabeth has gone on working at her dreary job to keep them in the stuff that Robert likes – good wines, for example. And travelling. Not the two of them, just him. He always has an excuse – a conference or something – but actually I think he just likes going to these wonderful places.

Elizabeth does absolutely everything for Robert. She does all the domestic stuff. She organises his travelling – even types up his itinerary, like she's his secretary or something. She taxis him about – Robert has never learned to drive; she buys his clothes; and if he is working at home she literally tiptoes around the place so as not disturb his concentration.

All of that would be all right if Elizabeth seemed happy. But she's not. Over the years we have watched her get greyer, and pinched, and sort of mean. Depriving herself has become such a habit that she can't do anything else and I hate having to watch it. And there is some kind of resentment brewing under the surface. Once I was staying there when Robert was due back from a trip. It was atrocious weather and his plane was delayed so he missed the last train back. He phoned Elizabeth and I heard her saying that she would drive out to get him – it was a round trip of about six hours and would mean her being up all night and then having to go to work in the morning. I told her: 'He can't possibly expect you to do that', but she was half way out the door before he was off the phone.

But her car wouldn't start so she had to call him back and tell him to get a hotel for the night. We had a couple of glasses of wine and then Robert rang again to say he couldn't get into a hotel and was going to have to stay in the station and wait for the first train. It was like 'Mummy! Come and get me!' It made me giggle and that set her off too. But there was real malice in her laughter that made me feel quite uncomfortable. 'He's only got a lightweight jacket,' she said, 'and short-sleeved shirts.' And then she opened a bottle of wine that he'd been saving for a special occasion.

– A. R.

ROLE PLAYERS

The personalities in this group started as acts or roles that the person adopted to deal with particular situations. At first they were worn like costumes or masks, but as they became learned they grew into fully fledged personalities. Role players were all useful at some time, and many of them retain their original purpose.

The Success

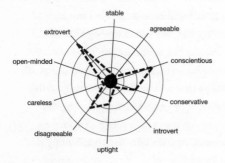

What it says
'I am a winner!'
'I can do anything I turn my hand to.'
'Success comes easily to me.'
'I always finish on top.'
'Nothing can hold me back.'

What it does
Success is usually created to keep up appearances in a culture where failure is not an option. It is an act which was initially adopted to persuade the external world that the person presenting it was triumphant in a particular arena. It makes us attempt to take the lead in all situations, raises our expectations of ourselves and causes us to put a good face on

all situations. If it is allowed to develop a life and momentum all of its own, the Success personality is prone to believing its own publicity.

Strengths

It boosts confidence, urges everyone in the family to live up to its expectations and often turns belief ('I'm a winner!') into reality.

Weaknesses

The danger with Success is that its claims and beliefs do not match reality so it misleads us into thinking we are doing better than we are and may make the person seem absurd, conceited or even deceitful. It may mistake style for substance; it can substitute glossy self-advertisement for genuine accomplishment. And if it does those things, it can backfire on us spectacularly by making us appear to other people as emptily boastful.

Recognise/expect it

In any competitive or potentially competitive environment.

Questions to ask it

'Is this the right time and place to project a successful personality?'
'Are you keeping tabs on the situation?'
'Do you need to emphasise what might already be obvious?'

Success can be very attractive. But it can also drive people away:

I was good at school. I finished top of the class all the way through primary school, and in high school I passed most exams without trouble and was more than useful at sport. So in my final year, I fully expected to be made head boy and was both disappointed and surprised when I wasn't. I couldn't understand it.

I couldn't help feeling that they'd overlooked something; that maybe my obvious qualifications hadn't been properly recognised. I suppose that's when the self-advertisement started. Throughout my late teens and twenties, through university and into my first job, I had this irresistible compulsion to 'talk myself up'. When I look back now I cringe. It's not as if I didn't have enough going for me, without shouting about it all over the place. And, of course, it had the opposite of the intended effect. I must have been pretty well unbearable. My conversation with almost anybody, almost anywhere, revolved around me and what I had done. I guess people crossed the street when they saw me coming. It took me a long time to get over, a long time to suppress that boaster in me. But I still think I should have been head boy.

– Damien

The Professional

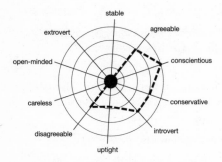

What it says
'If a job is worth doing, it's worth doing well.'
'Work is work and play is play and the two shouldn't be confused.'
'I don't have time for amateurs.'
'I don't bring my personal life into the office and nor should others.'

What it does
The Professional, like the Driver, is a doer – a personality that behaves in whatever way is appropriate for the job on hand. Very useful it is too, until it is time to stop work. The danger then is that the Professional refuses to step back and allow others to take over.

Strengths

Self-evidently, the more we concentrate on and enjoy our work, the more rewarding – in all senses of the word – that work will be.

Weaknesses

Nobody should be at work all of the time. If the Professional personality within us becomes too dominant it can ride roughshod over other essential roles in our lives. The workaholic father, mother, sister, brother or friend may be a good provider, but he or she is rarely an easy companion.

Recognise/expect it

In the workplace – its only legitimate habitat.

Questions to ask it

'Are you sure this is a working situation?'

'Might your work benefit from the input from other personalities?'

'Have you heard of "burn-out"?'

When it is coupled with the Driver, the Professional often fails to notice when it is time to pack up:

Looking back, I'd suppose I'd describe myself as 'dutiful'. I was a hardworking if not particularly inspired schoolgirl. I spent more time in the library than in the bar at college, and when I landed a good job with a public relations company I was determined to put in all the hours necessary to do a good job. And it worked – or it seemed to work. I went steadily up the professional ladder. I got a reputation for thoroughness and dependability. The fact that I was putting in eighty-hour weeks didn't bother me.

Then I reached my thirties and began to realise that not only was I chronically single, I didn't seem to have any friends. That wasn't because I'm unattractive. I'm not that modest – I know I can be fun to be with. It was because of my work. I was devoting so much time and energy to my job, which I continued to do extremely well, that I had nothing left over at the end of the day.

It was a vicious circle that took some time to break. At first, even when I'd made a conscious effort to put in fewer hours at the office and make myself some downtime, I couldn't properly enjoy it. There'd be a nagging voice in the back of my head telling me that I was wasting valuable time, that there were important phone calls to make, reports to write and clients to see. That voice has never really disappeared. It has just got a little quieter over the years. It lets me have a bit of time to myself, occasionally.

– *Jacqueline*

The Boss

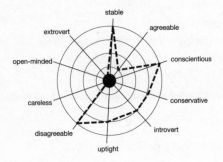

What it says
'I'm the only one who can run this show!'
'I know better than you do.'
'Get *on* with it!'
'If I don't take charge, no one will!'
'I'm in charge!'

What it does
The Boss is superficially similar to the Professional or – at worse – the Bully. Unlike the Professional, though, the Boss role has been developed primarily for other people, and is often paper-thin and collapses on

challenge. The Boss attempts to control every situation it finds itself in and every person it finds itself with. It calls the shots in even the most unlikely and unnecessary situations – such as dictating whose turn it is to buy the after-work drinks in a bar. It confuses the line between professional circumstances, where seniority counts, and domestic or social situations, where rank is less important.

Strengths
Some situations do demand a boss (which is how they are created) and many awards accrue to the person who steps up to take on that role.

Weaknesses
People who are used to bossing others around can find it hard to shake off the habit. They may – and do! – take their bossiness out of its natural habitat at work and impose it on others when it is unrequested and misplaced. This, needless to say, is a formula for resentment and ill-feeling.

Recognise/expect it
In situations where someone needs to take charge.

Questions to ask it
'Are you sure we are still at work?'
'Could you be overdoing it?'
'Might someone else be a better lead in this particular situation?'

The Boss, like the Professional and the Driver, may not know when to leave the stage:

I didn't realise I was doing it until it was pointed out to me. I don't suppose anybody does, or they wouldn't act that way. I'd been a teacher for fourteen years and a headmistress for the last five of them, and I guess I'd just got used to ordering people around!

The thing is, at work they were very young people who actually looked to me for instructions and orders. At home they were my family, several of whom didn't look to me for much instruction and

one of whom – my husband – didn't look to me for any orders at all!
I was told that I was being bossy, of course. My friends told me and
my older children weren't shy about making it clear. But I'd got into
a kind of mindset that was difficult to shake off. Once I could come
out of the school gates and become a 'normal' person again, but in
recent years I seemed to carry my headmistress personality with me
everywhere I went.

It wasn't the end of the world, of course, nor even the end of my
marriage – my husband actually said that he found a little bit of
bossiness quite appealing! But it was awkward. It was awkward at
times for me, so I can guess what it must have been like for other
people. She just needs watching carefully, that headmistress inside
me!

– Geraldine

The Clown

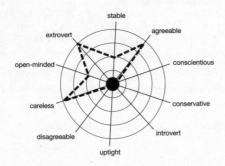

What it says
'I don't care if people think I'm a fool.'
'Life's too short to be serious.'
'I will do almost anything if it gets a laugh.'
'Must keep them laughing.'
'Me? Upset? Never!'

What it does

The Clown has several functions and may have been created to fulfil any or all of them. One is to draw attention to the person in whom it lives. It may have originated in a child's need to get parental attention without displeasing them. Another is to distract attention from another one of the internal family which may otherwise court disapproval. For example, a child may develop a Clown to distract people from a personality that feels it is failing to fulfil adults' expectation. A third function is the obvious one: to keep other people happy.

Whatever its function, the Clown carries a heavy weight of responsibility both to its own inner family and to others. It is frightened that if it ever stops fooling about something calamitous will happen: either it will be neglected, or scorned, or allow sadness to take over the world.

Strengths

Everybody likes and needs to be amused. People who are prepared to go out of their way to be amusing can therefore be attractive, and in some circumstances genuinely helpful.

Weaknesses

The Clown is driven to hog the limelight because it is scared that if it ever stops clowning something dreadful will happen. If other personalities are not strong enough to take over when there is serious business to be done, the person may be taken for what the Clown would have them believe is the case – a fool.

Recognise/expect it

In situations where you feel uncomfortable and might go to unnecessary lengths to 'break the ice'.

Questions to ask it

'Why are you coming out now?'
'Are other personalities trying to come out?'
'Is there a hint of desperation here?'
'Have they seen it all before?'

If it is kept in its place the Clown is a role worth preserving:

Telling jokes and acting the clown was what I was good at when I was younger. Teenagers need a kind of niche, don't they? Some are good at football, some are good at fighting, some are just plain cool, and some are funny. I was the funny one. And it made me popular. Even the teachers liked me. But I realised that after a while nobody took me seriously for very long – even if I put my hand up in class, the teachers expected me to make a joke. And away from other people I was actually quite a serious and studious youth. So I learned to trim the act back a bit.

It was pretty much a teenaged thing, though, and I thought I'd put it away when I got older. I had to. I became a bank manager, and a bit of gravitas is expected in that job. You can't really go mugging and gurning to customers and colleagues while discussing overdrafts and interest rates. Not all the time, anyway.

At home it was different. We had a big family and I love hamming it up at kids' parties. It is as though there is this whole other part of me that isn't much use most of the time – or particularly funny, for that matter – but on certain days in the year it really came into its own. So now it gets brought out, dusted down, does its job, and put back in the box again. And everybody's happy.

– *John*

RELICS

Relics are minor personalities that were created for some long-ago purpose and have been frozen in that role, unable to move on. Although they may gain new information each time they come out many of them never seem to mature – perhaps because their behaviour is such that they always succeed in recreating the sort of situation in which they were created and so the world always looks to be the same to them. Many relics are children with childish attributes and limitations such as the inability to see properly things from others' point of view, or to articulate their more complex ideas through language.

The Abandoned Child

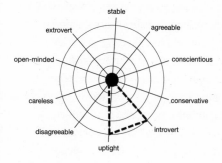

What it says
'I am all alone.'
'I'll always be alone.'
'Why have they left me?'
'I am frightened.'

What it does
The Abandoned Child is embedded in a clutch of emotions dating from an episode (or episodes) in infancy. Babies initially show distress when they are parted from their mothers (or other familiar caregivers) but if the mother returns within a short period of time all is forgotten. Children who are left alone for prolonged periods, however, give up crying and searching and lapse into a state of resignation, cutting themselves off from their own fear and loneliness. Those emotions nevertheless register in the child's brain and may stay with it for life as an Abandoned Child minor.

Strengths
The Abandoned Child is a 'classic' minor in that it is created by the brain's clever trick of carving out intolerable emotions and placing them in a separate compartment so that they will not 'pollute' the major

personality. This character has no strengths of its own, but its creation was a masterpiece of situation management at the time.

Weaknesses
The Abandoned Child, if it is activated in later life, can make the adult emotionally needy and insecure. Part of its personality is the conviction that there is nothing that can be done to regain security, so it does not even act as a spur to action.

Recognise/expect it
When someone you love has gone away, or perhaps just at times when you are alone without choosing to be.

Questions to ask it
'What are you so worried about? Do you think we will die if we remain alone?'
'Is he/she really deserting or just busy elsewhere for a while?'
'How about asking for reassurance in an adult way?'

Young children cannot project themselves into the future. A very short separation from the people who give them security may therefore feel to them like permanent abandonment:

It was a craze during the fifties, if you remember, to whip out the tonsils and adenoids of every child as soon as they sniffled. I had mine done when I was just three. To say it was traumatic would be an understatement. I don't mean the operation – I mean being dumped, as it seemed, in hospital.

I remember the first night in the children's ward, being in a cot by the window. I could see the cars passing below and I was sure one of them – the next one or the next one – would be my parents coming to take me home. But the whole long night went without them and I just wept myself dry. In the morning I remember a parcel turning up from my mother with clean pyjamas and my teddy. This made me feel worse because I knew she must have been into the hospital to leave it and I couldn't understand why she hadn't come to see me. Now I didn't just feel abandoned, I was convinced my mother couldn't even be bothered to walk into the ward and see me!

She explained later that it had been almost as bad for her as for me. Apparently the hospital issued instructions to the parents saying they should not try to see their children on the ward because the children 'settled' quicker if they weren't visited. Mothers' visits just set them all off crying again, apparently. She said she was beside herself with frustration, not being able to come and see me – the parcel was the nearest she could get.

I wouldn't say the incident scarred me for life or anything. But I do know this. If my husband is late home – even just half an hour, I go frantic. He is the most reliable, devoted man and I know perfectly well that he will not ever leave me, but I become absolutely convinced that he has. Permanently. I told him, right at the beginning of our marriage, that I had an irrational fear of him being in a car accident, so please would he call immediately if he was held up. He usually does. But on those isolated occasions when he hasn't been able to I am right back there in that ward, counting the cars.

– Annie

The Mule

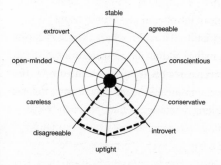

What it says

'No, I will not do that!'

'No!'

'Not likely.'

'If I appear rude, I am actually doing nothing more than defending my own independence.'

'Nope.'

What it does

The Mule manifests in stubborn truculence or refusal to cooperate. Most Mules originate in childhood, from the child's battles with those who had power over them. Straightforward refusal was then just about the only resource on hand. Hence when the Mule emerges in an adult it is usually a sign of weakness – the person feels they have been transported back to a state of childhood impotence, where debate or a more dignified and reasoned form of refusal is beyond them.

Strengths

Although negative, in style, its behaviour is often surprisingly effective. Mulishness, when appropriately applied, can prevent an adult as much as a child from being exploited.

Weaknesses

It blocks debate, cuts off alternative paths of action and makes you very unpopular!

Recognise/expect it

When you are feeling exploited, or in a situation where there is potential for exploitation, or when people in authority are pressing you to do something you are uncomfortable about. In circumstances of actual threat, obstinate and even truculent mulishness can be a positive defence mechanism and a means of asserting self-respect.

Questions to ask it

'Is this request so unreasonable?'

'Might it use less energy simply to comply rather than refuse?'
'If I do what they want, will any real harm be done?'

The Mule is usually created quite early in childhood. The more it triumphs then, the more likely it is to stick around into adulthood:

My parents had me late in life – after my brothers had left home – and they totally indulged me. I never had to refuse to obey them because they never insisted I did anything much. I just had to ask to get. But when I was about six my mother got seriously ill, and my father hired a succession of au pairs and then properly trained child carers to look after me.

I was already used to getting my own way and I certainly wasn't going to be told what to do by these people. At first I'd throw a tantrum. Later I'd just threaten a tantrum. Later still they simply stopped trying to get me to do things I didn't want to do. Finally I was sent away to school and a lot of that was hammered out of me. But a residue certainly remained and as I reached adulthood I became very good at throwing what I suppose you would call 'a wobbly' whenever anything came up that I didn't want to do.

It was ridiculous. If my mates wanted to go down the pub and I wanted to play football instead, I'd occasionally work myself up into a fit bordering on rage. It was utterly disproportionate – I'd yell and call people all the names under the sun. And then after an hour or two, it would all be forgotten by me – but not by my friends. So it was all pretty destructive. One day a mate sat me down and talked long and hard to me about it. I think that helped. I began to recognise this wobbly-throwing me that had a habit of springing up out of nowhere. I can't say he's gone away for ever. But at least now I know to look out for him. If he begins to surface, these days, I bite my tongue very hard indeed, or I just leave the room!

– Declan

CREATIVES

Creativity is a fundamental human faculty and Creative personalities are the vehicles in which it is conveyed. People brought up surrounded by creative endeavour are naturally more inclined to be creative themselves because situations *make* personalities. But even those who have been deprived of that sort of experience (happily, very few today) will find a way to express their inherent creativity – perhaps through a hobby like cooking, or inventing, or gardening.

The Artist

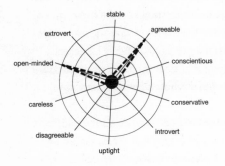

What it says
'I can see it in my mind's eye.'
'I could make it into reality.'
'I will make that.'
'How shall I do it?'

What it does
The Artist is essentially a doer. Not only does it see things to be made, it also works out how to make them and actually sets about making them.

Strengths

Apart from the fruits of its creativity – which may or may not be valuable – the Artist's viewpoint constantly refreshes the entire family's way of seeing the world and therefore allows them all to interact with it more flexibly.

Weaknesses

Few. Even failed attempts to create can be, to some degree, laudable – and at the very least are harmless.

Recognise/expect it

Anywhere and everywhere – the artist may emerge in the home, when you are struck by a desire to rearrange the furniture; in the kitchen, when you see a new way to combine two ingredients; in the garden, when you place one plant next to another for visual effect, and whenever you find yourself spinning a story for someone's entertainment.

Questions to ask it

'Are you doing this often enough?'
'Are there other forms of creation and art which you could explore?'

If the Artist does not emerge spontaneously it may need encouragement from outside the family:

I was the last person you'd expect to play in a band. I was a workaholic. I had my job in the daytime and my kids at night. I had no time at all to myself. My day consisted of feeding and dressing children, working, feeding and undressing children, then falling asleep on the couch. Also, I had no musical aptitude or inclination at all – I didn't even listen to it.

Three of my colleagues at work put me up to the idea. They'd started a small country music band just for fun. They played guitar and drums and fiddle, met once a week, and apparently had a whale of a time. And they told me they needed a singer. I just laughed! Even if I could sing – and I'd never tried – where would I get the time?

Well, they sorted a baby-sitter for me one night and I went along.
They played a few tunes, very nicely I thought, then they gave me the
song sheet and I tried out the vocals. Weirdly, I liked it! I found I was
able to hold the tune, and as we did it more I was able to put a bit
more expression into my voice. The two hours, those first two hours,
passed in a flash. And when I got home I wasn't in the least tired – I
was exhilarated! I couldn't wait for the next session. So things just
went on from there. I wouldn't miss those sessions for the world.
They've progressed a bit now – we play occasional gigs in bars, and
I've even started writing one or two songs of my own. And most
astonishingly – it makes the rest of my life better! I've got more
energy with the kids and at work. I think I'm better company all
round.

– Chrissie

The Dreamer

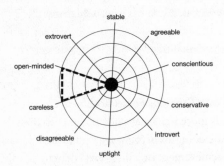

What it says
'I can see it in my mind's eye.'
'I could make it into reality . . .'
'. . . and I will . . . when I've got time/finished this current project/learned
a bit more about it/get free of my responsibilities.'

What it does

The Dreamer shares the Artist's ability to see how things *could* be, rather than how they *are*. But it does not have the drive and practical skills to see the transformation through. Its projects remain dreams. The Dreamer comes from a similar source as the Artist – from our native compunction to think 'outside the box', to imagine schemes and artefacts which will enhance and enrich our lives. The Dreamer may possibly be more protean in his or her ideas – they may encompass a much broader scope than creations of purely artistic beauty and merit. The Dreamer is capable also of imagining new inventions, labour-saving devices, money-making initiatives. The Dreamer's flaw is implicit in her title – she may dream of whole new worlds, but never actually create or explore them.

Strengths

Dreaming is an essential precursor to artistic activity. If it can find the Artist in the family, and merge with it, the combination will be stronger than each alone.

Weaknesses

The Dreamer is usually pretty harmless and has entertainment value. But it can also be a time-waster and a drain on thinking resources that could be put to better use by other personalities.

Recognise/expect it

The Dreamer may emerge to fill the cracks between active pursuits, which is where it belongs. It is more irritating when it comes to life at a time when we really should be doing something practical, when it may interfere with a flow of real achievement or a discussion of actual projects.

Questions to ask it

'Is this a practical idea or are you just enjoying playing with it?'
'What would actually be required to put it into practice?'
'Are you stopping someone else from doing something more productive?'

The Dreamer can often be traced back to a period of boredom or lone-liness during childhood when its distractions were welcome and harmless:

I was a real live wire at my first school – always the first to put my hand up, first to be changed and ready for gym, always engaged and active. But when I got to my secondary school I was put into the top class and for the first time I wasn't able to keep up. Instead of trying all the harder, what I did was retreat into my own head. I had always had an active imagination but up until then I had channelled it into stories and art and things. Now I just used it to entertain myself and to get out of what I suppose might have felt like an uncomfortable situation – me, the dunce at the back of the class.

It started to spill over into my time at home. I'd spend long hours at school living in a world of my own spinning increasingly elaborate narratives in which I was the central character. Then I would continue them as walked home – I can remember getting quite upset if anyone tried to talk to me because I was so wrapped up in my own little world. I became antisocial – not because I didn't like people or wasn't popular but because my dream world was more interesting and exciting than anything I could do with other children.

Of course I fell behind at school as a result of this. And that was when I started to dream about being a success. Instead of actually working for exams I would spend my time pretending to myself that I had already passed them! So of course I didn't get the exam grades I needed to go to university, and in the end I had to take this dreary job my dad fixed me up with.

I'm still doing it. But I'm not going to be doing it for life. As soon as I've saved up enough money I'm going to take time off work and go back and do the exams and get myself a university place as a mature student and then I'll be back on the right road.

– *Peter*

As you can see, the life events that create personalities are not necessarily traumatic. Majors tend to be formed by the slow accretion of everyday experiences, while minors are more likely to come into being through a sudden shift in perception which produces a new way of behaving. The extent to which newly formed personalities maintain their separation depends on whether their view of the world can bind with personalities that already exist, and their survival depends on the recurrence of the situation – or type of situation – that brought them into being. Personalities are often born out of necessity – they arise to suit the occasion. Ideally they come and go according to circumstances.

Sometimes, though, our personalities do not heed their cues. One might refuse to hand over to another when it should, or refuse to come forward when needed. Or two might try to come out at the same time, engaging in a fight for dominance which prevents the energies and talents of either being projected into the outside world. The next section is designed to help you to see how your personalities act and interact, and encourage them to do so for the good of you all.

CHAPTER 8

Working Together

Visualising your selves

This exercise is for those who prefer a more intuitive approach to the rather formal 'framing and charting' technique described so far. Essentially it involves conjuring up one or more minors and externalising them, much in the way that novelists experience the characters they create as being 'out there' rather than inside their heads, and children experience Imaginary Companions, complete with clear physical attributes.

Visualisation of this sort is used very widely as a tool in various kinds of psychotherapy, and a lot of people probably do something very like it whenever they want to transport themselves speedily into the world of their imagination. This particular exercise, however – using visualisation to clarify our inner beings – was originally devised by the founder of psychosynthesis, Robert Assagioli (page 4).

This type of exploration will come more easily to people who are quite high on the dissociation spectrum. This is closely correlated with the multiplicity spectrum because dissociation is one important way that personalities are created (Chapter Three). So it is likely that people who find it works well for them will also discover more minors than people who find it difficult. (NB: Before starting it, please make sure you have read the warning advice on page 70 and answered the questions on page 117 relating to MPD.)

The exercise begins with the 'framing' routine described for the Personality Wheel exercise.

- Relax, get into a neutral or relaxed state of mind and then allow thoughts and memories gradually to seep in. If memories of a holiday come to you, think of yourself in 'holidaymaker' role. If you find work problems pressing in, think of yourself as 'worker'. If a seemingly irrelevant thought pops up – the idea of fixing a meal, say, don't act on it directly but encourage yourself into the role of 'hungry' or 'nurturer' or 'mother' or 'hostess' – whichever seems most appropriate.

- Close your eyes and become really aware of the thoughts, memories and feelings that come up when you slip into this frame. Imagine how this personality looks – it could be an image of you, either as you look now, or perhaps as you were as a child, or last year, or even in the future. Or it could be an object or, indeed, anything. Let it emerge, do not force it and do not censor it. Trust the process.

- Keep observing the image, letting it reveal itself; try to make contact with the feeling coming from it. Be aware that it may change as you are observing it – let this happen.

- Let the image speak to you and hear what it is saying. Objects are allowed to speak as well as people – you are, after all, working in an imaginary world and it is a *private* world, so don't worry about anyone thinking you are silly.

- Encourage conversation. Try to find out who this personality is. What does it want? Does it have a name for itself? What makes it happy, what sad? What does it think of the other personalities in the family? Who does it get on with it, who does it disagree with? Why?

- When it feels right, stop and open your eyes. Record in your journal everything that happened. First, give your personality a name if it doesn't already have one. If it has given you a name which is different to the one you expected, go with that. Now write about its character, habits and quirks.

If you feel clear about this personality you may like to map it on the Personality Wheel along with the others. The shape may match one that you have already drawn, in which case you may be seeing the same personality from a new perspective, effectively 'fleshing it out' so that you will recognise it more easily when next it emerges.

Kate

When Kate did this exercise she found that what came to mind was a tendency she had to let others do things for her that she could perfectly well do for herself, such as booking tickets, making travel arrangements and keeping in touch with mutual friends. It was obviously a line of thought that was 'on the back burner' and as soon as she relaxed it bubbled up into her consciousness. As this happened she saw a tiara emerge. Realising it was symbol for a personality, she called it 'Princess' and started to talk to it.

Princess, it seemed, felt 'entitled' to use others to indulge her own laziness. Their reward, according to the Princess/tiara, was her company and friendship. She could not see why her attitude was sometimes met with resentment, because she regarded herself as 'special'. The minor was, she came to realise, one that had emerged when she was a little girl, spoiled and petted by indulgent parents. In fact, her father's nickname for her had been 'Princess'.

Bob

Bob found that he could not shake off a feeling of irritation that had seeded in him earlier that day during a lunchtime conversation with his friend Jacob. Jacob had recently become a teacher and he seemed to Bob to have developed a patronising manner towards his old friends, treating them as though they were his students. Bob had felt this at lunchtime when he had joined Jacob for lunch in a new restaurant which featured some quite obscure dishes from northern Spain. Jacob took it upon himself to tell Bob about them – how they were cooked, what went into them and so on – and even took over the ordering.

At the time Bob could only think about how conceited Jacob seemed, but when he came to do this exercise he found an image of himself coming to mind. It was of him as a small boy being subjected to his father's 'wisdom', which tended to take the form of long rambling lectures on subjects that didn't really interest him. He called the image 'Reluctant Student' and concentrated on how it felt. The main thing he realised was the desire to move about – he felt pinned to the spot, unable to leave despite increasing boredom. It was this – rather than the lecturing itself – that created a sense of tension.

Turning back to the lunchtime incident Bob realised that he was really rather interested in the food at the restaurant, and that it was actually he who had suggested they went there by way of an experiment. Jacob had made the effort to research the dishes, not to impress Bob but because, as he had told Bob when they made the arrangement, he happened to have a book on Spanish cuisine.

In the event his irritation had prevented Bob from taking in what his friend said – indeed, it had stopped him from really appreciating the meal. And the reason, he realised, was not that he felt he was being patronised, but simply that the situation – sitting still while someone else talked – reconstituted the frustrated little boy who couldn't wait to get down from the table.

Julia

The image that arose in Julia's mind was of herself and her partner playing tennis: 'The game was always the same – like a video loop. I would serve the ball over the net with all my energy and my partner would sort of lift up his racquet and let the ball hit the strings – but he would make no effort to hit it back. The ball would just fall to the ground and dribble away. So I would serve again and the same thing would happen. As it went on, time and again, I started to feel exhausted and less and less inclined to serve the ball. So I started just making it drop over the net so he would have to run to get it. He still wouldn't hit it back, but I got some satisfaction out of making him move. Then I started deliberately hitting it to the very edge of the court, where he couldn't get it. And that gave me even more satisfaction.'

Julia had little trouble recognising that the Tennis Player was echoing the role she played in her relationship. She was endlessly trying to engage her partner in a dialogue, but finding that he blocked all her invitations to communicate. The tennis ball was like the 'ball' of conversation – it flew in one direction only. By concentrating on how the Tennis Player felt, Julia realised that she was rapidly getting exhausted by this one-sided game, and that she was starting to take pleasure out of, as she put it, 'prodding him' with remarks intended to provoke rather than to produce a real exchange of views. It started her thinking about whether the relationship was worth preserving.

Know your triggers

Have you ever had the experience of seeing a photo of yourself, remembering precisely what you were thinking and feeling at the moment it was taken and being startled by the contrast between the remembered experience and the way you feel now? Whenever this happens you are effectively bringing two personalities face to face – the one in the photo and the one looking at it.

This exercise is designed to help you discover what situations bring out which of your minors. You will need a photo album, paper and pencil.

■ Divide the paper into three columns.
■ Go through the pictures in your album until you find one of you which you clearly remember being taken. Ideally it should be one that 'leaps out at you', releasing sudden memories that contrast sharply with your current situation.
■ In the left hand column of the paper write down the situation in which it was taken. This does not mean the sort of thing you might

scribble on the back as a reminder ('Portugal, August 2000, waiting for ferry'). Rather you should write down what the situation was for *you*. If you were on holiday, for example, was it a holiday in which you were in charge, or having an adventure, or being looked after? Were you with your family? If so, were you, at that moment, being a son/daughter, partner, sibling or parent? If you were with friends were they close friends? What was your position within the group? Were you the one who made sure everyone had got their passports, or the one who nearly made everyone else miss the plane? If it is a work photo, were you in charge, part of a team, in competition with others, in uniform, on duty? If it is a party photo, were you the host or guest? Was it an intimate party or a big impersonal occasion?

- Now turn to the *inside* situation, as you remember it. In the next column write down what were you were thinking, feeling and most sharply aware of at the precise moment that snap was taken. This might not have anything obvious to do with the situation as seen by an outsider. Although the photo might have been taken on holiday, for example, your inner situation might have been boredom or irritation or exhaustion. You might have been thinking, I am anxious because my son's asthma has come back and we are a long way from home, or I am jealous because my partner is flirting with that girl again, or I want to go home. You might be in pain, or too hot, or engrossed in a book, or feeling sexy, or worrying about work.

- Match that inner state with one of the personalities you have already identified or, if it doesn't match with any of them, create a new name for it and write it alongside your description of the external and internal situation.

- Move on to another photo and do the same. Continue until you have dealt with at least a dozen photos this way.

- Look back at the list and see if you can see a pattern emerging. Does a particular sort of *external* situation bring out a particular *internal* situation – in other words, a particular minor? If so, what are the essential connections and which are merely peripheral? For example, do those photos taken of you with your family – whether they are at your children's sports day or on the beach – consistently produce an internal state equivalent to your 'Parent' or 'Caretaker' or 'Witch' or 'Indulgent One'? Do parties correspond with 'Flirt' or 'Princess' or 'Loudmouth'? Do photos taken at work always seem to be of 'Sulky Sue' or 'Little Miss Tidy' or 'Boss Man'?

■ Note which situations bring out which minors. In particular, make a note of situations which seem to activate two or more minors, or which bring out a minor which is clearly inappropriate. For instance, do parties bring out an introvert minor rather than an extrovert? Does work bring out a rebel rather than someone more conscientious? Does being with a particular friend, who you know to be kind and caring, bring out a sulky or bad-tempered minor? These are the potential battle-zones which we will focus on in the section 'Getting it Together'.

Stocktaking

You may find, having done the Personality Wheel and the visualisation exercises once each, that you have identified all your minors. If you scored fairly low on the multiplicity scale (page 122–4) this may indeed be the case. But if you feel there are still things that you do, feel or think that cannot be accounted for by the personalities you have found so far, repeat the exercises from time to time, ideally over quite a long period and in as many different situations as is practical.

When you feel fairly certain that you have identified all your minors, do a 'stocktaking'. Write down the names of all of your personalities and then use the examples I have given as a template to arrive at a profile showing:

■ What each one says/thinks (favourite phrases, telltale attitudes, reflex comments).
■ What it does (its function in your life, the way it manifests).
■ Its strengths (what does it add to your life, has it a use?).
■ Its weaknesses (does it hold you back or spoil other personalities' plans?).

- Questions to ask it (designed to increase its self-awareness).
- Try also to think of how the minor has manifested in your life generally, rather as the life stories I have placed against each of my examples show this.

Then look down the list and see if you can spot any obviously opposing pairs. Have you discovered, for example, a 'Chicken' who tries to stop you taking any risks and a 'Go For It!' who would have you bungee-jumping off Niagara Falls? A 'Devoted Dad' and a 'Wish I Was Free'? A 'Miss Obliging' and a 'Mule'? Place these pairs together on your list – later they will be talking to one another.

Leave a gap of a few days before going on to the next section and during that time just keep your personalities in mind. Note when you slip into one or the other, jot down their thoughts and sayings as they occur, think about when one or another has been particularly active and dictated a course of action in your life. Try to think of what might have happened had another minor taken charge. Listen to their thoughts and get familiar with the particular voice that each personality uses. Learn to recognise characteristic phrases which alert you to whoever is active. Generally try to distinguish each one clearly in your mind and get to know them. Once you are familiar with each one move on to the next, final set of exercises.

Building the team

The previous chapters should have helped you to acknowledge and identify your minors and get an idea of what they do and why. Your own personalities will probably include some of the examples I have given, but by now I would expect that you have also found many that are unique to you. I would also hope that you have started to see how they might conflict with one another, and how these disputes cause problems in your day-to-day life.

The first set of exercises that follow are designed to get your personalities talking to one another. Later ones will help you to change your 'characterscape' – strengthening minors that are generally helpful, curbing those that have got too strong, creating new ones where necessary and transforming those that are a nuisance. Finally we will deal with those personalities that might be better off out of the family altogether and see how that might be achieved.

The purpose of getting minors to communicate is not to bind them together into one. To do that would be to throw away the adaptive advantage that multiplicity is designed to give. Rather the idea is to allow them to preserve their individual characteristics and make the best of them by ensuring they come out when, and only when, they are suited to the situation. It is, if you like, internal team-building.

Let sleeping dogs lie

Among your cast of personalities you will have some that are complex, active and dominant (your major or majors); others which are distinct but fairly narrow in scope (the Worker, the Clown); and some that are too shadowy even to name. Among these skeletal minors you may have got a glimpse of one or two that are unhappy or frightened or angry.

If a minor is emerging spontaneously you may need to see where it came from in order to work out how best to move it along – away from its original miseries or resentments. It is possible to change minors even if they seem at first to be hopelessly 'stuck'. But what is required is that you activate them at the same time as a more optimistic or stable personality who can talk to them and encourage them to see things from a different perspective. What is *not* helpful is simply to go over their pasts while entirely 'being' them. You need to develop a degree of co-consciousness, and if you find this impossible it may be best to avoid working with negative minors altogether.

The reason for this is obvious when you consider how memories are encoded in the brain (Chapter Three). Personalities *are* memories, and every time a memory is recalled it becomes more firmly and more widely connected to others and thus more likely to be jogged into consciousness. Reactivating a traumatised personality, just for the sake of it, is therefore going to strengthen its influence rather than weaken it. This has been widely recognised for more than a decade, and hence psychiatry has largely abandoned therapies which depend on rehearsing old hurts in the expectation that this alone might take away their sting.

If you come across a minor that produces bad feelings, go on to another personality or stop the exercise altogether and do something routine that will flip you back into your default (major) personality. If the minor seems to be lingering, even when you stop trying to activate it, seek out a personality that will eclipse it by 'framing' yourself in the positive personality's role. Or go back to the visualisation exercise in the last chapter, but instead of allowing just anyone to come to mind, dismiss any negative minors that come up and zone in on one that is generally upbeat and happy.

If you find that a negative minor repeatedly intrudes and that you cannot easily slip out of it, you may prefer to pursue a formal course of therapy, either through one of the courses which use a multiple personality model similar to this (for contact details see pages 251–2) or through a more conventional route.

Making conversation

To carry out these exercises you need to create a state of mind that borders on the co-consciousness we looked at earlier (Chapter Two). For most of us our normal state is to 'be' one or another personality almost completely – the only hint we get of the others in us is what you might call 'breakthroughs' when a backstage minor stirs into consciousness for a moment and throws in some contradictory thought or surprise emotion, or momentarily takes over the action causing a 'Why did I do *that*?' moment. Hence most instances of having more than one minor active are rather confused or uncomfortable and our brain – which is constantly trying to smooth over rough moments – tries hard to avoid them.

These exercises, however, depend on nurturing communal consciousness rather than stifling it. The idea is that if you can get two personalities (or more) to be active at the same time it is possible for them to talk directly to one another, to exchange ideas, iron out misunderstandings and agree on future behaviour.

It is useful, in these sessions, to use one personality as a sort of chair or host, to oversee and keep control of proceedings. In many people this will be their major or 'default' personality. Normally a major tries to take over completely, but here the idea is to get it to retreat a little and tick away gently while allowing minors to come and go. Some majors are not suitable for this role, however. They might be bullies, or too anxious or controlling to let others speak freely, or they might insist on overlaying the words of the minors with thoughts of their own. Your major might be totally skewed in its own thinking – a Critic that has got out of hand, or a Driver that can't relax enough to allow its mind to roam. Or it may think this sort of thing is quite simply silly.

If this is the case you may do better to find a more appropriate minor that you can activate to play this role. For those who are aware of having one (and most of us do), the Wise Friend is a good candidate because it is by nature more distanced, cool and objective than most minors. Or you might like to look at the shapes on your Personality Wheel and see if you have already identified one that is both open-minded and stable who you can bring in to do the job.

Before you begin try to clear the stage of all but the personality that you want to chair proceedings. If this is not your major, 'frame' yourself into the minor that you have chosen for this role. Then:

- Refresh your memory of each (other) personality by reading back through your stocktaking list. Add any more minors that you have come across since you drew it up and flesh out the descriptions with any new insights.
- Look at which situations bring out which minor. Start with those in which more than one minor seems to be active – where it is clear that two or more personalities are trying to get the upper hand.
- Get into the frame by imagining yourself in that situation, much as

you imagined yourself in a specific role (father, worker, councillor, gardener, etc.) for the Personality Wheel exercise. Use the photos from the last exercise in the previous chapter to prompt your memory.

- Once you are in the situation listen very carefully to the thoughts that occur. Most of our thinking is done in words and these may be so distinct that they really sound like voices. (The difference between imaginary voices and hallucinatory voices is less to do with the way they sound than a certain absolute *knowledge*, in the first case, that the words are being generated from inside your skull and not coming from outside). At first they might seem very indistinct or babbling, as though several people are talking at once (which in a way, they are). But if you tune in carefully you will start to find that you can untangle the voices into separate strands.

- Identify the strands and write the name of the minor who is speaking against each one. This might be a personality you have already identified and who you expect to be active in this situation. But it might also be someone you have not encountered before. If you are in doubt, think of a title – any title – and label it. If it turns out to be an inappropriate name you can change it to something more fitting later.

- Write down what they say. The ideal way to do this is to write it as you hear it, but if you find this difficult, or find that you are lagging too far behind the voices, abandon it and write it down afterwards. Do not censor it. This is absolutely essential – throughout this exercise the big 'I' (Chapter Two) will constantly attempt to edit what is going on and reduce your multiple threads of thought to one. Try to resist this. Listen carefully to the fainter voices, go with what they say and do not try to put words, so to speak, into their mouth. You might find that what you hear is a complete surprise to you.

- Go on until you feel you have got a useful amount of dialogue to work with . . .

You should now have quite a bit of writing, comprising speech from at least two and maybe many more voices. Read it over and note how it sounds. Do your minors shout at one another, or tease or plead or just squabble in a dreary way? Do they listen to each other or simply ignore what the other is saying? Do two of them gang up against a third? Are they struggling to do fundamentally different things or just disagreeing about details? Does it leap out at you that one of them, quite obviously, is sabotaging the situation while another is trying to make it work?

Example

You are at home with a group of friends. You have been celebrating and you have produced a fantastic dinner that everyone has enjoyed. Now you are sitting round the table and you are meant to be relaxing. But the voices in your head are not.

Party-Goer: This is great. I'm really enjoying today.

Inner Critic: You burned the meat. They said it was nicely done but it was burned.

Party-Goer: Not now, please.

Little Badly-Done-By: I have done all the work up to now and nobody has even offered to clear the dishes.

Party-Goer: Oh no, not you too! Not *now*!

Smugness: I'm pretty damn wonderful. Did all that on my own!

Outer Critic: D. wolfed down two helpings of pudding and she just can't afford to, she's falling out of that top as it is!

Leave-Me-Alone-Please: I can't keep this smile up much longer . . . when are they all going home?

Party-Goer: I'm just not going to listen to all these miseries.

Love Everybody: These people are wonderful. I am so lucky to have them as my friends.

Outer Critic: No, they're not. They are boring.

Inner Critic: You just see them that way because you are boring yourself.

Love Everybody: It doesn't matter if they are boring. I love them.

Smugness: Aren't I wonderful for thinking that, even though they are boring?

Leave-Me-Alone-Please: These get-togethers are exhausting. I wish I could slip off and read my book.

Now look at the sentiments expressed by each minor and determine which are directly opposed to one another. In the example above, for example, Party-Goer is clearly at odds with Leave-Me-Alone-Please, Inner Critic is diametrically opposed to Smugness and Little-Badly-Done-By is hardly on the same wave length as Love Everybody.

This is the point at which your 'chair' personality needs to insert itself in the conversation. The aim is to alter the direction of the dialogue so that, instead of simply reiterating their opinions, the personalities start to *exchange* ideas and therefore influence each other instead of existing in their own little worlds. The important thing here is for the chair to resist driving the conversation. Instead it should nudge it along, generally allowing it to go in the direction in which it is drifting without hitting the buffers of old conflicts or disappearing down some dead end.

Very often you will find that the conflict or puzzle or contradiction that seems at first to need sorting out is not the crucial one, or that a minor which seems at the start to be peripheral floats into the centre and becomes the focus of the session. If that starts to happen, let it. Continue with the conversation until you feel you have arrived at a notable shift in opinion, or a single negotiated settlement, or some other natural junction. Stop at this point, even if the original conflicts you identified remain unaddressed.

Below is how the earlier conversation might go. The words in italics come from your Wise Friend, or whoever is acting as chair.

Party-Goer: This is great (etc.).

Inner Critic: Yeah, *except* that you burned the meat. They said it was nicely done but it was burned.

They said it was good. Why don't you believe them?

IC: Because you always get something wrong when you cook. You just can't do it.

Oh really? Smugness? What do you say to that?

Smugness: I think Inner Critic should shut up. Everything he says is rubbish.

IC: No, it's not. How about that pasta that came out in a solid lump last week? One of your guests asked for a knife to eat it with, remember? How about the salmon that was still frozen in the middle? How about . . .

Smugness: Sorry, I can't take this (fading). I think I'm going . . .

No! Smugness, stay a minute. Didn't anyone else think we did a good thing today?

Little Badly-Done-By: If it was that good people would have been more appreciative.

Maybe they didn't realise you wanted help because you seemed so competent.

LBDB: They can't have done – you heard what IC said.

How about listening to Smugness instead?

Smugness (brightening): Quite right!

LBDB: Smugness is just embarrassing. She has no place here at all.

Smugness: I make you all feel good, though, don't I?

LBDB: Hardly the point . . .

Why not? Maybe you could all do with a bit of Smugness's feel-good?

IC: We don't deserve it.

Smugness: Yes, we do!

IC: No, we don't!

Smugness: Yes, we do! (etc.)

Shh! Who else thinks we deserve some credit for today?

Outer Critic: At least we did something except sit on our backsides and eat!

Love Everybody: Don't be so mean! It was so kind of everyone to come. We should be grateful.

Do you think they came because they were doing us a favour, then?

IC: Can't think of any other reason.

OC: How about they like being waited on?

Leave-Me-Alone-Please: I wish you would all shut up so I can get back to my book.

Hallo! Are you sure you should be here? This is a social occasion after all.

LMAP: But I *always* come to social occasions.

Everyone: Why?

Maybe you're not so welcome at these times – have you thought of staying away when other people are about?

LMAP: But the whole point of me is that I come to social events.
What for?
LMAP: Because I've always been at them.
How come?
LMAP: Because I don't want to be there.
Then why are you there?
LMAP: Because I have always been there.
When else do you come out?
LMAP: When the others start organising things.
You mean, you are there even before the party starts?
LMAP: Yup! Right at the start.
Do you try to stop the others making their plans?
LMAP: Not really. I know it's hopeless.
But you sort of invite yourself along in advance?
LMAP: Oh yes. I'm the first to arrive.
But why? Why do you go?
LMAP: Because I have always been there.
IC: Give up! She's beyond hope. You never get anywhere with her. She's just determined to ruin things.
LBDB: No, she's not. She has a miserable time. She talks to me at parties so I know. She doesn't want to spoil things at all – she can't *help* being there, that's all!
Leave-Me-Alone? Do you remember being at parties when you were little?
LMAP: You bet! I was the only one to go to parties then.
You mean, the others weren't active at parties when you were little? They weren't at them?
LMAP: That's right. It was just me!
What about Party-Goer?
LMAP: She wasn't even born then.
So why didn't you just not go to parties?
LMAP: It wasn't allowed, was it? Birthday parties, Hallowe'en parties, egg-hunts, gymkhanas, you had to go or you were thought of as sad or weird.
But you don't have to go now.

Party-Goer: And we would rather you didn't.

LMAP: But I've *always* been there . . .

How about if Party-Goer gave you permission to stay asleep during the party?

Party-Goer: Done!

LMAP: I think this is a trick.

It is. But try it. Just once – see how it goes.

LMAP: OK.

Putting agreements into practice

When your conversation gets to a natural junction, ask everyone to get on with their own business – go back to sleep (i.e. become unconscious) or carry on as normal, as appropriate. Try to stop the conversation cleanly at this point, but put it on hold so you can pick it up again at this point at a future time.

Write down the main points as clearly you can, using the language of the minors themselves. Don't be tempted to tidy up or 'correct' what the personalities say because the way they speak is a very good clue to what they are about. Leave-Me-Alone-Please's circular and limited thinking, for instance, and the childlike repetition of a nonsensical statement point to her origins as a Relic – a child who is still trapped in the schooldays parties which she hated, but which are jogged into recollection by the very different parties she attends today which the other members of her now greatly extended family thoroughly enjoy.

When you have got a complete record of the conversation – or as complete as you can make it – read it back and take note of any clear agreements that have been made. Note these separately and think about how they can be turned into concrete acts.

The agreement made by Leave-Me-Alone-Please sounds fairly straightforward – basically it is that she won't pop up at the next party. But this is not going to happen automatically because the party will jog those early party memories of which LMAP is an intrinsic part. However, the arrangement was specifically between LMAP and a minor who will also quite definitely be at the party: Party-Goer herself. These two are in almost direct opposition. One way to eclipse LMAP, therefore, is to ensure that Party-Goer is at full strength when you arrive at the next party.

To do this it would be worth having a 'private' word with Party-Goer before the next social event. You would start first by getting into the 'chair-person' mode, and then bringing on Party-Goer through the framing technique. The conversation might then proceed like this:

Leave-Me-Alone-Please has promised to sleep this next do out. Remember?

Party-Goer: Leave-Me-Alone-Please? Never heard of her. Can't we put some music on? What do you have to do to get a drink round here? (etc.)

Calm down, we're not there yet. Leave-Me-Alone-Please is the one among us who always wants to slide off somewhere quiet. She's the one who made us all climb out of the bathroom window to get away from that wedding reception, remember? She says things like 'I don't want to talk to these people' and 'I want to be at home in bed'.

Party-Goer: I remember her.

Anyway, she's promised you that she'd sleep this one out.

Party-Goer: Good thing too.

But you may have to remind her.

Party-Goer: I never talk to her.

That's the point – on this occasion you must.

Party-Goer: OK, I'll tell her to buzz off.

I don't think that will help. It will make her even more active. If you want her to carry out her side of the bargain you'll have to give her something in return. How about agreeing that if she will stay quiet until, say, midnight, you will leave the moment she asks you to after that?

Party-Goer: I might be too busy to listen.

Then Wise Friend will remind you.

Party-Goer: I don't listen to Wise Friend.

Well, maybe you should start . . .

As you can see, conversations with, and between, minors do not necessarily go in the direction that any of you may want. It is like the 'orchestra' of the brain – there is no conductor so the various instrumentalists take their cues from one another rather than from any external director. The Wise Friend or 'chair' can nudge and suggest, but is not in a position to control things any more than the others. Hence, changing the behaviour of minors tends to be a long and uncertain business. One personality – whether it be the person's major or another minor – cannot just command another to do something. Indeed, if one personality did get that sort of control in the family it would be overstretching its remit, because, as we have seen, each minor was originally created for a purpose and many of them are still valuable. Even Leave-Me-Alone-Please – born out of the misery of attending parties as a child which she did not enjoy – has a limited role still, if only to keep Party-Goer under some kind of control and get everyone home before dawn. You may only discover a minor's function after getting to know them very well and exploring how they interact with others.

The empty chair

If you find it difficult to get your minors talking to one another just by thinking about it, you might like to try this famous technique which was originally developed by Frederick Perls, the pioneer of Gestalt Therapy. Perls used it to explore the duality of mind which he believed to be a driving force in much of neurosis. He would sit in one chair and have two other empty chairs beside him. The client would start off in one of the chairs, and imagine another part of themselves – say the Parent or the Child – sitting in the other. These 'parts' are in some ways similar to minors and the physical separation of the two chairs, although it may seem artificial to begin with, may help to clarify the voices of your various personalities.

- Arrange two chairs or pillows a few feet from one another. Have extra chairs/pillows nearby to bring in if another personality arrives unexpectedly and wants to join in.

- Frame yourself into the personality – major or minor – that you have chosen to chair. Spend some time establishing yourself in that mode, but do not get taken over by it completely.
- Now frame yourself as one of the minors you want to work with. Don't try to bring in any others yet – just stick with that one.
- Externalise this minor in the way that you did with the visualisation exercise – that is, imagine it as a physical entity outside yourself. Sit it in the empty chair/pillow and re-frame yourself as chair (*person*, that is, not the actual piece of furniture).
- In that mode, say hallo to the chair with your minor in it. Don't be embarrassed. No one can see you but you and your minor and they will be pleased to be acknowledged.
- Now ask it a question. Anything will do. 'How are you today?' 'What have you been up to?' Or perhaps: 'Have I got your name right?'
- Shift into the other chair. Frame yourself as the minor and respond in that mode.
- Thereafter, shift chairs back and forth, according to who is speaking. Try to hold both speakers in mind as you do it, but shift your attention from one to another so that you respond in their voice.
- If another minor pipes up, bring in another chair and invite them to join in.
- Stop, as before, at a natural juncture. Write down the conversation.
- Proceed as before, to secure future agreements/shifts in attitude.

Drawing up an agenda

As you get to know your personalities better and become more prac-tised at initiating discussions between them you may find it useful to devise an agenda to determine what you want to achieve. Using your stocktaking list as a base, write down the names of your personalities together with the ways that they benefit or disadvantage your family as a whole. Then consider how they might be changed for the better. For example:

Personality	Strength	Weakness	Desired change
Inner Critic	Keeps smugness in check Gives reality check on performance	Undermines others' confidence Judgement too harsh and non-helpful	Speak up only if it can give positive criticism – i.e. some way of improving performance
Party-Goer	Generates pleasure and fun	Reckless – e.g. undermines health by binge drinking	Should occasionally stand aside for Leave-Me-Alone-Please
Leave-Me-Alone-Please	Potential to secure social 'down time' for quiet activities and relaxation	Comes out at wrong time	Learn to emerge when its desires are practical possibilities
Little-Badly-Done-By	Alerts others to possibility that they are being treated unfairly	Often sees unfairness when there is none there	Check with a more objective personality: 'Should I really be here now?' before launching into usual moan

Personality	Strength	Weakness	Desired change
Smugness	Makes everyone in the family feel good	Makes people outside feel bad and may cause them to dislike us	Currently too easily seen off by Inner Critic. Should be prepared to engage in dialogue with IC designed to test which of them should be uppermost in any situation
Love Everybody	Makes us, and everyone outside, feel wonderful	May invite others to take advantage of us	Should develop dialogue, as above, with Outer Critic
Outer Critic	Prevents us being taken in by/taken advantage of by others	Is too harsh and unforgiving – crushes Love Everybody and makes others dislike us	Learn to see others' faults without blaming them for them. Needs to talk more with Love Everybody

A helping hand

As you can probably see from the preceding exercise, once you start listening to minors talking it is almost inevitable that you will start to learn about their origins. Minors are embedded in memories – indeed in a sense they *are* memories – so whenever they are active they are bringing into the present some part of the past.

As I have said, there is no benefit to be had from simply digging out the origins of a troublesome or unhappy minor – all that is likely to do is make the personality more active. Going back to the 'birthplace' of a minor can be useful, however, providing you can do it while *also* 'being' one of your wiser, most adult or stable personalities. If you can do this – effectively achieving a state of co-consciousness – the happier minor can act as a 'helper', urging the unhappy one to overlay its original responses with ones which are more appropriate to the present situation. If you can do this consistently the unhappy minor may be transformed, merge with another, or perhaps just fade away.

The Helping Hand technique, as I'll call it, requires that a hurt or troublesome minor is first brought to mind and, for the reasons given earlier, I do not recommend deliberately activating such characters. This exercise should only begin, therefore, when a minor pops up spontaneously and starts to give you problems.

By now I hope you will recognise when this is happening. Typical examples are when you find that you are having 'second thoughts' about a plan of action that earlier seemed to be without flaws, or when you are 'in two minds' about something. You might hear a voice somewhere deriding your performance or warning you about some imaginary peril. There may be an argument going on inside you, or you may be in a bad mood for no reason you can see. There are countless different ways that unhappy or unreasonable minors can cause problems and only you can learn to recognise when it is happening.

You may recall Gail, from Chapter Five, whose shopping trips were haunted by the anxiety of being mistakenly accused of shoplifting. She traced the fear to an incident that happened to her as a child, when she took another child's flag from the top of their sandcastle and was roundly punished for it. The shamed and angry child that she was at that moment remained frozen in time in her mind, and leapt into consciousness whenever Gail was in a situation where a false accusation of theft might conceivably be made. But it was only when she saw a picture of a sandcastle in a store one day that she remembered the event that gave birth to her troublesome minor.

The fact that Gail maintained her adult consciousness while at the same time feeling the child's distress made it possible for her adult self to get a dialogue going with the child. 'I was able to tell it, effectively, that the sandcastle had been swept away years ago – there was really no need still to be upset,' she explains. 'After that I started to deliberately recall the sandcastle incident whenever I entered a store and to talk to the child. I told her it had all been a silly mistake, no one was at fault, no more blame, no more unfair accusation. Bit by bit the message got through – the child started to realise that it *was not going to happen again*.

'Now when I shop, instead of going through my pantomime of innocence I force myself to behave normally. I pick things up, put them back. I might take an item of clothing to a window to see the colour in the light; try on a jacket. At first it was uncomfortable. Little Falsely Accused, as I started to think of her, would agitate, "Put it down! Let go! It's not *yours*!" But slowly she has got to realise that it is not going to happen again. The outrage is subsiding. One day I could even start to enjoy shopping.'

A second example comes from someone I know well who was getting into trouble on account of an argumentative character almost directly the opposite of her usual agreeable self. Maggie does a high-profile public job, which requires her to look confident – more confident than she actually feels. This is her story:

There are times when all my swanky front just evaporates and I feel myself shrinking. It almost seems as though I am literally becoming smaller, like a child. It happens mainly when I am with people who I know – or suspect – are cleverer than me, or more successful, or have some sort of expertise that I don't share. I'll go in feeling chatty and cheerful and just fine, and then someone will say something that could be taken to be just a tiny bit unfriendly, or start talking about something I'm ignorant about, or it might be anything. And I collapse inside.

When that happens, later in the evening I often have a blazing row with someone! I'll spend all evening feeling pathetic and tongue-tied, and then suddenly the conversation will turn to something I know something about and I just – take over! If anyone tries to challenge me I go for them ferociously. I won't give an inch. I just have to win the argument.

One day I picked one of these fights with someone who I was meant to be chatting up for funding for the organisation I work for. At some stage in the evening he made some political comment which I didn't agree with and I was away! Afterwards he complained to my boss and I thought, Well, I've got to get this under control. But I couldn't – the same thing happened less than a week later. As I banged the table and shouted I actually thought to myself, Hey! You said you weren't going to do this! But I couldn't stop. You know that phrase: 'I don't know what got into me'? Well, that was how it felt exactly – as though something had 'got into' me.

The way that Maggie described her argumentative behaviour – as though something 'got into' her – made me think that this might be the emergence of a minor personality. Although she was sceptical about it, Maggie agreed to attend a single session of ego-state therapy (page 4) and report back to me. Ego-state therapy uses hypnosis, and the therapist began by putting Maggie into a light trance:

The therapist just told me to relax, to think about being in a garden, then about walking through it, visualising the flowers, going down some steps. It wasn't like going into a deep trance or anything. I just felt relaxed. But I do know that, in any other circumstances, I would certainly not have talked like I did then. The therapist asked me to indicate, by raising a finger, if there was anyone other than me who would like to say something. I thought that sounded rather silly, but I kind of felt like going along with it, so I raised my finger. Then she asked me who was there.

I was already aware of the shy, terrified 'me' of course, as well as the argumentative 'me', but I had never really thought of it as a separate person. As I sat there, though, I had this absolutely clear image of a child in a school playground, feeling terrified of all the other children and trying to melt into the wall. I believe this was a real memory because I recognised the school as being the very first one I went to – I was only there for a few months so I would have been just five. The feelings were real anyway; for a few moments I felt exactly what that child was feeling and saw the world – terrifying, noisy, threatening – through her eyes.

The hypnotist asked me what was happening and I remember not answering. She went on talking to me gently and I just didn't respond. It was weird: I was too shy to speak! Then she said, 'What's your name?' and I answered: 'Child'. Normally I would feel absolutely stupid saying something like that, but I said it. Then the hypnotist said, 'Do you want to talk to me?' and I shook my head.

Then – I can't remember what happened in between – after a while I think the hypnotist asked me if there was anyone else there. And I raised my finger again. As I did so again I had an absolutely clear picture of a teenage boy arguing like crazy against a bunch of adults. I wasn't 'in' this character, rather I was watching from the other side of the table. But I knew that this was the out-of-control warrior I had come to get rid of. I told the hypnotist I saw this person and she said: 'What's his name?' and I said, 'Anthony'.

Now this was the strangest thing of all because, as far as I can think, I don't know, nor have I ever known anyone significant called Anthony. The name has no particular attraction to me, no resonance. I have absolutely no idea where it came from. Yet I said it without hesitation and with absolute certainly that this was the boy's name!

The second strange thing – which was also utterly unexpected – was I realised that Anthony was not a bully at all. He was protecting

Child. He wasn't at all sure he was up to it, and the only way he could do it was to put up a shield of words so the adults couldn't turn their scorn on the kid. If they had a relationship it was of big brother to little sister, but that wasn't clear.

I can't actually remember how the session ended. I suppose the hypnotist had a chat with Anthony or something. Anyway, the things is, daft and New Agey and embarrassing as all this *should* be, it wasn't. And it was terrifically helpful because now when Anthony starts agitating I find I can sort of talk to him. I take a moment out and say internally: 'Oi! What are you doing here? This person isn't threatening! I can cope!' And when I do this he slides away.

Apart from stopping me arguing, it has made me feel better about myself because I realise that what I thought was a bully was actually nothing of the sort. It was another rather nervous kid, trying hard to be heroic. And I rather like myself for that!

Making a minor

The previous section looked at how a minor might be transformed, encouraged to merge with another or discouraged from muscling in when it is not needed or wanted. Here we see how you can deliberately create a new minor when the existing family seems to be short of a member that could be of use.

Minors, as we have seen, are made by situations. They are learned responses to the things that happen to us. Hence people who have encountered a very wide range of situations, each quite different from the other, are likely to have a correspondingly large number of personalities. People who have lived a very 'samey' life, by contrast, may just have a Single Major who is there morning, afternoon and evening.

Creating personalities is child's play – literally. Practically every game of make-believe involves making believe that the player is someone they are not and every act of pretence brings a little minor flickering into life, at least for the duration of the game. Most of these are almost instantly forgotten, but some will be revived again and again, and some of those will become complex and well enough entrenched in the memory net to stay around for many years, if not for a lifetime.

As we get older our ability to create new personalities in response to new situations decreases. We tend to 'set', like jelly, into our existing major and various minors and struggle to make them cope with any new challenge that comes along rather than responding afresh. In today's fast-changing world this is often a great disadvantage. Many middle-aged people find it difficult to keep up with new technology, for instance, because as children they were not showered with gadgets that created a gizmo-friendly minor. Those of us who learned to drive before our roads were studded with speed cameras may not have the 'Look-Out' minor who was created in younger drivers as soon as they first took the wheel. A person who grew up thinking gay relationships were perverse is unlikely to have a personality that is comfortable with sexual diversity.

This exercise is designed to help you to spot any gap in your 'cast-list' of personalities, and to create a new minor to fill it.

- Divide your life into manageable blocks such as Work/Home/Social.
- Using a separate sheet of paper for each category, list your strengths and weaknesses in each one. A work-sheet might, for example, look like this:

Strengths	Weaknesses
Reliability	Getting on with colleagues
Getting things done	Coping with complaints
Attention to detail	Initiating new projects

■ Now identify the qualities which give you your strengths. You may like to do this by using the Personality Wheel. In the case above, for example, your strengths (solid line) and weaknesses (broken line) would give you a shape something like this:

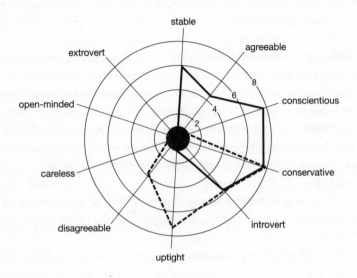

You can see clearly from this which characteristics are missing from the personalities who come out in you at work. You would benefit by creating one that was more extrovert (to get on better with your colleagues), open-minded (to initiate ideas), and agreeable (to cope with complaints).

Do the same for each major area of your life. You might find it helpful to use the Personality Wheel, but if not just think carefully about the areas in which you are weak. You may also like to think of areas of life in which you feel you do not engage because you don't have the where-withal. For example, you do less travelling than you would like to because you don't have a partner or friend to accompany you. In that case it might be useful to create a 'Lone Traveller' – adventurous, open-minded, savvy, self-contained but extrovert enough to make new friends along the way.

List the characteristics that your new minor should have. Start with general statements like 'carefulness' or 'extroversion' and then become increasingly specific, e.g. you might write:

Carefulness – care with regard to other people – always friendly – smile first – don't wait for them to smile – remember names of people's children.

Search out people who display the characteristics you wish to incorporate into your new minor. Look for them among people you know, people you see on TV or read about in newspapers, fictional characters from plays, films and books.

Observe the people you have identified very thoroughly. Note the precise expressions, gestures and deeds that mark the characteristics you want to make your own. Do they display friendliness, say, by the way they smile? The way they listen? By what they say or do? Note also the characteristics that you do *not* want to be part of your creation. After all, you are not trying to replicate this person – your minor is a *new* personality, not a weak copy of someone else.

New minors may be created in many different ways. The main ones by which it can be done deliberately include:

- Absorption: if it is feasible and socially acceptable, try to spend as much time as is reasonably possible in the company of the person or people who possess the characteristics you have targeted (but make sure you are welcome!). If it is a celebrity you want to emulate, do the usual fan thing of collecting photographs and reading interviews – but remember, you are not out to worship this person, you merely want to incorporate certain of their characteristics.
- Mimicry: once you have identified how your desired characteristics are manifested in the person you are using as a guide, copy them. Copy the smile, if it is the friendliness you want; the walk, the phrases, the gestures.
- Fronting: build up your personality in cyberspace using an avatar (see Chapter Five). Identify with your online character and gradually introduce it into your offline life.

■ Externalise: Write down the personality you want to be. Give it a name and talk to it in your head. Initially you will have to make an effort to imagine what it will say but in time you will find it will answer for itself and gradually it will take its place in the family line-up.

Saying goodbye

I started this book by inviting you to become aware of inner conflicts caused by squabbles among your various personalities. Anyone who drew a blank on that is unlikely to have got this far, so I assume that you know how it feels to be a battleground for warring minors. I hope that reading this book and doing the exercises in it have enabled you to identify the main players in your particular internal drama, and to start them talking in a way that will eventually lead to greater harmony between them.

On the way, though, you may have identified some characters who just do not want to play. They might be ancient Relics who refuse to depart from their narrow, negative brief or Punishers who loathe the others in the family and are determined to do them down. Critics may have developed such harsh views that they are beyond modification and Defenders may not have the sense to see that their actions are actually destructive.

You have probably also discovered a number of unhelpful 'micros' (Chapter Two) – fragments of personalities that are too skeletal to have self-awareness and have not (yet) managed to latch on to a more substantial personality that would lend them a sense of self. They might manifest as destructive habits such as smoking or bingeing, or as apparently ungrounded fears or seemingly causeless moods. Some of them are just knee-jerk reactions – brain habits that have never been questioned. If you catch yourself saying something like: 'I never wear blue' and then find that you cannot answer the question 'Why?', you have probably stumbled upon a micro.

Then there are the seriously undesirable minors and micros: unhappy, traumatised or destructive entities formed by some extraordinary situation which – though long past and never to be repeated – continues to cloud the present so long as they are there to revive it. These may include intrusive memories of horrifying events such as accidents, sudden bereavement or crippling humiliation.

No one needs characters like these in their family. Once you are satisfied that they have no redeeming features and are beyond transformation it is time to tell them that – to put it in corporate-speak – you have to let them go.

'Letting go' of a well-established personality is hard. Once it has been 'learned' a minor becomes part of the brain's hardware, as well as the software of the mind (page 47). Take a skeletal minor (or micro) that consists just of the desire and habit of smoking. Other personalities may overrule it so its activity is curbed. But if the smoker is well learned – in other words, if it is a full-blown addiction – it will remain encoded in the brain in the form of neural linkages that correspond to the smoker's desire and behaviour. So long as the neurons that make up the smoker remain quiescent, its thoughts and feelings (Where can I get a cigarette?, etc.) will be silenced. But if those neurons are jogged into action the smoker will come back with a vengeance, as millions of recidivist quitters can testify.

Over a long period, unactivated neural patterns may degrade and eventually fall apart. This, essentially, is forgetting, and it is what you need to aim for if a troublesome minor is to be eliminated from the fold. Deliberately forgetting something, though, is notoriously difficult because the very act of trying not to think about something inevitably brings it to mind. In one episode of the classic British TV comedy *Fawlty Towers*, German visitors come to stay and the hopelessly inept Basil (played by John Cleese) frantically instructs his staff: 'Don't mention the War!' Subsequently, of course, Basil himself finds it impossible not to mention it. Indeed, he ends up goose-stepping around the dining room – compelled to draw attention to the very thing he wants most to keep under wraps.

So it seems to be with all of us. Simply trying to suppress thoughts often leads to them popping up even more frequently than they might have done otherwise. In one experiment, for example, volunteers were asked not to think about a particular subject, but to ring a bell if the forbidden thought did come to mind. On average the participants rang the bell an average of seven times during a five minute period.[1] Furthermore, participants who were first asked to suppress a thought and then later asked to think about it experienced a rebound effect: they reported the thought many more times than those who were asked to generate the thought without first having suppressed it.

There is, however, another technique – Directed, or Intentional, Forgetting – which does seem to help people to prevent certain thoughts and feelings from becoming conscious. It seems to work by manipulating attention away from the things that are to be forgotten and attaching it to another set which are categorised as 'to be remembered'. It probably does not stop the thoughts from being activated *un*consciously – and minors can still have influence even when they are operating only at this level. However, banning them from consciousness should act on them as a sort of tranquilliser, making them more and more sluggish until, with luck, they will go into a permanent coma.

This, then, is the final exercise – a practical guide to saying goodbye:

- Select from your stocktaking list the minor/s you want to forget (then deal with one at a time).
- Note some telltale sign about them – a characteristic phrase or a particular habit by which you can recognise them quickly when they emerge.
- Make a note to yourself that when you become aware of this telltale you should resist being 'taken over'.
- Instead, deliberately frame yourself into the Wise Friend (or similar chairperson) so that you can hold the unwanted minor in co-consciousness.
- Try to clarify the minor's thoughts, e.g. I am useless; I shall never be any better; Everyone hates me, etc. Write them down as a list in coloured ink (say green).
- Now make up a list of *directly opposing* thoughts. If they jog a more positive minor into life, all the better. Write them as a list in another coloured ink (red).

- Reframe as Wise Friend (or other chair personality).
- Instruct yourself to remember the list of phrases written in red ink and to forget those in green.
- Repeat the phrases in red until you can say them by heart. Do not repeat those in green.
- If a 'green' phrase subsequently pops into your mind, immediately chant the 'red' phrases to yourself.
- Eventually you should find that the green phrases are 'drowned out' by the red ones. Your minor's attempt to tell you, for instance, that you are universally hated will immediately trigger an even louder statement asserting your universal popularity. Do not expect to *believe* these phrases at first, just aim to learn them.
- Once the minor has given up and gone to sleep – as eventually it will – do not on any account be tempted to have a memorial service for it. Thinking about a minor you have finally put to sleep is like giving cardiac resuscitation to someone with a terminal illness – it is kinder to them, and to the rest of you, just to let it go.

Families in families

One of the most frequent stories I heard while researching this book came from adults who told me how they regressed to childhood or to being a teenager whenever they were in the company of their parents or siblings. Some said that the time-warp occurred unfailingly as they entered their childhood home. 'The smell does it for me instantly – there's some kind of polish my mother alone seems to use and it never fails to transport me,' says one friend. 'It's the way my sister *always* manages to make me feel inferior,' says another. 'I'm a very confident person usually, but I felt bad about myself as a child because Toni was prettier than me and cleverer too. Now I find myself feeling exactly the way I used to within minutes of meeting her, even though she is usually in a tracksuit with baby-milk stains on it while I'm the one with the big job and the nice clothes.'

Some people find these transformations happen even *before* they meet their folks, as though the child that they usually keep out of mind starts agitating whenever a family get-together is in the offing. The immediate effect of this regression depends, of course, on the original family dynamics. People who felt loved and cared for by their families and endured little serious conflict with them as children find their return visits comforting and relaxing. Indeed, many adults admitted to me that they like returning to their childhood home precisely because it gives their adult selves a rest. But those who fought their parents or felt resentment or anger with them as children are immediately pitched back into the same disturbing state, even when the original disagreements have long been put aside or even forgotten. Each member of the family slides into a relationship niche that might have been carved out decades earlier, reviving old patterns of behaviour.

Given that every member of the family may be animated during get-togethers by a personality that only appears on these occasions, their major personalities may barely be known to one another. Often there is no room in the family setup for anyone to change, so when some members develop new ways of being they can only live them when they are away from the other members. In this way adults and their parents often become creepingly estranged, with neither having much idea what is happening in the others' lives despite having an intense sense of familiarity while they are together.

It is not always a matter of offspring growing away from the parents. People continue to change throughout their lives because the human brain remains plastic; admittedly less so as people get older, but nevertheless quite flexible enough to create new personalities and lose old ones. Indeed, older people often change their inner families more than younger adults, because they are free of constraints which tend to prevent major change, such as the need to provide a stable environment for young children. People past the traditional retirement age are now among the most travelled and exploratory groups and – as we have seen – if you throw yourselves into new situations you will almost certainly create new personalities to deal with them.

Discovering a new or newly-apparent adult personality in your mother or father can be uncomfortable. 'When I went through my father's things after the funeral it was like intruding on a stranger,' a 40-year-old woman told me, 'I found emails between him and some woman I didn't know which showed that he discovered with her a serious interest in opera. My Dad!!! At the opera! It was so unlike him I couldn't bear it!' That woman still regrets not getting to know her father better while he was alive. The estrangement was because she never met him as her adult self (who is also an opera buff) but only as the self-absorbed teenager she had been when they had both suffered the sudden loss of her mother. They were so stuck in the roles they adopted during that traumatic period – both of them concerned only with her needs and feelings – that she never discovered the other people in her doting father.

For families to evolve and for each individual really to get to know the others it is therefore important that their interactions do not become ritualised. While it is true that you may need to keep some of your personalities out of the family arena you do not want to meet the family as the same infant or truculent teenager they have always known. While it may be too late (or too disruptive) to start changing the dynamics of long-standing family units, the position is easier if you are yourself growing a family. If, for example, you have young children, you may occasionally benefit from sliding off the personality you usually adopt when dealing with them and bringing on another. Find (or develop) an adult personality which can fulfil the necessary nurturing and safekeeping activities due to your children while at the same time showing them other characters – the clown, or worker, or professional. Encourage the children to do the same. You might perhaps introduce a game in which, for a while, 'big brother' adopts the role of the younger one and vice versa. Or even encourage the children to try out the role of parent. If nothing else you may discover that they do not see you the way that you think they do!

In the workplace

Traditional employment selection forces people to present a narrow slice of their potential personality range at the outset. Simply by defining the employee by a particular type of skill: manager, artist, engineer, designer or whatever, most workplaces put a huge amount of their employees' potential out of bounds from day one. Then, once established in a particular job, employees are generally expected to do just the one thing they have been hired for. If they extend their remit there is a risk that other workers, and sometimes their managers too, will be put out. Colleagues may feel that the person who is straying from their job description is challenging them for their own job, seeking undeserved recognition, or just trespassing. Bosses may feel threatened as well – either because they too fear for their own position or feel that keeping people in well-defined boxes gives them power over the captives.

The result of this is that work is often less satisfying for those doing it than it would be if it allowed them to use more than one of their personalities. Employers, too, lose out by failing to tap into a huge reservoir of largely hidden abilities within their workforce. The constraints may even cause some employees' minor personalities to close down or die off, taking with them their potential abilities. Minors which are deprived of life may become wreckers, forever usurping the Major's efforts as well as those of people outside the individual. Worse, they may become silent but powerful critics, making themselves known only as small black holes of negativity.

Providing they are not completely mismatched to their work, people with strong Major personalities tend to do well in traditionally segmented workplaces – the sort where engineers do engineering, designers design and tea-makers make tea. Nevertheless, even the most integrated person is likely to have peripheral interests and talents, some of which could usefully be imported into the work environment. I know a plumber, for example, who, in his spare time, makes tiny train-set components for his children, who have an elaborate toy railway system in their attic. His day job makes no use at all of the delicate touch he has developed for working in miniature, and his skill came to light only when he saw me trying, unsuccessfully, to mend a piece of shattered jewellery and offered to help. A plumber would be the last person I would have thought of asking to do such a pernickety bit of manipulation, but it turned out that he had precisely the talent needed for the job.

How many 'extra' abilities of this sort might there be in a roomful of employees? And how might a company find out about them and encourage their use?

Given the near-infinite variety of work requirements, types of profession, companies and management structures it is impractical to try to answer that question here. It seems likely, though, that the recognition of multiplicity and the incorporation of diverse personalities could benefit every workplace, whether it be the boardroom of a vast multinational corporation or a cluttered kitchen table.

More broadly, I hope this book has convinced you that recognising and learning to know, understand and deal with the personalities that make up our selves can help us function to our fullest capacity in every endeavour. I have tried to show that what has conventionally been regarded as a potentially harmful pathology is actually a sign of inner diversity created by our species' wonderful ability to adapt to changing circumstances. In our quick-changing and uncertain world, the essential multiplicity of the human mind will I hope, come to be seen as a ubiquitous and precious faculty rather than a curious and rare eccentricity.

Notes

INTRODUCTION

1 Diederen et al., 'Neuroimaging of voice hearing in non-psychotic individuals: a review', *Frontiers of Human Neuroscience*, 9 May 2012, pp. 6–111

2 Kompus et al., 'The Role of the primary auditory cortex in the neural mechanism of auditory verbal hallucinations', *Frontiers of Human Neuroscience*, 24 April 2013, pp. 7–144

PART I

Chapter One: A Brief History of Our Selves

1 Robert Ornstein, *Multimind*, Macmillan, London, 1986, p. 25.

2 Simone Reinders et al., 'One Brain, Two Selves', *NeuroImage*, 2003, 20, 2119.

3 *New Scientist*, 29 October 2005.

4 Onno Van der Hart, Ph.D. and Barbara Friedman, M.A., M.F.C.C., 'A Reader's Guide to Pierre Janet: A Neglected Intellectual Heritage', *Dissociation*, 1989, 2(1), pp. 3–16.

5 Cited in H. F. Ellenberger, *The Discovery of the Unconscious*, Basic Books, New York, 1970, p. 127.

6 Morton Prince, *The Dissociation of a Personality*, Longmans, Green and Co., New York, 1906.

7 Helen H. Watkins, 'Ego-State Therapy: An Overview', *American Journal of Clinical Hypnosis*, April 1993, Volume 35, No. 4, pp. 232–40.

8 Joan Acocella, *Creating Hysteria: Women and Multiple Personality Disorder*, Jossey-Bass Publishers, San Francisco, 1999.

9 The leading researcher in this field, Elizabeth Loftus, details her work in *The Myth of Repressed Memory,* St Martin's Griffin, New York, 1996.

10 James V. Haxby et al., 'Distributed and Overlapping Representations of Faces and Objects in Ventral Temporal Cortex', *Science*, 28 September 2001.

11 Simone Reinders et al., 'One Brain, Two Selves', *NeuroImage*, 2003, 20, 2119.

12 G. Tsai et al., 'Functional Magnetic Resonance Imaging of Personality Switches in a Woman with Dissociative Identity Disorder', *Harvard Review of Psychiatry*, July/August 1999.

13 Joseph Ciorciari, 'EEG Coherence and Dissociative Identity Disorder', *Journal of Trauma and Dissociation*, 2002, Volume 3, Issue 1.

14 *Collins English Dictionary*, Third edition.

Chapter Two: The Landscape of Mind

1 J. Rowan, *Subpersonalities – The People Inside Us*, Brunner-Routledge, London, 1990.

2 A. G. Morgan and R. Janoff-Bulman, 'Positive and Negative Self-complexity: Patterns of Adjustment Following Traumatic and Non-Traumatic Life Experiences', *Journal of Social and Clinical Psychology,* 1994, No. 13, pp. 63–85. For an overview of research see John Altrocchi, 'Individual Differences in Pluralism in Self-Structure', in John Rowan and Mick Cooper (eds), *The Plural Self*, Sage Publications, London, 1999.

3 Marjorie Taylor, *Imaginary Companions and the Children Who Create Them*, Oxford University Press (USA), 2001.

4 Marjorie Taylor and A. Kohanyi, 'The Illusion of Independent Agency: Do Adult Fiction Writers Experience Their Characters as Having Minds of Their Own?' *Imagination, Cognition and Personality*, 2002/3, No. 22, pp. 361–80.

5 For more on this see Rita Carter, *Mapping the Mind*, Weidenfeld and Nicolson, London, 1998.

6 S. Harter, 'Self and Identity Development', in S. S. Feldman and G. R. Elliot (eds), *At the Threshold: The Developing Adolescent,* Harvard University Press, Cambridge, Mass., 1990, pp. 352–3.

7 K. J. Gergen and S. J. Morse, 'Self-Consistency: Measurement and Validation. Proceedings of the American Psychological Association', 1967, pp. 207–8.

8 Stanley Milgram, *Obedience to Authority*, London, Tavistock, 1974. http://www.stanleymilgram.com also gives details of these and other Milgram experiments and links to other sources.

9 Walter Mischel, 'Continuity and Change in Personality', *American Psychologist*, 1969, 24(11), pp. 1012–8.

10 http://www.prisonexp.org

11 Susan T. Fiske, Lasana T. Harris and Amy J. C. Cuddy, 'Why Ordinary People Torture Enemy Prisoners', *Science*, 26 November 2004, Vol. 306, No. 5701, pp. 1482–3.

12 Tara Pepper, 'Inside the Head of an Applicant', *Newsweek*, 21 February 2005.

13 Daniel Druckman and Robert A. Bjork, *In the Mind's Eye: Enhancing Human Performance*, National Academy of Sciences, New York, 1991.

14 M. Kennon et al., 'Trait Self and True Self: Cross-Role Variation in the Big-Five Personality Traits and its Relations with Psychological Authenticity and Subjective Well-Being', *Journal of Personality and Social Psychology*, 1997, Vol. 73, No. 6, pp. 1380–93.

Chapter Three: Mechanisms of Mind

1 Ronald C. Petersen, 'Retrieval Failures in State-Dependent Learning', *Psychopharmacology*, 1977, No. 55, pp. 141–6.

2 G. H. Bower, 'Affect and Cognition, Philosophical Transactions of the Royal Society of London (Series B)', 1983, 302, pp. 387–402.

3 Becker-Blease et al., 'A Genetic Analysis of Individual Differences in Dissociative Behaviour in Children and Adolescents', *Journal of Child Psychology and Psychiatry*, 2004, Vol. 45, No. 3, pp. 522–32.

4 C. A. Ross, *Dissociative Identity Disorder, Diagnosis, Clinical Features, and Treatment of Multiple Personalities*, John Wiley, New York, 1997.

5 Colin Ross, *Dissociative Identity Disorder*, John Wiley, New Jersey, 1997.

6 Marlene Steinberg and Maxine Schnall, *The Stranger in the Mirror, Dissociation – the Hidden Epidemic*, Cliff Street Books, New York, 2000.

7 Steven N. Gold, 'Fight Club: A Depiction of Contemporary Society as Dissociogenic', *Journal of Trauma and Dissociation*, 2004, Vol 5(2).

Chapter Four: Changing Times, Changing Selves

1 Population Trends, HM Government, 30 September 2004.

2 *Independent*, 17 November 2005.

3   P. W. Linville, 'Self Complexity as a Cognitive Buffer against Stress-Related Illness and Depression', *Journal of Personality and Social Psychology*, 1987, Vol. 52, pp. 663–76.

4   Cathy tells the full story of her depression and recovery in her book: *Life After Darkness*, Radcliffe Publishing, Oxford, 2006.

5   Catherine Harmer et al., 'Increased Positive Versus Negative Affective Perception and Memory in Healthy Volunteers Following Selective Serotonin and Norepinephrine Reuptake Inhibition', *American Journal of Psychiatry*, July 2004, No. 161, pp. 1256–63.

6   Shankar Vedantam, 'Prescription for an Obsession?', *Washington Post*, 19 March 2006.

Chapter Five: The People You Are

1   For evidence of this, see Judith Rich Harris, *The Nurture Assumption*, Bloomsbury, London, 1998.

2   'Ego Boundaries, or the Fit of my Father's Shirt – Mind-to-Body Ratio is not Always One-to-One', *Discover*, November 1995.

3   Interview, *Woman's Hour*, BBC Radio 4, 30 May 2006.

4   N. Ramirez-Esparza et al., 'Do Bilinguals H263ave Two Personalities?', *Journal of Research in Personality*, 2006, No. 40, pp. 99–120.

5   Margaret Shih et al., 'Stereotype Susceptibility: Identity Salience and Shifts in Quantitative Performance', *Psychological Science*, 1999, 10(1), pp. 81–4.

6   M. Inzlicht et al., 'Stigma as Ego Depletion – How Being the Target of Prejudice Affects Self-Control', *Psychological Science*, March 2006, pp. 262–9.

7   Interview with Grayson Perry by Trace Newton-Ingham: http://www.saatchi-gallery.co.uk/artists/grayson_perry_articles.htm

8   'Eating Disorders and the Search for Solutions', NIMH Publication 01-4901, 2001.

9   'The Prevalence and Correlates of Eating Disorders in the National Comorbidity Survey Replication', James I. Hudson et al., *Biological Psychiatry*, 3 July 2006.

10   'Wasting the Best and the Brightest: Substance Abuse at America's Colleges and Universities,' The National Center on Addiction and Substance Abuse at Columbia University, March 2007.

11   'Activity of Striatal Neurons Reflects Dynamic Encoding and Recoding

of Procedural Memories', Terra D. Barnes et al., *Nature*, 20 October 2005, 437, pp. 1158–61.

12 Marcia Degun-Mather, 'Ego-State Therapy in the Treatment of a Complex Eating Disorder', North East London Mental Health Care Trust, *Contemporary Hypnosis*, 2003, Vol. 20(3), pp. 165–73.

13 Virgin Money commissioned TNS to survey 2057 adults aged over sixteen between 10 and 15 May 2005.

14 Gareth McLean, 'When the Playboy Met the Liar', *Guardian*, 1 August 2006.

15 *Midweek*, BBC Radio 4, 18 January 2006.

16 'The Body Remembers: The Psychophysiology of Trauma and Trauma Treatment', *Psychotherapy Networker*, September 2004.

17 Robert Hof, 'My Virtual Life', *Businessweek.com*, 1 May 2006.

PART II

Chapter Eight: Working Together

1 D. M. Wegner, D. J. Schneider, S. Carter III and L. White, 'Paradoxical Effects of Thought Suppression', *Journal of Personality and Social Psychology*, 1987, 53, pp. 5–13.

Resources

Further reading

The Plural Self, John Rowan and Mick Cooper (eds), Sage Publications, London, 1999 and *The Multiple Self*, Jon Elster (ed.), Cambridge University Press, Cambridge, 1986.
Two excellent collections of essays by psychologists and philosophers about a pluralistic view of the self.

Subpersonalities, John Rowan, Brunner-Routledge, London, 1990.
Rowan is one of a very few psychologists fully to endorse the notion of normal multiplicity. This book details his own views about how they are created, how they work and how they manifest in everyday life.

The Myth of Sanity: Divided Consciousness and the Promise of Awareness, Martha Stout, Viking Penguin US, 2001.
Stout considers multiplicity to be pathological. However, she believes it to be so pervasive that it is effectively the 'norm' and manifests in everyday behaviour as well as in clearly dysfunctional individuals.

The Stranger in the Mirror, Marlene Steinberg and Maxine Schnall, Cliff Street Books/Harper Collins, US, 2000.
An informative and practical introduction to dissociation in all its guises.

The Society of Mind, Marvin Minsky, Pan Books, London, 1988 and *Multimind*, Robert Ornstein, Houghton Mifflin, Boston, 1986.

Both put forward the notion that individual minds are made up of many semi-autonomous brain modules, each of which has its own aims, talents and influence. Brain-imaging studies bring new confirmation of this every day.

Websites

Astraea's Web: http://www.astraeasweb.net/plural

This is an extraordinarily comprehensive source of information, insight and guidance to the whole field of multiple personalities, with emphasis on 'normal' multiplicity.

http://lists.topica.com/lists/darkpersonalities

A multiplicity discussion site for people who are interested in the topic generally, or consider themselves to be healthy and functional multiples.

Other multiplicity resources

Voice Dialogue (see page 4)

A therapeutic technique based on getting inner selves to talk together and also to strengthen what it refers to as 'the Aware Ego'. This is described on its website as 'a process where your usual ego becomes aware of itself, or rather of the selves that are a part of it, and is then able to *choose* which selves to express, rather than have the selves choose for you'. See http://www.voicedialogue.com and *Embracing Our Selves*, Hal and Sidra Stone, New World Library, California, 1989.

Ego-state therapy (page 4)

Uses hypnotherapy (mainly) to bring otherwise hidden 'ego-states' (what I refer to as personalities) into consciousness and thus to open them to interrogation and behaviour modification. See http://www.clinicalsocialwork.com/egostate.html and *Ego-States – Theory and Therapy*, John and Helen Watkins, Norton, New York, 1997.

Psychosynthesis
A somewhat spiritually inclined therapeutic system which is based on the idea that people are divided into subselves, but that they can develop a Higher Awareness that transcends the parts. See http://www.psychosynthesis.org

Dissociation – information and links to therapy
The site http://www.sidran.org is for people who are concerned about or interested in the dysfunctional or extreme form of multiplicity known as Dissociative Identity Disorder. The International Society for the Study of Dissociative Disorders website (http://www.issd.org) includes a list of therapists as well as a comprehensive book list and information about dissociation.

The Hearing Voices Network
The Hearing Voices Network offers information, support and understanding to people who hear voices and those who support them. Contact:

Hearing Voices Network (HVN)
c/o Sheffield Hearing Voices Network,
Limbrick Day Service, Limbrick Road,
Sheffield, S6 2PE
Email: nhvn@hotmail.co.uk
Phone: 0114 271 8210
www.hearing-voices.org

Multiplicity Training
An extensive training programme has been developed for individuals and organisations wanting to develop multiplicity to benefit their business. It is designed to help people find and use all their strengths, and to improve their ability – individually or as a corporation – to adapt to changing circumstances and to work together as a team for greatest possible success. The training comprises an introductory two-day programme with subsequent sessions aimed at in-depth knowledge and

further enhancement of personal happiness and team results. The follow-up trainings are tailor-made and presented in a modular form. For more details: info@multiplicity.eu or info@yellowyardscompany.com.

Index